THE CLASSICS
OF **WESTERN**
SPIRITUALITY

THE CLASSICS OF WESTERN SPIRITUALITY
A Library of the Great Spiritual Masters

President and Publisher
Paul McMahon

EDITORIAL BOARD

Editor-in-Chief
André Brouillette, SJ—Associate Professor of Systematic and Spiritual Theology, Boston College Clough School of Theology and Ministry, Boston, MA

Daniel P. Horan, OFM—Professor of Philosophy, Religious Studies and Theology, Director of the Center for the Study of Spirituality, Saint Mary's College, Notre Dame, IN

Andrew Prevot—Professor of Theology and Religions Studies, Amaturo Chair in Catholic Studies, Georgetown University, Washington, DC

Rachel Wheeler—Associate Professor of Theology (Spirituality), University of Portland, Portland, OR

Editorial Consultants
Rozanne Elder—Professor Emerita, Department of History, Western Michigan University, Kalamazoo, MI

Michael Fishbane—Professor Emeritus of Jewish Studies, Divinity School, University of Chicago, Chicago, IL

Karlfried Froehlich—Benjamin B. Warfield Professor of Ecclesiastical History Emeritus, Princeton Theological Seminary, Princeton, NJ

Moshe Idel—Emeritus Max Cooper Professor in Jewish Thought, Department of Jewish Thought, Hebrew University, Jerusalem, Israel

Bernard McGinn—CWS Editor-in-Chief Emeritus; Naomi Shenstone Donnelley Professor Emeritus of Historical Theology and the History of Christianity, Divinity School, University of Chicago, Chicago, IL

Seyyed Hossein Nasr—University Professor of Islamic Studies, George Washington University, Washington, DC

Sandra M. Schneiders—Professor Emerita of New Testament Studies and Spirituality, Jesuit School of Theology, Berkeley, CA

Michael A. Sells—John Henry Barrows Professor of Islamic History and Literature, Divinity School, University of Chicago, Chicago, IL

David Steindl-Rast—Spiritual Author and Hermit, Austria

David Tracy—Greeley Professor Emeritus of Roman Catholic Studies, Divinity School, University of Chicago, Chicago, IL

The Rt. Rev. and Rt. Hon. Rowan D. Williams—Master of Magdalene College, Cambridge, England (ret.)

CATHERINE OF SIENA

Selected Letters

Selected, translated, and introduced
by Diana L. Villegas

Paulist Press
New York / Mahwah, NJ

Caseside image: Painting of Saint Catherine of Siena by Sano di Pietro courtesy of Wikimedia Commons and the Bonnefanten Museum.

Caseside design by Sharyn Banks
Book design by Lynn Else

Compilation, translation, and introduction copyright © 2025 by Diana Lucia Villegas

All rights reserved. No part of this publication may be reproduced, stored in a retrieval system, or transmitted in any form or by any means, electronic, mechanical, photocopying, recording, scanning, or otherwise without either the prior written permission of the Publisher, or authorization through payment of the appropriate per-copy fee to the Copyright Clearance Center, Inc., 222 Rosewood Drive, Danvers, MA 01923 (978) 750-8400, fax (978) 646-8600, or on the Web at www.copyright.com. Requests to the Publisher for permission should be addressed to the Permissions Department, Paulist Press, 997 Macarthur Boulevard, Mahwah, NJ 07430, (201) 825-7300, fax (201) 825-8345, or online at www.paulistpress.com.

Library of Congress Cataloging-in-Publication Data
Names: Catherine, of Siena, Saint, 1347–1380. | Villegas, Diana, editor.
Title: Catherine of Siena: selected letters / selected, translated, and introduced by Diana L. Villegas.
Description: New York: Paulist Press, [2025] | Series: Classics of Western spirituality | Includes bibliographical references and index. | Summary: "This volume offers a fresh translation of St. Catherine of Siena's letters that are faithful to the oral, metaphor-filled language of an uneducated woman"—Provided by publisher.
Identifiers: LCCN 2024019974 (print) | LCCN 2024019975 (ebook) | ISBN 9780809106752 (hardcover) | ISBN 9780809188857 (ebook)
Subjects: LCSH: Catherine, of Siena, Saint, 1347–1380—Correspondence. | Christian saints—Italy—Siena—Correspondence. | Mysticism—Catholic Church.
Classification: LCC BX4700.C4 A4 2025 (print) | LCC BX4700.C4 (ebook) | DDC 282.092—dc23/eng/20240906
LC record available at https://lccn.loc.gov/2024019974
LC ebook record available at https://lccn.loc.gov/2024019975

ISBN 978-0-8091-0675-2 (hardcover)
ISBN 978-0-8091-8885-7 (ebook)

Published by Paulist Press
997 Macarthur Boulevard
Mahwah, New Jersey 07430
www.paulistpress.com

Printed and bound in the
United States of America

CONTENTS

Preface xi

Notes on Translation xiii

Abbreviations of Frequent References xvii

Introduction 1
    1. Catherine's Formation and Vocation 4
    2. The Letters: Numbering, Dating, Construction 15
    3. Essential Concepts of Catherine's Spirituality 23

1. Nuns 39
    Letter 73 to Costanza, Nun at Sant'Abbondio, Siena 39
    Letter 182 to Bartalomea, Nun at Santo Stefano, Pisa 43
    Letter 26 to Eugenia, Nun at Saint Agnes, Montepulciano 47
    Letter 86 to the Abbess of Santa Maria delli Scalzi, Florence 54

2. *Mantellate* and Close Lay Male Disciples 60
    Letter 99 to Neri di Landoccio Pagliaresi, Disciple 60
    Letter 132 to Multiple Sienese *Mantellate* 63
    Letter 125 to Nera, Prioress of Sienese *Mantellate* 66
    Letter 214 to Caterina and Giovanna, *Mantellate* 68
    Letter 49 to Alessa dei Saracini, *Mantellata* 72
    Letter 213 to Daniela, *Mantellata* in Orvieto 75
    Letter 186 to Neri di Landoccio Pagliaresi, Disciple 86

3. Friars and Monks 88
    Letter 41 to Tommaso dalla Fonte, Cousin and
        Dominican Friar 88

CONTENTS

Letters 127 to Bartolomeo Dominici and Tommaso d'Antonio
and 146 to Bartolomeo Dominici—Dominican Friars 91
Letter 134 to Bartolomeo and Jacomo, Hermits 95
Letter 36 to Novices at Monte Oliveto Monastery 99
Letter 51 to Felice da Massa, Augustinian Hermit 104
Letter 326 to William Flete and Antonio da Nizza,
    Augustinian Hermits 108
Letter 33 to the Abbot of Monte Oliveto Monastery 110
Letter 154 to Francesco Tedaldi, Carthusian 114

Raymond of Capua 122
    Letter 219 122
    Letter 267 126
    Letter 272 (Postscript) 131
    Letter 373 132

4. Ecclesiastical Authorities 140
    Popes 140
        Letter 185 to Gregory XI 140
        Letter 252 to Gregory XI 146
        Letter 305 to Urban VI 151
    Cardinals, Bishops 156
        Letter 181 to Cardinal Nicola da Osimo 156
        Letter 16 to an Important Prelate 161
        Letter 7 to Cardinal Pietro da Ostia 166

5. Civil Authorities 170
    Letter 149 to Piero Gambacorta, Pisan Official 170
    Letter 131 to Nicolò Soderini, Florentine Political Leader 173
    Letter 143 to Giovanna, Queen of Naples 177
    Letter 266 to Ristoro Canigiani, Florentine Political Leader 180
    Letter 358 to Andrea Vanni, Painter and Political Leader
        of Siena 187

6. Knights, Military Leaders 192
    Letter 374 to Bartolomeo Smeducci, Knight 192
    Letter 256 to Niccolò, Prior of the Knights Hospitallers 198

Contents

    Letter 347 to Alberigo da Barbiano, Captain of the Company of St. George 204

7. Other Laymen and Women 209
    Letter 130 to Ipòlito, Florentine Widower 209
    Letter 241 to Giovanna, Mother of a Disciple 212
    Letter 120 to Rabe, Wife of Francesco Tolomei 216
    Letter 95 to Young Men Mentored by Fr. Giovanni dalle Celle ... 219
    Letter 113 to Bandecca Salimbeni, Widow 224
    Letter 375 to an Unknown Layman 231
    Letter 307 to a Florentine Woman 232
    Letter 13 to Marco Bindi, Merchant 237
    Letter 300 to Agnesa, Wife of Francesco Pipino 243
    Letter 249 to Francesco Pipino, Tailor and Agnesa, His Wife ... 243

8. Family 248
    Letter 14 to Benincasa, Stefano, and Bartolomeo, Three Older Brothers 248
    Letter 1 to Lapa, Mother 250
    Letter 117 to Lapa, Mother, and to Monna Cecca 250

Appendix 1—ISIME Critical Text 255

Appendix 2—List of Letters in Numerical Order 259

Notes 263

Bibliography 293

Index 299

PREFACE

My attraction to Catherine of Siena started during my graduate studies and grew so that her teaching became part of my PhD dissertation, which explored her wisdom on discernment and compared it to that of Ignatius of Loyola. As the Fordham theology department did not have an expert on Catherine, my mentor, Ewert Cousins (for many years editorial consultant for CWS), recommended Suzanne Noffke[1] as an outside reader. It was Noffke's love of Catherine, her heartfelt encouragement, and her generosity in sharing her scholarship and her passion for this mystic that encouraged my ongoing study of Catherine's wisdom.

A lifelong scholar of Catherine's life and works, Noffke rigorously studied her linguistically, historically, and culturally, and furthered the interpretation of Catherine's contribution to theology and spirituality. This volume would not exist without Noffke's scholarship. The dating of the letters, historical context, and biographical summaries of Catherine's correspondents found in Noffke's four-volume translation of all of Catherine's letters have been foundational to this work. Indeed, this volume follows in Noffke's footsteps as she is the editor and translator of the CWS volume on Catherine of Siena's book, *The Dialogue*.

This volume came about as André Brouillette, SJ, my colleague on a committee of the Society for the Study of Christian Spirituality, informed a group of us about his new role as editor of the Classics of Western Spirituality and encouraged us to make proposals. I recommended an anthology of Catherine's letters using Noffke's translation, now out of print and published in four academic volumes. As we discussed this option, the idea of my doing a new translation arose.

CATHERINE OF SIENA

In doing a new translation, I benefit from the completion of the critical edition of *The Letters* by Antonio Volpato as well as from many more years of available Catherine scholarship. While Noffke, a fine writer, gave Catherine a very fluid and almost elegant style, I am offering a more literal translation that I believe better reflects Catherine's communication, which, as will be discussed, was that of a young medieval woman with no education but with a gift for passionate exhortation and creative use of language and images.

I thank André Brouillette for his encouragement and support in the creation of this volume. Rosemary Curran offered invaluable editing of composition and grammar.

NOTES ON TRANSLATION

In order to offer as complete and accurate a translation as possible, this translation was checked against Suzanne Noffke's and against a classical translation into Spanish.[1] Translations are from Volpato's online critical edition, Catherine of Siena. *Lettere, edizione critica e commento*. Edited by Antonio Volpato (Rome, 2016) https://centrostudicateriniani.it/santa-caterina-da-siena/epistolario/.

GENERAL

Biblical Translations

Catherine's biblical quotations are translated as they appear in the critical text; these are based on Catherine's recollection or internalization of a particular passage, so that the words do not usually correspond exactly to a contemporary translation of Scripture. For a few important passages, the NRSV translation is offered in the notes.

Gender

In fourteenth-century Italy there was clearly no attention to gender-neutral language, so I have made no attempt to change Catherine's usage as this would be historically inaccurate.

Pronouns

Catherine frequently changed the use of pronouns within a letter. For instance, she addressed the correspondent in the singular and then in mid-sentence she changed to the plural "we" to include herself in the advice and exhortation.

Soul and pronoun use. Catherine frequently refers to the person as "the soul," which is feminine in Italian. Accordingly, in letters to men, both the pronouns "she" and "he" will refer to the person addressed.

Capitalization of pronouns for God. Pronouns referring to God and Jesus are not capitalized except where it is necessary to make clear that the pronoun refers to God.

Paragraph breaks. I have used the paragraph breaks of the critical edition, which often differ from those created by Noffke in her translations.

PARTICULAR WORDS OR PHRASES

Affetto

Affetto has a number of related meanings in medieval spiritual writings. As a translator of works of the twelfth-century Cistercians tells us, *affectus*, the twelfth-century Latin version of the Italian *affetto*, cannot be translated by a single English word.

> *Affectus*, precisely because it is at the center of our life, can clothe itself in the various nuances of the powers (virtues) and faculties of our soul. In its tending to goodness, the *affectus* can be a movement of piety, or perception, or faith, or hope, or love, or thought, or will, and so on. Under an unusual influence and penetration of grace, the *affectus* can "be" the Holy Spirit.[2]

This paragraph could be applied to Catherine's use of *affetto*, which will be left in Italian, with notes indicating the meaning in a particular context.

Notes on Translation

Charity

By *charity* Catherine means *love* rather than the offer of assistance or altruism to another; accordingly, *charity* is translated as *love*.

Crusade

In Catherine's day, the crusade was referred to as *santo passaggio* or just *passaggio*, where *passaggio* had the connotation of pilgrimage; this is a medieval usage, as today *passaggio* has a number of meanings that do not include "crusade" or "pilgrimage." *Santo passaggio* is thus translated in this work as "crusade pilgrimage" or "holy crusade pilgrimage," as for Catherine the crusade was, indeed, a holy pilgrimage, a most significant form of spiritual journey.

Monna, Messer

These titles have no equivalent in English, so I have left them in the original. They are a form of address for a woman or man usually combined with the first name and are not equivalent to Ms., Mr., or Mrs. For instance, Catherine also uses *monna* to address abbesses. These titles function more as do *don* and *doña* in Spanish today, where one might address a woman as doña María, while Señora María Perez would be equivalent to Ms. or Mrs. Maria Perez.

Name

Besides Catherine's, Raymond of Capua's, and a few key, well-known names, such as those of the popes, names are kept in the original, which includes medieval Sienese versions of Italian names.

Person

The word *person* is used for Catherine's frequent phrase, *creatura che ha in se ragione* (creature who possesses reason). This set of words alludes to persons created in the image of God and capable of choice, a meaning for which there is no simple English translation. *Creature* used alone would have connotations that are not implied in Catherine's language.

Remain in the Holy, etc.; Remain, etc.

When Catherine shortens her closing greeting, "Remain in the holy and tender love of God," using "etc.," I have translated it literally. Noffke's translation inserts the complete phrase.

Selfish Self-Love

This term is used for a number of different expressions that Catherine uses with the same meaning or similar connotation, namely, *volontà sensitiva, dispiacimento di sé, amare sé sensualmente, amore proprio di sé, sensualità coperta con l'amore proprio.*

Unbelievers

I have translated this term literally as it is the historically appropriate term. It referred to anyone who was not Christian, and particularly, in the context of the crusade, to those of the Islamic tradition.

ABBREVIATIONS OF FREQUENT REFERENCES

Noffke, I:13n   Indicates volume, page number and note number in *The Letters of Catherine of Siena*. Translated and edited by Suzanne Noffke. 4 vols., Tempe, AZ: Arizona Center for Medieval and Renaissance Studies, 2000–2008.

Dialogue, 1:43   Indicates chapter and page in Catherine of Siena. *The Dialogue*. Translated and edited by Suzanne Noffke, New York: Paulist, 1980.

INTRODUCTION

Catherine of Siena has caught the imagination of many in the twenty-first century as the young woman who spoke truth to power in the fourteenth century and as one of the great Christian mystics. Her 383 letters reveal her personality, aspects of her story in her own words, and the wisdom she taught.[1] Her wisdom reflects her closeness to God, and the essential elements of her teaching express the core of the Christian message in a way that remains valid today, seven centuries later. Her formulations rang true to many of her own generation and have continued to ring true to many over time. Catherine's wisdom as gift of the Holy Spirit was highlighted when she was made a doctor of the church—one of five women given this honor.[2] Unlike other doctors of the church,[3] Catherine was an uneducated, barely literate young woman who learned about her faith orally, digesting this wisdom in prayer.

One of the unique characteristics of Catherine's letters is the variety of people to whom she wrote, revealing a notable dimension of her spirituality, that is, the inner authority she assumed to advise a wide variety of persons, even though she had no formal role or authority. Through her relationship with God, she arrived at a certainty that she was in touch with God's wisdom and acquired a clarity that her mission was to share this. In this respect, her vocation was prophetic, that is, she was called to proffer the word of God to others.[4] She exhorted and advised high ecclesiastical dignitaries including two popes, as well as prominent temporal authorities including kings and queens. She also wrote to knights, leaders of city-states, lawyers, notaries, artisans, and others. One third of her letters were sent to other women, including noblewomen, her lay followers, abbesses, and nuns. And of course, she had a wide correspondence with monks and friars. André Vauchez, prominent medieval historian, considers Catherine's letters the most important letter collection by a medieval woman.[5]

This volume offers a selection of Catherine's letters, which, though small relative to the corpus of 383, includes a comprehensive selection of types of correspondents and covers most topics of her teaching, since she repeats essential elements of her spirituality throughout her letters. This volume further offers the first translation based on the critical text, completed in 2002.[6] It is innovatively organized by chapters according to type of correspondent, and arranges the organization by date of the categories of correspondents,[7] covering a full range of dates.

Catherine's letters offer a comprehensive source for her views on theology, spirituality, and the ecclesiastical politics of her day; they offer glimpses into the piety and customs of the Tuscany of the second half of the fourteenth century. Though her letters offer insights into who she was apart from the hagiography that has shaped the narrative about her even into our own day, she does not focus on her own experience; rather, she exhorts others based on that experience. Only very few letters to Raymond of Capua—the Dominican friar who became her mentor and friend—and to close companions, include descriptions of her mystical experiences of God.[8]

Catherine's letters are difficult for the twenty-first century reader to interpret because of their style and language as well as cultural and historical differences. Accordingly, through this introduction, introductions to each letter, and notes that offer historical and cultural context, this volume is edited to aid the reader in gaining the fullest possible appreciation of Catherine's teaching. As described in detail below, Catherine dictated her letters in a style that is practical, authoritative, very creative, but not smooth or elegant and at times obscure; it is the orally based communication of a poetic, very wise and inspired yet uneducated young woman. This translation re-creates Catherine's style as closely as possible, with no attempt to make it more elegant, literary, or smooth. The power of the Spirit working through her—witnessing to her surrender to and union with God—are revealed in the authority and force of her communication despite her unorthodox style, which lacks elegance. In its imperfection, then,

Introduction

her style reveals an aspect of Catherine's own spiritual journey. Accordingly, this translation differs significantly from the earlier English translation of Catherine's letters,[9] which imparted a smoother, more elegant style to Catherine's communication and translated some of her awkward metaphors and language into English phrases. For instance, Catherine tells a nun that she is "cell" and frequently uses the term *she-who-is*. (Both of these will be addressed below). In this volume these expressions are translated literally and explained, as they convey significant insights into Catherine's spirituality and reveal her originality.

It is important to keep in mind that interpretation is a major factor in all readings of historical texts and life stories. This is even more the case with medieval sources, especially material on Catherine's life and experience, most of which is based on hagiography and legend. This volume is written from the perspective of Christian spirituality and theology, and therefore, interpretation of Catherine's life and writings reflects this disciplinary lens. At the same time, material from the extensive studies of Catherine by medieval historians and literature scholars is included, as some of it is critical to the interpretation of Catherine's life and writings. For instance, historians have studied the medieval upbringing of female children, ideals and models of piety particular to fourteenth-century Italy, and the changing lifestyle models for women who wanted to dedicate themselves to God. Historical realities such as these are important for understanding Catherine's vocation and wisdom. Literature scholars have studied Catherine's style, her use of metaphors and other rhetorical devices and have delved into the authority and authorship of medieval women mystics. While material from history and literature are very important to the interpretation presented here, I indicate instances when the interpretation from Christian spirituality differs significantly from that of history or literature.

Part 1 below highlights the historical-cultural realities that shaped Catherine's formation, with an innovative presentation of her formation and vocation in three stages, each significant to the shaping of the wisdom we find in her letters. Part 2 offers literary and historical tools for reading the letters, and part 3 presents a summary of the essential elements of Catherine's spirituality so that the reader can fit into the overall perspective particular aspects found in any one letter.

1. CATHERINE'S FORMATION AND VOCATION

Catherine was the daughter of a wool merchant, part of the emerging medieval merchant class—comparable to today's upper middle class—one of a pair of twins, the last born to parents who had twenty-four children. Families were large and extended families lived in contiguous spaces. Thus, Catherine grew up in a large extended family, learning at home how to be a useful part of this family with the assumption that her main role in life would be eventually to run such a family of her own. Like other medieval girls who did not belong to the nobility, she was not taught to read and write or offered any structured formal education.[10]

Her earliest religious education came through family instruction and devotional practices at home. In addition, it was customary for mendicant friars to visit families, spending time socializing and offering religious formation. Catherine's family lived a short walk from a Dominican church, and her family was known to have close ties to some of these friars; Catherine was undoubtedly present during such informal communication about the faith. Laypersons and especially women attended recitation of the Liturgy of the Hours (Divine Office) during the day. While the official liturgical services were in Latin, sermons and devotional instruction were offered in the vernacular during this attendance at church. Since most people did not know how to read or write, they were taught about the faith through these talks associated with liturgical celebrations.[11] Catherine would have attended Mass and the recitation of the Liturgy of the Hours with her family, thus benefitting from this formation on the part of the Dominican friars.

Catherine's vocation unfolded in three parts: a period at home, emphasizing a life of prayer, asceticism, and as much solitude as possible; a period when she began to offer pastoral ministry within Siena; and her public engagement in the ecclesiastical politics of her day.

Introduction

Childhood and First Vocation

Highlights

- March 25, 1347. Born at home, a twin, the twenty-fourth child of her parents. Her twin died as a baby.

- Age 6. When out in the fields with her brother she had a vision of Christ; this vision marked the beginning of her desire for a relationship with the God of love she experienced in her vision.

- Age 15. After a favorite sister died in childbirth, Catherine cut off her hair to give a definitive message to her family that she would not marry; she wanted to be free to focus on a relationship with God, to be the bride of Christ according to the devotional imagery of the time.

Catherine's story is associated with exceptional mystical experiences beginning at the age of six. Though much has been written about her early visions, information about them is based on hagiographies and legends with interpretations of these accounts based on the piety of Catherine's time and the goals of portraying her as extraordinary and holy.[12] What is clear is that Catherine experienced God's presence, love, and communication with her since her childhood, and as a result of this experience she was led to give herself to God.

In response to her experience of God, Catherine wished—with all the passion of her personality and youth—to give herself to God totally and absolutely. Influenced by the spirituality of her day, she interpreted "giving herself to God" as requiring commitment to prayer, ascetical practices, and solitude. While most hagiography about Catherine sees this response as extraordinary, Catherine would have seen these ideals publicly lived by penitents in Siena.

Ascetical Models Followed by Catherine

Catherine lived at a time when there was a shift in the practices of women who wished to give themselves to God, and these shifts were a major influence on the way Catherine interpreted and lived her call from God. In the thirteenth century the church began to tighten regulations about women's religiously dedicated lives. For instance, in the twelfth century there were still women solitaries who informally attached themselves to men's monasteries, as did Jutta, the anchoress to whom the eight-year-old Hildegard of Bingen was apprenticed.[13] However, in 1298 Boniface VIII passed laws about the tight cloistering of women in their own monasteries. This led to the development of new lifestyles for women who did not want to marry or were widowed and wanted to dedicate themselves to God without entering a monastery.[14] Many women became a sort of urban hermit, seeking solitude in their homes or building small hermitages in public places. They practiced prayer and asceticism, living on contributions from the community or their families, were considered close to God, and were sought out for intercessory prayer and words of wisdom. We know that as a child Catherine wanted to run off to join such women living just outside Siena, seeing them as examples of persons totally given to God. As she grew up, she implemented this model within her home.

Ministry in Siena, Dominican Penitent Spirituality

Highlights

- Age 16. Persuaded her mother to support her joining the *mantellate*.

- Age 16–19 approximately. Lived mostly in solitude and contemplation in a small room of her family home, spending time in her "inner cell," where she learned the foundational spiritual lessons of her life.

- Around age 19. Began to offer care to the sick at the hospital and elsewhere.

- Early 20s. Became involved in mediating conflicts among Sienese families and shared her wisdom with a few who followed her as she went about caring for the sick.

- Age 20–21. Began to offer wisdom to other *mantellate* and people she knew around Siena.

Penitent Spirituality—Mantellate

The second stage of Catherine's vocation was becoming a *mantellata*, a hard-won choice first objected to by her family. Joining this penitent group of women was a further choice to cement the fact that she was not going to marry and wanted to give herself to God.[15] The *mantellate* were a penitent lay association affiliated with the Dominican Order; theirs was a form of lay religious life without a contemporary equivalent. They were not a religious order or a third order as we understand these today. Penitents were one of the emerging forms of lay religious life evolving at the same time as the solitary women, the "urban hermits" described above. Penitents were mostly widows, a few single women, and, rarely, married women. In Italian cities of Catherine's day these women mostly continued to live in their homes, though some would eventually live together. The *mantellate* of Siena were a penitent group who sought spiritual guidance from the local Dominican friars.[16] They were not an official part of the Dominican Order, nor did they make vows. Yet the *mantellate* penitents were allowed to wear the Dominican habit and were placed under the direction of a friar with whom they met once a month; this assigned friar acted as a mentor, formator, spiritual guide, and confessor. There was an informal rule that offered guidance regarding liturgical and devotional practices. Service to others was not a formal part of penitent orders—there were no "active" service-oriented orders of women at this time—but the *mantellate* of Siena became involved in caring for plague victims.[17]

After joining the *mantellate*, Catherine's formation was deepened and strongly shaped by the spirituality of the Dominican penitents, so that important themes of her spirituality and the interpretation of her experience of God were directly shaped by this teaching. This is a significant fact, for some of the emphases and themes of Catherine's wisdom were expressions and adaptations of her formation as *mantellata* rather than original to her.[18]

CATHERINE OF SIENA

In terms of her daily practice and occasions for listening to preaching, as a *mantellata* Catherine would have been more likely than before to regularly attend the celebration of the Liturgy of the Hours and Mass at her local church, where she would have listened to preaching and teaching by the Dominican friars, and where she would have been steeped in oral exposure to scripture, especially the psalms.[19] In addition, the friar assigned to the *mantellate*, as well as other Dominican friars who might have informally met with some or all of the *mantellate*, would have imparted guidance and formation.

The central focus of Dominican penitent women's spirituality was the life and passion of Christ, a focus we find in Catherine's letters. Part of devotion to Christ included mystically becoming a bride of Christ and receiving a ring in mystical prayer in order to seal the woman's complete giving of self to Christ. Catherine lived this experience together with many others. When the Siena *mantellate* became involved in helping those who were abandoned and sick, they interpreted this work as serving the suffering Christ present in those in need. Indeed, Catherine's first ministry outside her home involved assisting the sick, and she was most active during epidemics.

Imitating Jesus in his suffering, a central theme, was the motivation for ascetical practices common to penitents, including fasting and physical scourging—forms of piety not uncommon in the Middle Ages—though the Dominican penitent's rule suggested moderation.[20] "Penitents did not conceive of their pain as an ordinary affliction....The ascetic life of penance thus gave women an opportunity to celebrate Christ's victory over death and victoriously transcend the limits of their bodies in the anticipation of the life to come."[21] Catherine is known for her ascetical practice, especially fasting; though Catherine was not moderate in her own practice, she advised others to be moderate.[22]

Devotion to Christ's passion was very concrete, including visualizations and meditations about his physical suffering, focusing on his wounds. "The extreme concreteness with which Dominican penitent women celebrated Christ's passion set them apart from many other religious lay groups."[23] We will see in Catherine's spirituality a strong focus on Christ's suffering on the cross, and visualization of his wounds.

Introduction

In line with Dominican spirituality—the Dominicans popularized the Rosary—the penitents also highlighted devotion to Mary, often through visualization of Mary with the child Jesus, and specifically as a mother nursing her child.[24] Catherine's letters refer on many occasions to Mary's motherhood and to images of nursing based on this devotion.

Community Ministry: Role of Noblewomen in Formation and Ministry

After Catherine's period of asceticism and solitude in her own home, she began to experience in prayer a call to become involved in helping the poor and sick of Siena. At this time, several *mantellate*, local members of the nobility, became Catherine's friends, sponsors, and patrons, and they played a major role in the unfolding of Catherine's vocation and formation.[25] Some of these women supported her work with the sick and introduced her to their families so that Catherine began to preach informally to these small groups to the point that she developed a following, as did other penitents or urban hermits who acquired a reputation for holiness, effective intercessory prayer, and wisdom.[26] Indeed, apparently Catherine sometimes escaped from her home to avoid the large number of people seeking her ministry.[27] In this respect, Catherine was not unusual, for at this time in medieval Italy laypersons considered particularly holy ministered to their fellow townspeople.[28] "Hermits gathered in the grottos above the hilltown; clusters of recluses settled at the city gates; permanent clerical and clairvoyant guests resided in the affluent household;…charismatic itinerant preachers, often recent converts, dramatically disconnected their listeners from material and familial ties."[29]

Through her connection to *mantellate* who were members of leading local families, Catherine's reputation continued to spread in Siena. She was effective in challenging young men to conversion[30] and eventually was called upon to mediate among persons or families engaged in conflicts with one another.[31] Catherine's summons to appear in Florence before the Dominican superiors that eventually led to her broad public involvement and correspondence was in part due to the fact that she became known to ecclesiastical authorities, almost certainly through her ministry to the ruling Sienese classes.

The noblewomen who befriended Catherine also had a significant influence on her formation and her letter writing. In medieval Italy only girls of the nobility were taught to read and write, so they read religious literature themselves and read aloud to others. To provide this reading material, there was a production of translations into the vernacular of psalters and Books of Hours; the latter often included devotional reflections and formative religious narratives. Books of Hours were considered the most popular books among medieval women.[32] Indeed, noblewomen contributed to the creation of such books by commissioning them for themselves and their households.

Since women were expected to read devotional literature, it is not surprising that they played an important role as instigators of vernacular translations from the Latin and of vernacular literature in general. Nor is it surprising that an upsurge of such translations occurred in the twelfth and thirteenth centuries together with the development of Books of Hours.[33]

Writers such as the Dominican friar Domenico Cavalca in early fourteenth-century Pisa produced works in the vernacular that were widely distributed.[34] For instance, Cavalca produced translations of works of the desert mothers and fathers, inserting his informal commentary. In his *Mirror of the Cross*, he offered reflections about Jesus's crucifixion based on passages from the Gospels. Catherine would have listened to such vernacular works read aloud by her fellow *mantellate* and by friars that ministered to them and to her family. Antonio Volpato has shown Cavalca's influence in Catherine's letters.[35] In short, after she became a *mantellata*, Catherine would have been exposed to much more reading from the psalms, from the Books of Hours, and from devotional books written in or translated into the vernacular. Her letters reflect these influences.

Catherine was also exposed to theological formation from monks or friars who were theologians and ministered to the families who were Catherine's friends. For instance, she befriended William Flete, to whom Catherine eventually wrote seven letters (see Letter 326 in this volume).[36] He was an English Augustinian who had stud-

Introduction

ied theology at Cambridge and then came to live as an Augustinian hermit near Siena.

Political Engagement and Letter Writing
Highlights

- Age 27 (1374). Called to a meeting of the Dominican Order and assigned Raymond of Capua as mentor and spiritual advisor. She was tasked through Raymond to advocate for papal policies.

- Age 27–32. Active period of advocacy for papal policies through frequent letter writing and travel, including a trip to Avignon to meet with Gregory XI.

- Age 27–32. Continued to minister to people in her community and to mediate between warring families in Tuscany. She wrote multiple letters offering advice regarding the spiritual journey.

- Age 30. Dictated *The Dialogue*, her book.

- Age 32. Moved to Rome, continued her letter writing, and advocated for the papacy of Urban VI, elected in 1378.

- Died in Rome at 33, April 29, 1380.

The year 1374 marked the start of a new phase of Catherine's vocation. This shift was due to a new relationship with the Dominicans. They took her under their wing, not just as a *mantellata*, but individually and in a unique way. Through the recommendation of high church authorities, she was placed under the mentorship of Dominican friar Raymond of Capua, who was well educated in canon law and theology and formed part of the leadership of the Dominican Order. During a period of almost four years, he spent much of his time accompanying Catherine in her travels around Tuscany and on her trip to Avignon. While Raymond was her official mentor and confessor, he and Catherine became close collaborators and friends, and in due time, Catherine advised him and exhorted him regarding his spiritual journey.[37] Through this close relationship, Catherine deeply furthered her theological knowledge, which undoubtedly informed her letters, most of which date from the time after she met Raymond.[38] During this last period of her life, Catherine was also formed through the personal and epistolary dialogue she held with a number of learned monks and friars.

Through Raymond's guidance Catherine began her vocation as advocate for papal and ecclesiastical policies that she considered good for the church. She became convinced that the pope should reside in Rome and not Avignon, that a crusade should be fought in order to recover control of the Holy Land,[39] and that the Tuscan independent city-states should be in alliance with the pope and the Papal States. When two popes were elected in 1378, she promoted the legitimacy of Urban VI.[40]

These points of view regarding ecclesiastical politics were shaped mostly by Raymond, who undoubtedly prompted Catherine regarding particular actions and particular persons to lobby through her correspondence. Catherine acted out of her own conviction, but she was intentionally guided and formed by Raymond to further a particular ecclesiastical outlook. While the full argument regarding Raymond's influence on this final stage of Catherine's vocation cannot be made here, two facts give us a flavor. Raymond indicated that he was named as Catherine's mentor "for the saving of souls, the Crusade, and other business of the Holy Roman Church"[41] In other words, his mission was to form Catherine and guide her into action for the benefit of the church. Catherine's letter to Cardinal Nicola da Osimo, secretary to Gregory XI, offers another example of Raymond's influence. Catherine recommended that the pope name a particular Dominican as general of the order.[42] Given that Raymond had served in Rome with Stefano della Cumba, the proposed candidate, we can assume this suggestion came from him.[43] Clearly such a recommendation could not have come from Catherine herself.

The good of the church, as Catherine came to understand it, became her central passion, a focus of the mission that she felt God had given her. She advocated for the causes described above through her correspondence and through personal pleas. She travelled to Pisa, Lucca, and Florence to lobby for the crusade and to seek peace

Introduction

between the Tuscan city-states and the papacy. She traveled to Avignon, France, to meet with Pope Gregory XI to advocate for peace on behalf of one of the governing factions in Florence.

Most of all, Catherine engaged in intensive letter writing. She considered that there was an urgent need for the conversion of pastors at all levels, from the pope on down. She was well aware of the worldly life led by many, a life guided by desire for power and wealth rather than concern for pastoral care, for the preaching of the gospel, or for sacramental ministry. Catherine was certain that only with a transformed heart, capable of love—that is, capable of care for the good of the other—would the pope and other pastors be able to look after their sheep and the church. Therefore, she exhorted all correspondents first and foremost to conversion and transformation, after which she would either issue orders outright or make strong recommendations regarding what should be done.

Her letter writing ministry was not limited to ecclesiastical issues. By this last period of her life, Catherine had clearly come to consider it her vocation to work for the conversion and transformation of others, and not just within Siena, and she had discovered that her gift for exhortation could be pursued through letter writing.

Consciousness as Writer

Historians and literature scholars have debated about Catherine's consciousness as a writer and her self-understanding regarding the goal of her letter writing.[44] I contend that Catherine did not think of herself as a writer, as a woman making history by writing to ecclesiastical and temporal authorities in the vernacular (where Latin was the official and literary language).[45] Rather, we can glean from the content of her letters and knowledge of the unfolding of her vocation that she learned she was effective at exhortation and her letter writing became an extension of this ministry for the transformation of others and the good of the church. Her experience with pastoral care offered to those in Siena had showed her that through her closeness to God, her words had power to work for the healing and conversion of others. She had learned that her authority came from God. Thus, she and her advisors took the step of communicating her words of exhortation in writing, and in this way, Catherine learned that the written word had a particular form of power and efficacy.

Her letters give evidence that she came to see the power of the written word to work God's will in others. We see this in the unselfconscious authority with which she advised and exhorted all sorts of people, from the pope and queens on down. The rhetoric of her letters and their content was blunt and commanding. She always started with her desire for her correspondent, a desire stated with the authoritative tone of "I am writing because I want you to...." Many of her letters, including those to the pope and high temporal authorities, state, "'io voglio,' (I want) you to do such and such." Often, in no uncertain terms and brooking no doubts, she tells others what God's will is for them.[46] The authoritative quality of her letters will be evident to the reader.

When she was close to death, she wrote to Raymond, "I would like to ask that you deliver by hand my Book [*The Dialogue*] and all writings of mine that you should find, to the Master and to Friars Bartolomeo and Tommaso. Together with messer[47] Tommaso—in whom I trust—please do whatever you think would be for the greater honor of God."[48] This testament shows that Catherine knew her writings were important for "the greater honor of God." In other words, she saw her letter writing as part of her God-given vocation.

Did Catherine Learn to Read and Write?

Much has been written about whether Catherine eventually learned to read and write, and the historical sources can be ambiguous. For instance, Raymond of Capua, her mentor, confessor, and eventually her hagiographer, does not focus on these questions; indeed, he does not cover Catherine's epistolary mission, though supported and guided by him. This is in line with his view of female holiness and his goal of producing a story that would lead to Catherine's canonization. Based on available scholarship and hagiographical testimony, I suggest that Catherine gradually learned to read in her late teens, most likely taught by her literate fellow *mantellate*.

As to her ability to write, Catherine herself ascribed this ability to a miracle close to the end of her life. She felt God gave her the gift

Introduction

of writing so she could have a release valve for the intensity of feelings and insights that were the fruit of her mystical experience. This account about learning to write comes at the end of Letter 272 (included in this volume), written when Catherine was twenty-nine years old. There are a number of interpretations from literature and history regarding this personal account.[49] From the perspective of spirituality, my interpretation is that Catherine's literate female companions and her very close male scribes had made efforts to teach her to write. She then had an exceptional mystical experience that empowered what she had learned so that she was able to take up a quill and form words that flowed into paragraphs in order to express the intensity of her mystical experience. In any case, as Suzanne Noffke summarizes, "Still, if she ever wrote any of her letters in her own hand (a few rubrics attest that she did), none of these have come down to us."[50] The central issue is that she intended her words to be sent out in writing as discussed above.

2. THE LETTERS: NUMBERING, DATING, CONSTRUCTION

Letter Manuscripts and Dating

There are 383 letters included in Antonio Volpato's critical edition.[51] Of those, twelve were written prior to 1374 (when Catherine was twenty-five). Most were written between 1375 and 1379. Only five were written in 1380 prior to her death at the end of April;[52] thus, Catherine dictated 366 letters in four years.[53] The bulk of Catherine's epistolary ministry, then, occurred during the last five years of her short life, and featured a mature expression of her wisdom and her theological and ecclesiological formation.

When reading Catherine's letters, it is important to keep in mind that they were dictated,[54] some while she was in ecstasy, and may have been dictated at great speed; indeed, those supporting her holiness for purposes of canonization reported that sometimes she dictated more than one letter at a time.[55] This would clearly affect the style of her letters, which include very long sentences, at times difficult to unravel, and that had to be trimmed in order to create a readable English rendition.

Catherine had a number of different scribes, which raises the question of fidelity to her actual words. Her earliest scribes were her fellow *mantellate* who could read and write, with the bulk of her letters dictated to male scribes who were also disciples and followers. The most frequent scribes were Neri di Landoccio Pagliaresi and Stefano Maconi, young Sienese men of prominent families, and Barduccio di Piero Canigiani, a Florentine layman who was by Catherine's side during the last months of her life.[56] Scholars concur that Catherine's scribes edited her words, for instance changing very specifically Sienese terms or spelling; they added and modified conjunctions to make her argument clearer; they added more precise biblical citations. At times they may have changed the order of her dictated ideas. There is evidence they may have censored sentences considered problematic, such as references to the crusade.[57] However, there is no evidence that Catherine's scribes inserted their own ideas or edited Catherine's words to create different meaning.[58]

Catherine's letters were copied many times to create collections for particular people or purposes.[59] One of the earliest significant collection was made by one of her disciples, the Sienese Dominican friar, Caffarini (Tommaso d'Antonio da Siena), for the purpose of promoting the cause of her canonization. Caffarini highlighted the variety of her correspondents and the depth of her doctrinal wisdom.[60] Many other collections were made during medieval times, with 350 letters collected by 1500. In 1721 Girolamo Gigli[61] published a printed collection of 373 letters, which became the major source of Catherine's letters until the nineteenth century. At that time, Robert Fawtier[62] and Eugenio Dupré Theseider[63] began the task of creating a critical text. Dupré Theseider only completed eighty-eight letters before his death, and it was his work that was taken over and completed in recent times by Antonio Volpato.[64] The translations in this volume are based on this critical edition. A multidisciplinary group of scholars under the direction of the Istituto italiano per il medio evo (ISIME) is currently working on a new critical edition of the *Letters*. The first seventy-six were published as this manuscript was

Introduction

completed.[65] See appendix 1 for a description of this effort and its relevance for this work.

Scholarship of the letters has included not only careful examination regarding consistent authorship by Catherine but has also addressed debates regarding the authenticity of parts of Catherine's letters, some of which are quite important, such as the postscript to Letter 272, which describes her mystical experience about learning to write. The conclusion of such scholarship is that, overall, the content of Catherine's letters—as we have them today in Volpato's critical edition—represents her intended teaching.[66]

Numbering. The letters were not numbered in any particular order until Gigli (1721) assigned numbers to his collection. In 1860 there was a complete edition of the letters numbered differently by Niccolò Tommaseo;[67] this numbering is used by Volpato in his critical edition and followed in this translation.[68] Dupré Theseider gave his own numbering to the eighty-eight letters of his critical edition.[69]

Dating. A few letters were dated in the foundational manuscripts. Fawtier and Dupré Theseider proposed dates for an additional small number. In the letters annotated in Volpato's critical edition to date (October 2023), he comments on dates based on Dupré Theseider's work, noting a couple of variations from the latter. It was Suzanne Noffke who dated all of Catherine's letters in her comprehensive English translation found in the four volumes published between 2000 and 2008. Noffke, whose doctorate was in linguistics, argued for a linguistic methodology in dating the letters, emphasizing that her method yielded a relative, approximate chronology which she further refined through textual-historical analyses.[70] I find Noffke's work persuasive and thorough.[71] Accordingly, the letters in this volume are organized in historical order within each chapter, using Noffke's dating. Where available, Volpato's dates will be included.[72] ISIME's dating is discussed in appendix 1.

English translations. There are no English translations in print. Noffke's four-volume translation is based on her direct work with key manuscripts, Dupré Theseider's notes,[73] and a few letters available to her from Volpato's critical work, because the complete critical edition was not yet available. Noffke's edition presents the letters in historical order with an introduction to each letter, including important historical context. Each volume contains valuable appendices. Volume 1 includes a detailed listing and description of all manuscripts of the letters and four appendices with data related to the linguistic methodology for the dating of the letters. All volumes offer a bibliography and an appendix with a list of major correspondents including brief biographical information about each. The introductions to the letters in this work rely in great part on this biographical data.[74] Volume 4 has a guide to the 383 letters in numerical order so the reader can identify the volume in which it is found.

Other English translations include sixty-four letters translated by Vida Dutton Scudder[75] based on Gigli's edition, and sixty letters, many abridged, appeared in a volume by Kenelm Foster and Mary John Ronayne,[76] which were translated from Dupré Theseider's edition.

Parts of the Letters

To fully appreciate and interpret Catherine's letters, it is important to understand their structure and the meaning of some of the language she repeats throughout her correspondence. The first line tells us who is the correspondent. The second line invokes Jesus and Mary; how one translates the preposition *al* in this invocation makes a statement about Catherine's spirituality. Former translations have translated the Italian *al* as "in," so this line reads, "in the name of Jesus Christ crucified and tender Mary." However, *al* actually means "to" and therefore *al nome di* literally means "to the name of,"[77] changing the line "to the name of Jesus Christ crucified and tender Mary." This interpretation expresses significant aspects of Catherine's spirituality. She is dedicating her writing to Jesus Christ crucified, evoking up front Jesus who loved us unto death, a theme that repeats itself in most of her letters, where just about every correspondent is exhorted to learn experientially about this love. Mary is always described as *dolce*, which literally means sweet—and has been previously translated as such—but which is really an expression of tenderness; accordingly in this work, *dolce* is translated as tender.[78] For Catherine had a maternal relationship with Mary, so that her spirituality involved trusting in the care and help of a tender, loving Mother.

Introduction

Thus, Catherine dedicated her letters *to* Jesus as Christ and *to* Mary as tender mother, and she did so as a deep expression of her belief in them and her gratitude for their help.

Catherine addressed her correspondents with the word *carissimo*, in its feminine, masculine, or plural forms depending on the correspondent. The Italian word-ending *-issimo* makes a term a superlative; thus, *carissimo* means "most dear." Catherine addressed all correspondents, from unknown dignitaries to family members as *carissimo*. For instance, she addressed the cardinal of Ostia as *carissimo e reverendo padre* (Letter 7) and her mother as *carissima madre* (Letter 1). *Carissimo*, then, is a formulaic word that can express respect and value, or it can express affection depending on the addressee; accordingly, it is important not to interpret "most dear" as meaning the person is particularly special to Catherine or that she has an emotional attachment to them.

Catherine addresses all her correspondents as brothers, sisters, mothers, or fathers "in Christ tender Jesus" or in "Christ Jesus." Thus, the cardinal of Ostia is "reverend father in Christ tender Jesus," and her mother is "mother in Christ Jesus." While this form of address is formulaic, it nevertheless expresses Catherine's very personal concern for each correspondent, but most of all, it asserts that her writing ministry and all her relationships—those dear to her and those to whom she wanted to minister—were all lived in Christ.

There follows another formulaic expression that exists in all her letters—with some variations in her earliest letters—namely, "I Catherine, servant and slave of the servants of Jesus Christ write...." The term *servant and slave* (and similar variations) come from Paul's letters[79] and was used by other monks, friars, and clerics. That Catherine would start her letters in this way—though she was a penitent and not a religious nor had any formal ecclesiastical role—reveals that she experienced herself as a servant of God, as did Paul, who considered himself "an apostle—sent neither by human commission nor from human authorities" (Gal 1:1). In other words, through her relationship with God, Catherine felt called directly by God to a special vocation as communicator of God's word and wanted her correspondents to know this. Antonio Volpato has asked the question, who were the servants of Jesus Christ to whom she was slave? I would summarize the answer as, all those who chose to follow Jesus Christ.[80]

Catherine then asserts that, as slave and servant, she writes "in [*nel*] his precious blood." While this was undoubtedly formulaic, as today some might end a letter with "in Jesus," I propose that this term was full of meaning for Catherine, not just a conventional formula. In *The Letters*, *The Dialogue*, and *The Prayers*, the blood of Christ[81] is a recurring theme of Catherine's communications. It is a metaphor for God's unfathomable love, for the redemptive love of God, and for the life of God in the sacraments necessary for salvation. With this expression, then, Catherine is signaling that her desires for her correspondents are rooted in her utter trust in the power of God's love.

Catherine next starts her advice and exhortation, usually expressing her desire regarding an aspect of conversion/transformation necessary for a particular task or for playing a particular role. The whole sentence then is, "I Catherine, servant and slave of the servants of Jesus Christ, write to you in his precious blood, with desire." For instance, she tells the cardinal of Ostia that she desires "to see you bound with the bond of charity, as you have been made Legate (as I have heard)" (Letter 7). To her mother, she writes with desire "to see you acquire true knowledge of yourself and of God's goodness in you. For without this true knowledge, you could not participate in the life of grace" (Letter 1). After her exhortation—the longest part of her letters—there is a much shorter part telling correspondents how they should act or what they should do, ending with, "I say no more," a formulaic way of concluding letters.

Yet, the latter formula is often not the end of the letter. Sometimes she adds greetings to people other than the correspondent and occasionally she includes a postscript. In most letters, her closing words enjoin her correspondent to observe the most important spiritual practice, namely, being conscious of the presence of God; she writes, "remain in the holy and tender love of God," followed by praise to Jesus, "tender Jesus! Jesus love!"

Introduction

Metaphors

The style of Catherine's letters is difficult for contemporary sensibilities for a number of reasons. Besides the historical and cultural differences between Catherine's world and—in this case—an Anglophone twenty-first century world, her communication is about experience of God and of reality from the perspective of God's love learned through mystical experience. And mystical experience is ultimately ineffable and therefore very difficult to render in words. Besides, since Catherine's goal was exhortation and formation, she wanted to cause an affective impact; she wished to stir and move her readers. It was not her goal to offer linear, logical wisdom, nor mystical knowledge based on formal philosophical and theological training, as did Bonaventure or Bernard of Clairvaux. Rather, with her passionate and intense personality, formed orally and lacking a formal education, Catherine expressed herself in long, intricate sentences with the hyperbole more typical of emotional expression in Latin languages. "In Catherine's writings passages of emotional intensity, doctrinal persuasion and eloquent exhortation at times alternate and at times are intertwined; but ultimately, they become fused together and an overall harmony prevails."[82]

Catherine was endowed with an imagination worthy of a poet, so many letters are filled with metaphors that can render her meaning quite convoluted. At times metaphors are so interlaced that one must pause to use one's imagination in order to unravel her teaching. She uses a number of rhetorical tools, most likely spontaneously. For instance, in the middle of an exhortation to the correspondent she will start addressing God, or she changes pronouns within a sentence from that of the correspondent to "we," thus suddenly including herself in the exhortation. The following paragraphs illustrate some of these characteristics.

> My dearest mother, we should act like a child who, wanting milk, takes the breast of his mother, placing it in his mouth so that he takes in milk through her flesh. We should act in this same way if we want to feed our soul. We

should attach ourselves to the breast of Christ crucified, in whom is the mother of love, and through his flesh we take in the milk that feeds our soul and its children the virtues. (Letter 86)

In this passage from a letter to an abbess, we see an example of intricate, overlapping metaphors. Catherine highlights that a child seeks the breast out of hunger and attaches herself to the breast, which means that the child is fed through the physical reality of her mother. Similarly, we should long for closeness to Jesus, where longing is the "hunger"; physical attachment evokes an intimate connection that can be experienced in concrete, human ways. That is, Jesus is a real person from whom we receive real nourishment, namely, love. The metaphor then becomes intertwined with another. Catherine tells us *in* Jesus is the mother of love. That is, milk/love obtained from Jesus is mother of those human qualities through which love is actualized. Thus, the milk or love we receive from Jesus makes possible the actualization of the virtues, which are the children of their mother, love.

In the next passage Catherine uses the metaphors of fire and heat interlaced with Christ's blood. We also see one of her unique rhetorical moves: in the middle of an exhortation, she starts addressing God, Jesus, or another character of the letter and, as here, putting words in that character's mouth. In other words, she uses a brief dialogue with God, Mary, or a saint to dramatize and thus emphasize one of her points.

Oh fire [God's love] that burns but does not consume!...This was the true heat that cooked the spotless Lamb on the wood of the most holy cross. Oh hardened, unjust hearts! How could you keep from being dissolved by such heat!... The saints raced to spread this blood, for they were not blinded by selfish self-love but were saturated in the knowledge of God's goodness and in the fire of his passionate love; like Lorenzo who could speak to the tyrant while standing on the grate from which emerged an overwhelming fire. So, Lorenzo, is the fire not hot enough? He

Introduction

would answer, "No, for the fire within is so hot that it puts out the outer fire." (Letter 134)

Fire is one of Catherine's most common metaphors for God's love. That it burns but does not consume suggests it is purifying and transforming but respects the identity and freedom of the person. Jesus "cooked" by the "true heat" of love offers a jarring image of Jesus giving his life as a result of love. How could someone's heart not soften and surrender, and want to receive God's love after recognizing the enormity of God's love in Jesus? In the midst of this metaphor-laden exhortation Catherine brings up St. Lawrence, martyr, who died by fire, and she starts a dialogue to emphasize her teaching. She plays with the contrast between a material fire that burns and destroys and the inner fire of love. Even though real fire can destroy, it is not as powerful as love, the inner fire, which is so powerful that it makes us capable of giving our own life in imitation of Jesus.

As can be glimpsed through these examples, the reader of Catherine's letters must stop and imagine the picture she paints with words in order to unravel the full meaning of some of her metaphors. In this respect, Catherine's words are not only exhortatory and instructive, but her metaphors can serve as images for contemplation and prayer. Was she conscious of offering images for prayer? Given that her own prayer included imagination and inner, pictorial dialogues with God, I suggest she is likely to have had such a goal in mind.

3. ESSENTIAL CONCEPTS OF CATHERINE'S SPIRITUALITY

This section offers a summary of the core themes of Catherine's spirituality[83] so that the reader of a particular letter can fit the wisdom presented there into Catherine's overall teaching. This teaching must be culled from all *The Letters* and *The Dialogue*, as she did not write in a systematic manner. The fullness of her thought on any given theme can be best understood through knitting together the metaphors and bits of wisdom shared with her multiple correspondents. Getting the full picture of Catherine's view about any theme is like looking at a multifaceted crystal; the whole is made up of different facets. Thus, facets of her wisdom found in certain letters would be one side of the crystal, while another set of letters would offer another facet or side of the same crystal. As stated in part 1, historical texts involve interpretation, and since Catherine's wisdom is not organized in one place in a systematic manner, there are a number of ways of organizing and presenting the ensemble of her spirituality. The presentation below is one possible approach.

Knowledge of God and Self

The fundamental concept in Catherine's spirituality is love. Following Augustinian and patristic theological anthropology common in medieval times—rooted in Scripture (Gen 1:26, 2 Cor 3:18 and 4:4, 1 Cor 11:7 and 15:49)—Catherine asserts that persons are made in the image of God, created out of love, for love.[84] Accordingly, the foundational goal of the spiritual journey is recognizing this reality at the level of one's deepest self, with one's emotions and spirit; and having recognized this reality, committing oneself to acquiring knowledge of God and self, thus enabling our transformation into our created capacity for love and relationship with God. All the rest of Catherine's wisdom flows from these core beliefs.[85]

Accordingly, a central and foundational dynamic of any spiritual journey involves acquiring knowledge of self, meaning knowledge of one's vulnerability to live short of one's calling as image of God, and knowledge of God, which is knowledge of God's merciful transforming love needed to empower and make possible our vocation as images.[86]

Knowledge of Self: Selfish Self-Love

Acquiring knowledge of self means learning that we are self-centered and that *we-are-not*. Self-centeredness or, as Catherine would say, selfish self-love, distorts the intended image of God that we are meant to be. Because of selfish self-love we are incapable of perceiving reality in terms of the common good and the good of the

Introduction

other, whoever that other may be—family member, neighbor, one's community, coworkers, or the earth. Selfish self-love means that if the good of the other is not perceived, then it is never sought. *Without recognizing our self-centeredness, we are unable to know that we are seeing and acting without love.* Thus, self-centeredness—or the view of reality and others through the lens of one's own interests without regard for others—is, for Catherine, the root of all sin and disorder because it prevents the person from seeing and acting with the eyes of love. Given these beliefs, Catherine almost always exhorts her correspondents to come to recognize selfish self-love and to allow God's love to transform it.

In *The Letters* Catherine often refers to her own sinfulness and she writes frequently and at times intensely about the sinfulness of her correspondents; this can seem contradictory with her doctrine about love. This is, however, congruent with her profound recognition—knowledge of self—that human persons are self-centered without God's grace and that overcoming human vulnerability to self-centeredness requires God's love—that is, knowledge of God.[87]

Knowledge of Self: *We-Are-Not*

Because we owe our being to God-Creator in whose image we are made, Catherine affirms that self-knowledge also involves the deep-seated recognition that *we-are-not*, and *God-is*; these expressions are her way of communicating the meaning she intuited about the Exodus text, "God said to Moses, 'I AM WHO I AM'" (Exod 3:14). Catherine's formulation undoubtedly comes from her mystical experience through which she intuited how much human beings need God to actualize who they are meant to be; she had a profound experiential comprehension of how much we need God simply to *be and become.*[88] Accordingly, Catherine frequently reminds her correspondents that knowledge that *we-are-not* and *God-is* is foundational to motivating a desire to change, to become transformed through a relationship with God and experience of God's love.

CATHERINE OF SIENA

Knowledge of God: God Is Infinite Abyss, Angelic Food

By knowledge of God Catherine most fundamentally means felt recognition that God is love and the ground of being (GOD IS), which we need in order to actualize our potential and be transformed. Such affective, deep recognition will motivate us from our deepest core to connect intentionally with God. In other words, the felt or affective knowledge that we need God whose love holds us in being creates the condition for conscious reception of God's love.

The full meaning of "knowledge of God" comes through Catherine's countless metaphors and rhetorical moves. For instance, knowledge of God is like coming to know an infinite abyss; that is, God's love is immeasurable and ineffable and can be discovered only through the practice of connection to God, "in the cell of the heart and soul. In this dwelling we will acquire life-giving treasure, that is, the blessed abyss of knowledge of God and self" (Letter 30). God's love is also "angelic food."

> "What is this angelic food?" My response is that it is God's desire, a desire that dwells in the *affetto* of the soul[89] and draws our desire to him so that the two desires become one [God's desire for us and our desire for God]. This is the food that makes the soul angelic, and the food is called "angelic" because the soul is able to taste God in his essence. (Letter 26)

Knowing God as "angelic food" means coming to the felt recognition that God actually desires to be in a relationship with us and to be known by us "in his essence." Such knowledge should motivate us in those spiritual practices that lead to ever deeper relationship with God. It is in that connection with God, Catherine intuits mystically, that God's desire for us and our desire for God unite. This union of desires is transforming so that, over time, we also become "angelic," that is, capable of love or care for the good of the other.

Introduction

Knowledge of God: The Cross

Knowledge of God's love also implies a profound appreciation that such love involves self-emptying, a radical giving of self for the good of the other in imitation of Jesus's giving his life for us. Such knowledge allows us to learn that loving others will involve a giving of self and at times an acceptance of suffering. This theme is repeated frequently in Catherine's letters. It is captured in the following metaphor about the tree of the cross being planted in the cell of the soul, meaning that consciousness of Jesus's self-giving love must be a central, permanent dimension of our knowledge of God.

> Make sure that the tree of the Holy Cross is always planted and standing straight in the cell of your soul. For from this tree you will harvest the fruit of obedience, patience and deep humility. You will die to selfish self-love; you will acquire a reputation for being a lover of souls. (Letter 52)

The Cell

Knowledge of God and self is acquired through connection with one's inner self, with attentiveness to the state of consciousness where we can tune in to our core, where the transcendent is experienced. Such experience requires time and space devoted to solitude, silence, and introspection, a practice Catherine learned early in her time of silence and solitude while living as a "hermit" in her parents' home. Catherine's metaphor for this experience was that of spending time in the inner cell. Knowing that the room of nuns and friars was called a cell, she considered her bedroom—and she had her own bedroom—her cell. This was the physical cell, and the inner space for encounter with God was the inner cell. In the inner cell, one could "hear" or inwardly perceive God's presence, communication, and inspiration.

Catherine uses a variety of metaphors for this concept of inner cell. At times it is the cell of self-knowledge, the house of self-knowledge, the cell of the soul, the cell of the side of Christ, and other word pairings. All of these terms refer with small nuances to the fundamental dynamic of spending time in silence, with consciousness focused inward, connecting to God's presence within.

In Catherine's letters, one encounters repeated exhortations to spend time in the cell. Indeed, as Catherine tells us in the first paragraph of *The Dialogue*, becoming accustomed to dwelling in the inner cell, that is, regularly taking time for such introspective inner experience, is a basic first step in the spiritual journey.[90]

Through a number of metaphors, we glimpse various facets of the way Catherine envisions time in the cell.[91] For instance, in a particularly rich passage, Catherine encourages Costanza, a nun, to

> focus on your bed, where you find rest. You should act in a similar manner when you reach the cell of self-knowledge where I want you to open the eye of understanding through affective love. Enter the cell and go to bed, where you will find God's benevolent goodness, which is within you, cell. (Letter 73)

Catherine is saying: "Notice that you seek your bed in order to rest; in a similar manner seek rest in inward consciousness, taking in God's love for you and learning about yourself through the lens of God's love." When Catherine tells Costanza that God "is within you, cell," she is communicating that the core of our being, the soul, is a dwelling place or space where God resides, a space we should "enter" to encounter God. In other letters Catherine exhorts her correspondents to spend time in the cell of the soul, a metaphor with a meaning similar to the foregoing.

Two Cells in One

Catherine underlines the importance of recognizing our sinfulness and need for God simultaneously with experiencing God's love. She tells Costanza, "I would like you to be aware of your negligence

Introduction

and ignorance and that *you-are-not*, but I do not want you to experience this because of darkness and disturbance; I want you to learn this through God's infinite goodness, which is within you" (Letter 73). In other words, knowledge of self and God are two sides of the same coin that are transformative when experienced together. Catherine highlights this through the metaphor of two cells in one, which she describes to Alessa, her friend and fellow *mantellata*.

> [These two forms of knowledge] give you two cells in one; when you dwell in one of these it is important for you to dwell in the other at the same time so that the soul does not become arrogant and muddled [spiritually disoriented]. If you dwell [only] in knowledge of yourself, you will become muddled, and if you dwell only in knowledge of God, you will become proud. So the two forms of knowledge should season each other and form a whole. In this way you will reach perfection. (Letter 49)

Through other metaphors and in direct exhortation, Catherine repeatedly advises spending time in the inner cell in order to learn about God and self, emphasizing that these two forms of knowledge must be experienced together in order to be effectively transforming.

Affetto, Desire, the Three Powers of the Soul

There are three interrelated concepts—the meaning of which is not obvious to twenty-first-century readers—which are frequently used by Catherine when exhorting to knowledge of God and self. These are desire, *affetto*[92] and the three powers of the soul. These concepts are part of Catherine's theological anthropology, which, as already stated, held that persons are created in the image of God; this means that by virtue of creation persons have a capacity for love and are created to be in relationship with the God of love. Accordingly, human persons inherently possess a drive toward God, a desire for God that might be summarized in Augustine of Hippo's well-known phrase that we are restless until we rest in God.[93] Desire, in Catherine's teaching, refers to this foundational drive to connect to God, to experience and know God, a desire that arises in the depth of our being.

Affetto. Catherine often interchanged desire for God with the word *affetto*, a term that appears in over half of her letters with multiple but crucial connotations for her wisdom regarding the spiritual journey. I will use this term in its original Italian as it cannot be translated by a single English word. (See Notes on Translation). *Affetto* most often means the motivation emerging from the core of a person's identity and being that, when ordered, moves toward God and the good. In other words, *affetto* originates in the human capacity for the transcendent, in Catherine's words, from the soul of the person. At the same time, given the belief that God is present by order of creation in the core identity (soul) of the person, *affetto* can also refer to God's love dwelling within us reaching out to our *affetto* or capacity for God. In many medieval texts *affetto* indicated the movements of the heart, which referred to all dimensions of one's being, including moral sensitivity, depth of feeling, and capacity to connect to God. At times Catherine referred to this connotation, which overlaps with the foregoing description.

Though created in the image of God, persons are vulnerable to sin, that is, to living contrary to our God-given identity. Thus, Catherine also used *affetto* to indicate disordered desire; that is, when the movement of our affectivity is directed toward that which is not in harmony with the law of love. We see in *The Letters* that Catherine frequently exhorts her correspondents to the transformation of *affetto*, meaning allowing God to transform the motivation that emerges from the core of our being.

Three powers of the soul. This term refers to the trinitarian structure of the human mind that makes possible relationship with God. Augustine of Hippo was one of the early Christian writers who argued that if persons are created in the image of God, then the trinitarian reality of God would be reflected in the spiritual capacities of persons. The mind, or human consciousness, the faculty through which God is encountered, is composed of memory, understanding, and will.[94] This conceptualization about the human person continued to influence the formulation of spirituality throughout medieval times and became one of Catherine's core beliefs.

Introduction

Memory refers to the capacity to be conscious of God. Such capacity allows persons to recognize God, because some part of their being has always known God, their creator. Memory also makes possible holding in awareness all the graces received from God. **Understanding**, which Catherine sometimes called the *eye* of understanding, enables recognition of who God is, both through experience of God's presence and through reflection on Scripture and on other sources that—with the infusion of grace—impart wisdom about God and reality in terms of God. Adding the metaphor of *eye*, Catherine emphasizes that understanding has to do with the capacity to see and to recognize what is of God. In other words, through understanding persons are capable of graced internalization of what is learned about God through formation and information. It is this faculty of consciousness that can recognize what is true and just in God's eyes and therefore a central power of the soul for discernment.

The **will** is much more than that which the contemporary connotation suggests. Will, as one of the powers of the soul, involves the capacity to choose and act moved by memory and understanding, where understanding has been empowered and motivated by desire and *affetto*. Catherine sometimes uses *affetto* to mean will in order to emphasize that she is talking about a capacity to act enabled by a deep knowledge of God and the related motivation to act out of this knowledge.

Catherine's wisdom about the three powers of the soul does not reflect a philosophical position, as in Augustine. In Catherine's case, the three powers of the soul are metaphors to express Catherine's intuitive mystical experience about who God is, who persons are in relationship to God, and how these conceptualizations help imagine and live out a spiritual journey. In *The Dialogue* she summarizes her wisdom about the three powers in words ascribed to Christ. "For I gave them memory to hold on to my blessings, and understanding to see and know the truth, and will to love me, eternal Truth, once understanding has known me."[95] In the passage below, she tells the mother of one of her male followers to spend time in the cell, using memory and understanding to know herself and God's immeasurable love; this will enable her to discern and act according to God's love and will.

My dearest mother in Christ tender Jesus, I want you to follow this advice. I want you to love God's goodness within you and his boundless love, which you will find in the cell of self-knowledge. In this cell you will find God, who as God holds within all that has being; and therefore, within yourself you will find memory, which is made to hold and holds the treasure of God's blessings. There you will find understanding, which makes possible our sharing in the wisdom of the Son of God, knowing and comprehending his will and realizing that he wants only our sanctification. (Letter 241)

In the following passage *affetto* is used to mean "will," to highlight that will is that part of consciousness empowered by the depth of desire. The will acts according to the law of love to the extent that, through knowledge of God and self, selfish self-love has been transformed, allowing the eye of understanding to see clearly. "Once love removes selfish self-love, the eye [of understanding] remains clear and sees well, and so it is important that *affetto* wake up and desire to love its benefactor [God]" (Letter 51).

In the next passage we see an example of Catherine's multifaceted use of *affetto* and desire. First, *affetto* is the depth of our motivation, affectivity, and desire; then, further in the passage, *affetto* means will, that is, the choice to love God.

So, we need to raise our *affetto* and desire with true knowledge of ourselves, and to open the eye of understanding, learning to know God's goodness within us, the immeasurable love he has for us. As the understanding comes to see and know this, it becomes impossible for *affetto* not to love, and for memory not to hold her benefactor in consciousness. (Letter 182)

Growth in Virtue

For Catherine, living out our capacity to love occurs through the practice of virtue; thus, the theme of growth in virtue, a common

Introduction

medieval theme, also appears throughout her letters. While Catherine would undoubtedly say that allowing ourselves to be transformed into our capacity to love will result in moral living, her reference to the virtues was not an articulation of a moral theology, but rather an exhortation to order one's life so that one becomes capable of love, that is, to give of oneself for the good of the other.[96] For instance, in the following passage (already cited), Catherine advises, "We should attach ourselves to the breast of Christ crucified, in whom is the mother of love, and through his flesh we take in the milk that feeds our soul and its children the virtues" (Letter 86). In another passage, she tells an abbot,

> How tender is this mother, who is love! Is there any virtue that she does not encompass? No….Love is a mother who conceives in her soul the virtues as offspring which she bears to benefit her fellow human beings for the honor of God. Her wet nurse is authentic, deep humility….Because of this self-knowledge her soul is humble….through this self-knowledge she feeds the fire of divine love. (Letter 33)

Humility. Humility is a central virtue in Catherine's spirituality—in line with medieval spirituality—where humility has the connotation of knowing the truth about ourselves, both that we need God and that we are created in the image of God. Most centrally, humility involves recognizing that without grace we cannot overcome our vulnerability to selfish self-love. It does not usually have a connotation of effacing ourselves before others (while occasionally it can have this latter meaning).

Patience is another central virtue because it allows us to bear suffering, disappointment, and persecution for the sake of the good of others and to further our spiritual growth. Patience, thus, involves the capacity to accept the cross. It is a capacity to "bear with" central to love. These themes can be seen in an exhortation to a merchant struggling due to losses in his life.

> With desire to see you rooted in true holy patience; otherwise, we would be unable to please God…which is why we

need patience, this glorious virtue. Since God is one who receives holy desires, he will give us this gentle, true virtue (patience) so that we can bear every difficulty with true, holy patience. When patience is acquired out of love and with the light of holy faith, you will be rewarded with the fruits of all your efforts. (Letter 13)

Catherine clarifies for her correspondent the importance of the virtue of patience and how it is acquired through faith, that is, trust in God's transforming love. Patience allows acceptance of the cross when it must be carried. In addition, patience allows discernment of God's providence and the ability to live in congruence with such providence.

Other Significant Themes in Catherine's Spirituality

Truth

Catherine's wisdom, as has been said, is intuitive and mystical and is expressed in a literary manner so that key themes are interrelated in a nonsystematic way; accordingly, one could highlight her perspective on the essential thrust of the spiritual life in more than one way. While I have highlighted love as the core motif and overarching theme of the spiritual journey in Catherine's teaching, others highlight truth as central to her spirituality—in keeping with truth as a charism of the Dominican tradition.[97] Indeed, Raymond of Capua in his hagiography, which influenced most interpretations of Catherine into our own century, argued that Catherine centrally elaborated a doctrine about the truth.[98] Whether you highlight love or truth is to an extent a matter of interpretation. Raymond, McDermott, and Cavallini, all Dominicans, may be influenced by their religious charism. While, in this introduction, I cannot fully make the argument for the centrality of love, I suggest that for Catherine, truth is an inherent dimension of love. Her anthropology, as we saw, asserts that we are created out of love and for love. While God is centrally love, God is also truth; love shines a light upon real-

Introduction

ity so that truth is revealed. Thus, that which persons see with the eyes of love, love ordered in God, will be true. For Catherine, the relationship of love and truth is highlighted in the first paragraph of *The Dialogue*:

> Deeply stirred with a most intense desire for the honor of God and the salvation of souls, a person has applied herself for a period of time to practicing the virtues. She has lived in and become accustomed to the cell of self-knowledge in order to better know God's goodness within herself. *For from knowledge follows love, and loving, she seeks to live and clothe herself in truth.*[99]

This foundational first paragraph of *The Dialogue* encapsulates Catherine's teaching.[100] She asserts the importance of spending time in the cell to acquire knowledge of God and self in order to be transformed in capacity to love; transformed through love, the person will then be "clothed" in truth and live truth. This interrelationship between truth and love will be found repeatedly in the letters.

Continuous Prayer

This term has biblical roots (Luke 18:1; 1 Thess 5:17) and was most developed in the monastic tradition. It literally meant "remembering God" but also refers to a way of being in life related to a life of prayer and transformation. The monk became capable of continuous prayer when he was easily able to tune in to God's presence. Such a capacity developed through a journey of transformation, so that continuous prayer also involved living according to God's love.

Catherine's wisdom follows the aforementioned monastic wisdom. She teaches that continuous prayer is not just a form of prayer, but also a way of perceiving and acting, a way of living consciously out of a desire to follow God and bring about God's kingdom.[101] This becomes possible as one acquires a facility for turning one's consciousness to God and to respond to God's guidance in living a life of self-giving and care for the good of the world, the environment, our fellow human beings, our families, and ourselves. In other words, continuous prayer is not just a form of prayer; it involves a transformed way of being in life, living according to God's law of love. Catherine tells us,

> One [form of prayer] is continuous prayer, to which all persons are obligated. This is the true, holy desire grounded in charity toward God and our fellow human beings such that all actions toward our neighbors are done in God's honor.... This is the prayer to which the glorious apostle Paul invites us when he tells us to pray without ceasing. (Letter 154)

Obedience

For Catherine obedience was centrally related to transformation so that many of her letters exhorted her correspondents to living this virtue. She understood obedience according to a prevalent theology articulated by Aquinas, which asserted that obedience to the superior in religious life was necessary for salvation; one of the signs the religious was advancing toward perfection was the capacity to practice obedience above and beyond the essence of the rule of the religious order.[102] Reflecting this conviction, Catherine teaches that obedience, whether in religious life or outside it, is a necessary aspect of a commitment to live according to God's love.

This is the case because Aquinas's theology and the related medieval beliefs were based on a particular interpretation of Jesus's salvific role. That is, Jesus obeyed God in accepting death on the cross for our salvation. Accordingly, obedience is an imitation of a central choice Jesus lived and one that was crucial for our redemption. We must keep in mind this theological interpretation when some of Catherine's passages about obedience seem extreme or jarring to our contemporary sensibilities.

Discernment

Catherine elaborated her teaching on discernment starting from the perspective of the monastic *discretio* tradition about the ordering of the virtues so that the right-ordered behavior is rendered

Introduction

to God, neighbor, and self. Catherine conflated this tradition with teaching about the transformation of the three powers of the soul so that the person is able to see, desire, and choose according to God's will. Ultimately, discernment in Catherine goes back to the transformation that ensues from knowledge of God and self, so that as the person is transformed, she is able to perceive and act with a heart and mind congruent to a greater or lesser extent with God's law of love.[103]

1

NUNS

LETTER 73

To Sister Costanza, nun at Sant'Abbondio Monastery near Siena
February to early May 1376 (Noffke); between mid-1375 and mid-1376 (Volpato)

Introduction

Costanza is one of a number of religious women and men to whom Catherine offered spiritual advice. That she was sought out despite her youth and even though she held no role of spiritual authority reveals Catherine's reputation for holiness and wisdom.

This letter offers an example of the richness of Catherine's teaching through metaphors that appeal to our affectivity and invite contemplation in order to fully grasp the message. Christ's blood, as symbol of his self-giving love,[1] is a primary theme. Catherine offers here two significant metaphors that elucidate her teaching on knowing the immensity of God's love and on the inner cell. The blood as love is also interlaced with love as fire; through this rhetorical move doubling down on symbolism, Catherine emphasizes the power of that love. As blood, love is like wine that makes us drunk (in this case a positive image), and as fire, it consumes self-centeredness. The fire of love also consumes the "fire" of fear; love as fire heals fires that harm. The blood is also love that heals and protects us from self-deceit.

The other complex metaphor is that of a bed, as the place where Costanza should rest in inner quiet and contemplation. On this bed can be found a table, an unlikely metaphor for the Father, but it is also the place where the Father, Son, and Holy Spirit gather to minister to us. The bed is covered with a red bedspread, meaning a bedspread soaked in the blood (God's love), thus tying together the metaphors of blood and bed.

❊ ❊ ❊

To the name of Jesus Christ crucified and tender Mary.

Dearest daughter in Christ Jesus, I, Catherine, servant and slave of the servants of Jesus Christ, write to you and wish you strength through his precious blood, with desire to see you submerged and bathed in this precious blood of the Son of God, since in bringing to mind[2] the blood we encounter the fire of most ardent charity.

Love leaves no room for sadness or confusion, and therefore I desire that the desire and motivation emerging from your core [*affetto*][3] be grounded in the blood. The blood will make you drunk; it will burn and consume all your selfish self-love; in so doing the fire of his [Christ's] love will douse the fire of fear and selfish self-love. Why is there fire in the blood? Because the blood was offered out of a most passionate fire of love.

Oh glorious and precious blood, you are a balm and cleansing fluid for our wounds! Truly, my daughter, He is a cleansing fluid, a bath where you will find the warmth, the water, and the place where fire is found. I tell you, in this glorious bath you will find the warmth of divine charity given out of love; you will find the fluid, blood, from which flows the fluid of grace; you will find the eternal Godhead, the place where the Word was also from the beginning; and you will find the wall that holds the place.[4] Oh infinite, benevolent Charity, you have taken on the wall (container) of our humanity, containing the ultimate, eternal, exalted Godhead—God and man; this is such a perfect union that nothing can separate it, not even death. There is such delight, refreshment, and consolation in the blood! For in the blood is found the fire of divine love and the virtue of the ultimate, high, eternal Godhead. For you know that the power of the blood of the immaculate Lamb is due to the divine essence. Know that if he [Jesus] had been only a man, without union with God, his blood would have had no power. However, because of the union God formed with man, God received the sacrifice of his blood. And so this glorious blood is a perfumed ointment that cancels the stench of our iniquity.[5]

He [Jesus] is a light that lifts the darkness, not so much the great outer darkness of mortal sin, but the darkness of disordered inner trouble that many times afflicts the soul under the semblance and guise of a foolish sort of humility. This inner trouble arises when thoughts surface from the heart saying, "Nothing that you do is pleasing and acceptable to God; you are damned." And as such inner trouble progresses, he [the evil one] penetrates this experience coloring it with humility and says, "You see, due to your sins, you are not worthy of grace and blessings." Thus, the person often ends up withdrawing from taking communion and from engaging in spiritual exercises. This is the sort of deception and darkness caused by the evil one.

If you, or anyone else, is submerged in the blood of the immaculate Lamb, you would be protected from such deceptions; and even if such deceptions should come to you, they will not take hold. They will be driven away by the living faith and hope you have placed in the blood. You can make a fool [of the evil one] saying, "I can accomplish anything through Christ crucified, who is within me and strengthens me. And even if I should merit hell, I will not miss out on my spiritual exercises." It would be great stupidity to allow yourself to be disturbed with threats of hell ahead of time.

And so, my dearest daughter, arise with the ardor of love and do not become confused, rather say to yourself, "What comparison can there be between my sinfulness and the abundance of the blood shed with such fiery love?" I would like you to be aware of your negligence and ignorance and that *you-are-not*, but I do not want you to experience this because of darkness and inner trouble; I want you to learn this through God's infinite goodness, which is within you. Be aware that the evil one would like nothing better than that you would only learn of your weakness without seasoning; for, knowledge of weaknesses should be seasoned with the condiment of hope in God's mercy.

You know what you should do? That which you do when you go into your cell at night to go to sleep. First you reach your cell, and once inside, you see your bed. You clearly know that you need the cell [as a space in which to sleep], but your eye and *affetto*-desire focus on your bed, where you find rest. You should act in a similar manner when you reach the cell of self-knowledge where I want you to open the eye of understating through affective love. Enter the cell and go to bed, where you will find God's benevolent goodness, which is within you, cell.[6] You will see clearly that your being was granted to you through grace and not out of obligation.

For you see, my daughter, this bed is covered with a red bedspread dyed in the blood of the sacrificed Lamb totally given for us; rest there and never leave. Notice that you have no cell without a bed nor a bed without a cell. Fatten[7] your soul on this goodness of God, because whoever is in this bed is richly fed, as this bed holds the table, the food, and the waiter; that is the Father is the table, the Son is the food, and the Holy Spirit waits on you and makes of himself a bed for you. Be aware that if you notice the bed and the table set for you without entering into knowing God in these, and instead focus on yourself while in confusion or inner trouble, you would not receive his peace and tranquility, but you would remain dry, sterile, and fruitless. And so I beg you, for the love of Christ crucified, remain in this loving, glorious bed. I am certain that if you immerse yourself in the blood, you will do it [stay in the bed]. And, therefore, I want to see you immersed and bathed in the blood of the Son of God. I say no more.

Remain in the holy and tender love of God! Place yourself on the cross with Christ crucified! Hide in the wounds of Christ crucified! Follow him in the way of the cross! Mold yourself onto Christ crucified!

Find joy in shame, sorrow, and torment, and in being scorned or treated disdainfully for the love of Christ crucified, remaining steadfast till the end of your life, always partaking of the blood that he shed on the cross!

Tender Jesus! Jesus love!

LETTER 182

To Sister Bartalomea della Seta, nun at the Monastery of Santo Stefano in Pisa
October 1377 (Noffke); February 1375 or later (ISIME)

Introduction

It is likely Catherine met Bartalomea during a visit to Pisa, but not much is known about the relationship between these two women, other than that Catherine wrote two letters to her. Accordingly, we can assume there must have been a significant enough connection between them so that either Bartalomea sought Catherine for spiritual advice or Catherine believed her spiritual advice would be particularly welcome.

This letter highlights the importance of safeguarding our capacity to love through the metaphor of a royal dress that is God's love; the royal dress is at the same time a garment of grace—another word for God's transforming love—and it is a garment of love of virtue. We recall that for Catherine the practice of virtue is the way of living out love (see general introduction). As in other letters, Catherine stresses that acting out of love will involve suffering in imitation of Jesus.

The letter also includes one facet of Catherine's wisdom about transformation of memory, understanding, and will, the three powers of the soul.

❦ ❦ ❦

To the name of Jesus Christ crucified and tender Mary.

Dearest daughter in Christ tender Jesus. I, Catherine, servant and slave of the servants of Jesus Christ, write to you in his precious blood with desire to see you clothed in royal dress, that is, in the attire of most passionate love; this is the garment that covers our nudity and hides our shame; it warms us and eliminates the cold.

I say that it covers nudity; I mean the soul created in the image and likeness of God possesses being, and without divine grace would be unable to live according to the end for which she was created. It is most important to possess the garment of grace received through holy baptism and mediated by the blood of Christ. Because of this garment, children who die as infants receive eternal life. In our case as brides who have time, if we are not clothed in the garment of love for our eternal spouse—thus experiencing his unfathomable love—we should consider that the grace received at baptism is naked. So, we need to raise the motivation emerging from our core [*affetto*] and our deepest desire with true knowledge of ourselves, and to open the eye of understanding learning to know God's goodness within us, the immeasurable love he has for us. As the understanding comes to see and know this, it becomes impossible for the will empowered by the movement of love [*affetto*][8] not to love, and for memory not to hold her benefactor in consciousness. In this way, love attracts love, and her nudity is covered.

I say shame is covered [by this garment] in two ways. One of them is that having come to abhor sin, she tossed out its shame. How has she done this? The shame experienced because of offending her Creator, led her to be restored [to grace] through the garment of love of virtue, thus participating in God's glory and becoming fruitful. For from all our actions and desires, God wants the flower of the glory, leaving the fruit to us.[9] So, you see, this covers the shame of sin.

I will tell you of another way shame is covered. That which appears shameful to our sensual self-centered love—attached to a worldly perspective—does not appear so to our will. For the latter has died to self with respect to self-centeredness and transitory [worldly] things. Indeed, the will comes to take delight in shame, torment, scorn, injustice, and false accusations; she welcomes being trodden by the world.[10] For God's honor, she takes comfort when those who are worldly persecute her with many falsehoods and insults, when the evil one persecutes her with many troubles and temptations, when the flesh tempts her to rebel against God's spirit. She considers herself undeserving of peace and serenity of mind. She is able to rejoice in all this out of loathing for self [the self-centered self] and desire to offer retribution [for her sins] in order to become conformed to Christ crucified. She is not ashamed to be scorned and mocked by these three enemies, that is, the world, the flesh, and the devil; for her sensual self-centered will is dead having been clothed with the garment of God's eternal will. Indeed, she receives these [attacks of the enemies] with due acceptance and love, recognizing that God allows this to happen out of love and not out of hate. We should receive these trials with the affection with which we recognize these trials are allowed; it is loving to desire that shame with which shame is eliminated. How blessed is the soul that has acquired this tender light, learning to loathe our [disordered] inclinations and those of others, at the same time learning to love the sorrows that we suffer due to those inclinations! I refer to the inclinations of our self-centered sensuality and to the persecutions of the world.

Consider yourself, my dearest daughter, worthy of suffering and unworthy of the blessings that come through suffering. These [troubles and suffering] will be the adornments you will place on your royal garment. You know well that the eternal Spouse did the same, that over his garment he placed his many sufferings, that is, flagellations, scorn, torments, and injustices, the last being the ignominious death on the cross.

I explained that it [the royal garment] warms us and eliminates the cold. It is warmed with the fire of passionate love, which manifests itself in consuming desire for God's honor in the salvation of others, enduring and bearing their faults. She rejoices with the servants of God who rejoice, and she weeps with sinners going through the mourning period [for having offended God]; she has compassion for their sorrow and feels bitterness for the way they offended God. She willingly endures all suffering and torment in order to help them return to being among those who rejoice because they are in love with true loving virtues.

I also explained that it [the royal garment] eliminates the cold. That is, it eliminates the cold of selfish self-love, for this love blinds the soul and prevents her from knowing herself and God and deprives her of the life of grace. Further, it [selfish self-love] generates impatience and allows the root of pride to produce shoots and branches. As a result of disordered motivation and desire [*affetto*], she offends God as well as her fellow human beings; she is unruly, always rebelling against her commitment to obedience. Selfish self-love is the cause of all this. But the true [royal] garment consumes and eliminates all of these [disorders] and makes it possible to remain in the light of divine grace.

She does not travel in darkness but travels in truth along the path of the immaculate, sacrificial Lamb; and through the door of Christ crucified, she enters into the wedding feast of the eternal Father. There she is held and rooted in God; so she has no fear that the world or the evil one or the flesh might separate her from him. There she finds life without death, fullness without distress,[11] and hunger without misery. So, no more![12] If you want to prevail until the end, move onward as though you had the back of a porter, without concern for the amount of weight you carry. It would be most unsuitable for the bride to go down a different path from that of her spouse. There is no other way to move onward except to be dressed as I have described; that is, I said I wanted to see you dressed in the royal garment of the eternal King's bottomless love. I say no more.

Hide in the side of Christ crucified! Bathe and immerse yourself in his most loving blood!

Remain in the holy and tender love of God.

Tender Jesus! Jesus love!

LETTER 26

To Sister Eugenia, her niece at the Monastery of Saint Agnes in Montepulciano
May 1379 (Noffke)

Introduction

Eugenia, Catherine's niece and a follower of her wisdom, became a nun at the monastery of St. Agnes in Montepulciano, near Siena. This letter was written about a year before Catherine's death and so reflects her mature spirituality. The goal of the letter is to encourage Eugenia to grow in a contemplative relationship with God and to focus on living a disciplined religious life.

This is a very important letter for understanding Catherine's experience and conception of union with God, which here she explains through "angelic food," a metaphor to communicate the indescribable. "Angelic food" is God's desire for connection with us; it is God's desire that persons consciously experience God's presence within them as love, a love that calls forth a response of love. Angelic food is also our desire for God. Thus "angelic food" also means the union of God's desire for us and our desire for God. As the person responds in prayer to God's love within her so that her capacity for love is united to God's love, she becomes transformed into someone living out of a constant, deep consciousness of connection to God, thus becoming more "angel like." As consciousness of the dynamic of mutual desire between God and humans becomes rooted and habitual, it results in continuous prayer, which involves acting consciously throughout the day in union with God's presence.[13]

Catherine here speaks of motivation arising from one's core (*affetto*) and the desire of the soul. Through these constructs she captures the insight that desire is a movement that emerges from the core of self, capable of love; this desire seeks union and closeness to that which is loved. In the core of the person both the person's own God-given desire and God's desire meet. This mystical insight is based on Catherine's anthropology, namely, that God's love dwells within each person, holding us in being, and this indwelling love draws persons toward God.

Catherine has no systematic teaching about types of prayer or progression in prayer. This letter is one of the few places where she speaks of progression in prayer and distinguishes between verbal prayer and mental prayer, which includes a form of complete absorption in God.

"Angelic food" is intertwined with another significant metaphor—one that appears in several letters—namely, that of the cross as a table set on high. This metaphor points us to reception of the Eucharist—food, saving blood—as an experience of union with Jesus. Such contemplation is a food eaten on the table of the cross, where the cross is at the same time a metaphor for our own experiences of limitation, need, and suffering.

❈ ❈ ❈

To the name of Jesus Christ crucified and tender Mary.

Dearest daughter in Christ, tender Jesus. I, Catherine, slave of the servants of Jesus Christ, write to you in his precious blood, with desire to see you savor angelic food. You are made for nothing else; that is, God ransomed you with the blood of his only son so that you might taste this food.

But consider, dearest daughter, that this food is not eaten on the ground but up high. And so the Son of God sought to be raised on high, onto the wood of the most holy cross, so that we would savor this food at this elevated table. You might ask, "what is this angelic food?" My response is that it is God's desire, a desire that dwells in the *affetto* of the soul[14] and draws our desire to him so that the two desires become one [God's desire for us and our desire for him]. While we are pilgrims in this life, this is a food[15] that draws toward it the fragrance of the virtues, which are stewed on the fire of divine love and are eaten on the table of the cross. This means virtue is acquired with effort and hard work, rejecting one's selfish sensuality, and with force and

Nuns

violence cutting off the reign of self-centeredness from one's soul. For one's soul is called "heaven" because God dwells within it through grace. This is the food that makes the soul angelic, and the food is called "angelic" because the soul is able to taste God in his essence when she separates from the body.[16]

This food fills and satisfies the soul so that nothing else is appetizing, nor can she desire anything other than that which allows this food to be preserved and increased; she loathes anything that goes against this goal. Since she is prudent, she gazes through the light of most holy faith, for this light is the eye of understanding[17] that is able to see [discern] that which is harmful and that which is beneficial. Depending on this discernment she loves or disparages. And so, she rejects her selfish sensuality—and all vices that flow from such disordered sensuality—and holds these tied up under the feet of the will [*affetto*]. She [the soul] takes flight from all occasions that could lead her to vice or that hinder perfection. And so, she drowns her self-centered will, the cause of all sinfulness, and places it under the yoke of holy obedience. This obedience is not only rendered to her religious order or superior, but also to the least important, if it is for the sake of God. She takes flight from all worldly glory and pleasure, and only glories in the burdens and sorrows of Christ crucified, such as insults, scorn, torments, and injustices; these are as milk to her, finding joy in being conformed to her spouse, Christ crucified. She renounces interchanges with others, when she sees how often these can present a barrier between us and our Creator; instead, she flees to her physical cell and her spiritual cell.

I invite you and the others to live as just described, and I order you, my beloved daughter, to always live in the house of self-knowledge—where we find the angelic food of God's consuming desire for us—and in the physical cell, holding vigils with humble faith and continuous prayer, stripping your heart and deepest desires [*affetto*] of all creatures so it is only clothed in Christ crucified. Otherwise, you would be eating on the ground, where I already told you we should not eat. Remember that your spouse, Christ tender Jesus, does not want a barrier between you and him; he is very jealous so that if he notices that you love apart from him, he would immediately leave you; and then you would become worthy of eating food for animals.[18]

Would you not be an animal and your acts food for animals, if you left the Creator for his creatures? If you left infinite goodness for fleeting things that pass by like the wind? If you left light for darkness or life for death? If you left that which clothes you with the sun of justice, the clasp of obedience, the bright light[19] of living faith, firm hope, and perfect charity, for that which strips you of all these? Would you not have to be really stupid to abandon that which offers you perfect chastity (for the more you get close to him, the more he perfects your chastity) for those things that often have the fragrance of the refuse that contaminates your mind and body? May God, in his infinite mercy, distance all this from you.

So that nothing may come between you and God, be attentive so that your troubles don't become so burdensome that they lead you to exclusive conversations[20] with laypersons or other religious; no matter with whom [this should happen] mind that if I were to learn of it and if I weren't as far away as I am, I would give you such a reprimand that you would remember it for your whole life. Be attentive to not give or receive things except when absolutely necessary. [In giving] assess equally the need of persons inside and outside [the monastery]. Remain firm and mature. Serve the sisters with love and with great alacrity, especially those that are in need.

When guests come and ask you to come to the grille,[21] remain in peace and don't go. These guests can tell the prioress whatever they want to say to you; you can, of course, go if told to do so by the prioress, in which case you should bow your head and remain as unsociable as a hedgehog.[22] Keep in mind the attitudes that the glorious virgin saint Agnes required of her daughters. Go there [to the grille] for confession, say what you need and then leave quickly, as soon as you receive the penance. Make sure the confessor is not someone with whom you were raised. Don't be surprised by my saying all this, since you may have heard me say more than once something that is very true, namely, that conversations with pious men and women who use negative and immoral language can do harm to the soul and to the practices and observances of religious life.

Make sure you don't allow your heart to be attached to anything or anyone other than Christ crucified, otherwise, when you want to break the attachment, it will be very hard to do so. I tell you that the soul that has tasted angelic food will have seen with the light [of understanding], that all I have described and more, is an impediment to consuming this food, and so she [the soul] very diligently avoids these hindrances. She loves and seeks that which helps her increase and preserve this food; she has seen that she is best able to taste this food through prayer made while conscious of knowledge of self; and so, she continuously seeks to pursue all those practices that lead her to get closer to God.

There are three forms of prayer. One is continuous prayer, which is continuous holy desire, a desire that prays to God in all that one does; for this desire offers for his glory all spiritual and corporal acts, which is why it is called continuous. It seems this is the prayer about which the glorious saint Paul spoke when he said, "pray without ceasing" (1 Thess 5:17). The second is verbal prayer, when one recites the Office or other [set] prayers; this is a form of prayer geared to lead into the third, which is mental prayer. The soul reaches this level when she engages in verbal prayer with humility and prudence, which means that while speaking with her tongue, she does not let her heart wander away from God. Instead, she should find the way to pause and focus her heart on *affetto* of divine love.[23] When she becomes aware that her consciousness is visited by God—when she is in any way led to be present to her Creator—she should abandon verbal prayer and focus her mind with her deepest desire united to God [*affetto* of love] on whatever God has placed in her consciousness. Afterward, when such an experience ends and if she has time, she can take up verbal prayer again, so that her consciousness is always filled and does not remain empty.

In prayer there are always many forms of struggles, and times of darkness and much confusion (through which the evil one wants to make us think that our prayer is not pleasing to God due to the many struggles and experiences of darkness). You must not stop praying because of these experiences; with strength and perseverance you should remain firm, aware of the wiles of the evil one to separate us from the mother of prayer.[24] God allows these experiences to test the strength and constancy of the soul and to lead her to learn through the struggles and darkness that *she-is-not*. In the ability of her will to be able to persevere, she experiences the goodness of God who is the giver and preserver of any ordered and holy will; a gift that is not denied to any who ask for it.

In this way she reaches mental prayer, the third and last form of prayer in which she receives the benefits of the struggles she endured during imperfect vocal prayer. She tastes the milk of faithful prayer; she is lifted up above her ordinary consciousness, which is above the sensual self, and with angelic consciousness she becomes united to God in *affetto* of love, and with the light of understanding she sees and recognizes truth and clothes herself in it. Thus, she becomes the sister of angels. She sits with her Spouse at the table of crucified desire, finding joy in seeking the honor of God and the salvation of souls, which she fully recognizes is the reason the eternal Spouse raced to his appalling death on the cross, thus fulfilling his obedience to the Father and obtaining our salvation. Truly this prayer is a mother that conceives virtue through God's love, and it gives birth to these virtues in the form of love for her fellow human beings.

Where do you exercise faith, hope, love, and humility? In prayer. For who would focus on seeking what they don't love? The person who loves always seeks to be united to that which she loves, that is, with God through prayer. Ask him for all you need; for through self-knowledge—the foundation of authentic prayer—you recognize your great need. You are aware that you are harassed by your enemies, namely, by that which is worldly when its pleasures come to mind, by the evil one with his many temptations, and by the strong rebellion of your flesh and the way it contests the Spirit.

You recognize that *you-are-not* and therefore you cannot help yourself, so with faith you run to *He-who-IS* [Exod 3:14]; for it is he [God] who knows of all your needs and has the desire and power to fulfill them; with hope ask for and expect his assistance. Prayer should be made with this desire to receive what you expect. When you pray in this manner, nothing you request, if just, will ever be denied by the divine Goodness. If you pray in some other manner, you will receive little.

Where will you experience the fragrance of obedience? In prayer. Where will you strip yourself of the selfish self-love that makes you impatient with suffering, injustice, or other suffering? Where can you dress yourself in the divine love that will make you patient and able to glory in the cross of Christ crucified? In prayer. Where will you experience the fragrance of chastity and the hunger for martyrdom, making you ready to give your life for God's honor and the salvation of souls? In this tender mother of prayer. She [the mother of prayer] will lead you to live an ordered life. She will seal in your heart and mind the three solemn vows you made at your profession and leave within you the desire to observe these until you die.

She [the mother of prayer] removes you from interchanges with others and bestows upon you conversation with your Creator. She fills the receptacle of your heart with the blood of the humble Lamb, and she covers it with fire, for the blood was shed out of fire of love. The soul welcomes this mother of prayer more or less perfectly depending on how much the soul nourishes herself on angelic food[25]—which is the true, holy desire for God—and rises up to partake of this food on the table of the holy cross. So, I told you I wanted to see you nourish yourself on angelic food, because I saw no other way for you to be a true bride of Jesus Christ, consecrated to him in holy religious life. Make sure you act so that I can see you as a precious stone before God. And don't waste time. Bathe and drench yourself in the loving blood of your Spouse! I say no more.

Remain in the holy and tender love of God.

Tender Jesus! Jesus love!

CATHERINE OF SIENA

LETTER 86

To the Abbess of the Monastery of Santa Maria delli Scalzi in Florence
September–November 1379

Introduction

 It is unclear how Catherine knew this abbess, whether she met her in person or if one of her trusted followers asked her to intervene. Catherine advised the abbess on how to be a good leader for her nuns. In this effort she uses a significant metaphor, namely, that of suckling at a mother's breast, and in this case, the breasts that offer the milk of transforming love are those of Christ. Catherine explicitly challenges her correspondent to see the humanity of Christ, God as human person offering a love that nourishes in the unique, primary manner in which mother milk nourishes an infant. While Catherine often conveys her teaching by appealing to the image of blood and its connection to Jesus's brutal death, here God's saving love through Jesus is the tender offer of milk taken in through suckling at the breast. Yet even as Catherine offers this tender image for God's offer of love, she reminds her correspondent that reception of God's transforming love leads to willingness to suffer as did Jesus. The metaphor of suckling at the breast also highlights the motherly role Catherine envisions for the religious superior, the abbess. She first needs to be transformed by attachment to God's love so that she can be a mother who feeds love and justice to her nuns.

 Another significant theme of this letter is that of continuous prayer, a biblical concept found in Paul. Continuous prayer involves the capacity to often become conscious of God's presence throughout the day and is also a way of being in life. Catherine's multifaceted wisdom on continuous prayer is discussed in the general introduction.

❋ ❋ ❋

Nuns

To the name of Jesus Christ crucified and tender Mary

Dearest mother in Christ tender Jesus. I, Catherine, servant and slave of the servants of Jesus Christ, write to you in his precious blood with desire to see you grounded in true charity so that you can nourish your sheep and be a true leader to them.

It is clear that we cannot feed others if we don't first feed our soul with true, authentic virtues; and one cannot be fed with virtue if one is not attached to the breast of divine love, for from this love one obtains the milk of divine tenderness. My dearest mother, we should act like a child who, needing milk, takes the breast of its mother, placing it in his mouth so that it takes in milk through her flesh. We should act in this same way if we want to feed our soul. We should attach ourselves to the breast of Christ crucified, in whom is the mother of love, and through his flesh we take in the milk that feeds our soul and its children the virtues; that is, [we are fed] through the humanity of Christ—who descended into human form and endured suffering—not through the divinity.

We cannot feed ourselves with this milk—obtained from the mother of love—without struggles, and these struggles occur in many forms. Sometimes through severe struggles due to the evil one or other persons; or suffering ensues due to many persecutions, false accusations, torments, and vile deeds. These struggles are true sufferings, yet not really painful for the soul that has attached herself to the nourishment of the tender, glorious breast from which flows love; [suffering is not really painful to the soul] who sees in Christ crucified the ineffable love God has revealed in his tender, loving Word. And through this love the soul has acquired loathing of her faults and of the perverse law within her that opposes the Spirit. In addition to other suffering experienced by the soul that has developed hunger and desire for God, she experiences crucified [anguished] and loving desires for the salvation of all the world. For this is what love does. It becomes ill with those who are ill, it is healthy with those who are well, it cries with those who sorrow, and is joyful with those full of joy. And she sorrows with those grieving in the state of mortal sin and rejoices with those in the state of grace.

[The person who lives out of this love] has attached herself to the flesh[26] of Christ crucified and through suffering carries the cross with him. This is not a suffering that torments and dries up the soul, but a sorrow that fattens, finding joy in following the footsteps of Christ crucified, and thus savoring the milk of divine tenderness. How did she take in this milk? With the mouth of holy desire. Her desire for this milk is so great that even if it were possible to drink it without struggles and with it give birth to the virtues—virtues acquire life from overwhelming love—she would not accept it. Rather she chooses to take in this milk with suffering out of love for Christ crucified, because she doesn't believe that fragile persons should just stand under him who is crowned with thorns; rather they [his followers] should bear the thorns together with him, suffering as did their leader and not according to their preferences. Yet, it is the head, Christ crucified who bears the thorns. Oh how tender is this tender mother love! She[27] doesn't seek her benefit—in other words, she doesn't seek herself for her benefit but for God's! Whatever she desires and loves, she does so in him; she wants nothing that is not in him. No matter what her life situation, she [mother love] spends her time according to God's will. If she is a layperson, she wants to be perfect in this lifestyle; if she is a member of a religious order, she is a perfect angel in this earthly lifestyle, without desiring or loving anything worldly, or wanting wealth and particular possessions. For in the latter case, she would be acting against voluntary poverty, which she promised to observe in her [religious] profession.

She does not desire nor take pleasure in conversations with those who would want to get in the way of her vow of chastity. Indeed, she flees from them as though they were poisonous serpents; she accepts the protection of the grille and the parlor and avoids the familiarity of the pious.[28] As a legitimate and true spouse, she retreats to the cell, her home, and there comes to the breast of Christ crucified in vigils and in humble continuous prayer. Not only the eye of the body, but also the eye of the soul should be focused on acquiring self-knowledge, recognizing past weakness and moral fragility while seeing God's tender goodness within her and the ineffable love with which she is loved by the Creator. The virtue of humility is a product of this self-knowledge, as is overwhelming desire, which is that continuous prayer that Paul taught, saying that we should pray without ceasing [1 Tim 5:17]. [Such] holy desire is followed by good, holy actions; the person who prays without ceasing does not cease to act with goodness.

In the cell she makes a home with the eternal Spouse, embracing whatever sufferings and humiliations are allowed by God; she disdains the pleasures, honor, and status of the world, drowning out her own inadequate will, focusing on obedience to Christ crucified who through obedience to the Father and for our salvation ran to the shameful death on the Cross. Through Christ's obedience she is made obedient.[29] In this way she keeps the third vow, that of obedience; she is never obstinate about being obedient, nor does she question the will of whoever is in charge, but she simply observes obedience. This is the way a truly obedient person behaves, while the disobedient person wants to question and to know the why and wherefore of an order. Such a person is not observant of the Order but a violator of it. The obedient person holds obedience before her as a mirror and would choose death rather than violate it and so is a perfect disciple [of the Order].

If she must govern, she will be perfect in the role of authority given that she first feeds her soul at the breast of Christ crucified. If she has been a good disciple and is then called to govern, she would then be good at feeding her daughters. In her shines the bright light of justice and she exudes the perfume of honesty, offering her daughters an example of a holy, honest life. And since love cannot exist without justice—the soul is just to the extent that she justly possesses love—she renders to each what she is owed,[30] and to herself she renders disappointment with herself and loathing [of her selfish self-love]. With *affetto* of love she renders to God praise and glory to his name. She renders kindness to her neighbors, loving them and serving them in whatever way she can. To those under her she renders what each needs according to their situation. In the case of the perfect, she helps them to further build up their virtue. To the imperfect she dispenses more or less severe correction and punishment according to their capacity to tolerate these and depending on the severity of the fault. But she never leaves faults unpunished, for with love and not out of displeasure, she wants to punish their faults in this life and not wait until these are punished in the life to come.

Imagine what would happen if she had not fed her soul—as explained—she would not be filled with the bright light of justice but would lead her life with much injustice. She would act as a thief taking what is God's and giving it to herself, and she would act in similar fashion with what belongs to her neighbor. She would love her neighbors only because of their usefulness to her. She would govern her daughters only according to her pleasure and creaturely preferences; and to avoid displeasing them, she would pretend not to see their faults. If she called attention to their faults just verbally, she would do it superficially rather than in a heartfelt manner with a firm heart; and because her life is not ordered she would inspire servile fear[31] and her correction would not be heeded.

And so, I see no option but to attach yourself to the breast of Christ crucified; for as I said, this is the way to take in the milk of divine charity, making this your foundation. So, considering that there is no other solution or remedy, I told you that I wanted to see you rooted in true, perfect charity. I beg you, then, for the love of Christ crucified, to act in this way so that you govern your sheep while giving example of a good and holy life. In this way the sheep that are out of the sheepfold of virtue will return to their sheepfold. Encourage them to spend time in the cell and pull them away from chitchatting; make them arrive promptly in the choir and refectory as a community and not individually. If you do not use your authority with justice, God will call you to account, and you will have to take responsibility not only for your faults but also for theirs. And so, dearest mother, don't stay asleep but arise from the slumber of negligence. I say no more.

Remain in the holy and tender love of God.

Gentle Jesus! Jesus love!

2
MANTELLATE AND CLOSE LAY MALE DISCIPLES

LETTER 99

To Neri di Landoccio when he was at Asciano
Lent 1372 (Noffke and Volpato)

Introduction

Neri di Landoccio Pagliaresi was a nobleman and poet from Florence who moved to Siena and there held various public offices. He is an example of the highly placed single men who were attracted to Catherine's teaching and became her followers and assistants. In 1372, Neri officially sought to become one of Catherine's followers and soon became one of her scribes. He was one of those who collected and disseminated Catherine's letters after her death. He ended his life as a hermit.

In this letter, welcoming Neri as a follower, Catherine offers a summary of key aspects of her wisdom about the dynamics and goal of the spiritual journey, showing these were already worked out in 1372, two years before the beginning of her active letter writing ministry and eight years before her death. Catherine articulates the goal of the spiritual journey as becoming conformed to Christ crucified, letting go of all that is worldly, and addresses the importance of transformation away from selfish self-love through the metaphor of a knife that cuts out selfish self-love. In this letter, this dynamic is tied to the capacity for continuous memory or prayer, underscoring that as persons grow in knowledge of God and self by spending time in the cell, they become more and more capable of accessing the presence of God within.

Mantellate *and Close Lay Male Disciples*

In offering to be a "guarantor" for Neri, Catherine exemplifies her deep belief in intercessory prayer and its effectiveness for the transformation and redemption of others.

❊ ❊ ❊

To the name of Jesus Christ and tender Mary.

Very beloved and dearest brother and son in Christ Jesus. I, Catherine, servant and slave of the servants of God, write to offer you strength in the precious blood of the Son of God, with desire to see you united to Christ Jesus, transformed and conformed to him.

My most beloved son, the soul cannot become perfectly conformed to Christ unless she becomes detached from conforming to that which is worldly. For what is worldly is contrary to God and God is the opposite of what is worldly; they do not conform to each other. It is truly the case that he who was God and Man chose perfect poverty, insults, scorn, torments, injustice, hunger, and thirst; he did not value human honors or glory. He always sought the Father's glory and our salvation, always persevering with true, perfect patience. In him there was no pride but rather perfect humility.

Oh boundless, loving charity! You are certainly opposed to what is worldly![1] The worldly seek glory, honors, and amusements; they suffer pride, impatience, avarice, hatred, resentment, and selfish self-love. All this fills their constricted heart so there is no room to give of self to others for God's sake. Oh how deceived are those foolish persons that have become conformed to this evil world! They want honors but are insulted. They want riches but experience poverty because they do not seek true riches. They want happiness and pleasures but experience sadness and bitterness because they are devoid of God who is ultimate happiness. They do not want death or bitterness, yet they succumb to death and bitterness. They want strength and stability, yet they distance themselves from the living stone. So you see, dearest son, what a great gulf there is between Christ and what is worldly.

Recognizing that what is worldly has no correspondence to Christ, the true servants of God assiduously take care to not conform in any way to what is worldly. Instead, they loathe and dislike it, coming to love what God loves and becoming enemies of what God loathes. Their only desire is to become conformed with Christ crucified, submerged in and in love with true virtue and following always in his footsteps. They choose for themselves that which they see Christ chose for himself; in return, having chosen poverty and disdain they will always be honored; they will have peace, love, joy, happiness, fullness of consolation, and they will not suffer sadness. I am not surprised by this choice for they are transformed and conformed to the ultimate eternal truth and goodness of God, where all goodness resides and where true holy desires are fulfilled.

It is best, then, to follow him [Christ] and to free and cut yourself off from this sorry life. Pure love of God together with the knife of dislike for and loathing of selfish self-love will cut you off. I tell you, my dearest son, this knife and the loathing [of selfish self-love] would not be available to you without continuously keeping God in mind;[2] especially continuously keeping in mind the abundance of blood with which the Son of God bathed us. For with abundant fire of passionate love, he made himself vulnerable, letting himself be sacrificed on the wood of the holy cross. Here[3] you will acquire the knife of loathing [of selfish self-love] because Christ died out of abhorrence for and sorrow for sin. Love holds Christ on the cross, for as the saints said, neither the wood of the cross nor the nails would hold him if it were not for the bonds of divine charity. I want your eye of understanding[4] to be always focused on watching this [truth], for this shall lead you to discover and fall in love with true virtue; you shall thus acquire such perseverance that no person nor the evil one will be able to separate you from virtue and the related will to be submissive and to give yourself to persons with true, perfect humility for God's sake. When you are present to the blood,[5] the world and all its works will seem boring and repugnant. You will come to consume and relish souls[6] who are the food of the servants of God. I advise you and beg you always to delight in such food. If you think you are failing, do not relent, for God pays more attention to our good will than to our failures. For I tell you, our soul is purified through love of neighbor for God's sake.

To purify your soul well, help friar Bartalomeo as much as you can while he is there; remove him from the power of the evil one. If I could go and help you, I would gladly do it; however, it does not seem to be God's will. For now, there is little time so we will do what God permits. Know, my brother that what I can't do while present, I do spiritually.[7]

You asked me to receive you as a son.[8] Though [I am] unworthy, and inadequately inadequate,[9] I have already received you, and I receive you now with affectionate love. I commit myself now and in the future to be a guarantor for you before God, for your sins of the past and future.[10] However, I beg that you fulfill my desire to conform yourself to Christ crucified, removing yourself from involvement with worldly ways, as I described above. Unless you do so, you cannot be conformed with Christ. Please, please do clothe yourself in Christ crucified, for he is the wedding garment[11] that will fill you with grace in this life and will then place you before the table of everlasting life to eat with those who truly savor food. I say no more.

Remain in the holy love of God. Bless and offer strength in Christ Jesus to friars Bartalomeo and Simone.

LETTER 132

To monna Giovanna di Capo, monna Giovanna di Francesco, monna Cecca di Chimento, monna Caterina dello Spedaluccio, and other *mantellate* of Saint Dominic in Siena
December 1375 (Noffke); November 1375 (Volpato)

Introduction

This brief letter gives us insight into Catherine's care for her fellow *mantellate*. She had come to identify herself as their "mother" (addressed by her followers as *mamma*) and had taken on the ministry and responsibility of spiritual guide for those who were part of her "family," as her followers referred to those who were close disciples. Catherine took on this role as guide even though the *mantellate* had a Dominican friar assigned as mentor. This reveals that Catherine had acquired a reputation for holiness and great authority among her followers. Her sharing with fellow *mantellate* about the progress of ecclesiastical policy for which she was advocating indicates the unique role she had in being privy to such policy.

Indicating that she writes for support and encouragement, Catherine exhorts the *mantellate* to growth in detachment from their own will so that they can respond speedily to God's will and teaches them that progress in the virtue of patience is central to the acceptance of God's providence.

❈ ❈ ❈

To the name of Jesus Christ crucified and tender Mary.

To you my most beloved and cherished daughters in Christ Jesus. I, Catherine, servant and slave of the servants of Jesus Christ, and your mother in Christ's love and in God's love within us that unites to our capacity to love [*affetto*], write to comfort you in the precious blood of the son of God, who was the meek, immaculate Lamb. He shed his blood not due to the force of the nails or the lance, but due to the power of the immeasurable love he had for his creature.

Oh, love of our God, love beyond words! Oh most benevolent love, you have taught me and demonstrated [your wisdom] with more than words, for you say you are not pleased with many words; you say rather that you are pleased with the acts you expect from your servants. What is it that you have taught me, uncreated Love? You have taught me that as a patient lamb I should endure not just harsh words, but also harsh blows, insults, and affronts. Through this you wish me to be spotless and innocent, that is, that I would not harm any of my brothers or fellow human beings; this applies not just to those who do not mistreat us, but also to those who abuse us; you want us to pray for such

Mantellate *and Close Lay Male Disciples*

persons as if though they were special friends who offer us good, abundant benefits. And you want us to be patient not only with respect to insults and temporal harm, but also with regard to all that is contrary to our will; and so imitating you who wanted your Father's will to be done and not your own. How could we, then, raise our head against God's goodness, desiring that our distorted will should be done rather than God's will?

Oh Jesus, most benevolent love! Make it possible for your will to be always done, as it is always done in heaven by your angels and saints. My beloved daughters in Christ, this is the docility that our Savior wishes to find in us; that with a fully peaceful and tranquil heart we should be content with everything he arranges and works in our lives, accepting not our views of time and place, but God's. And so, the soul devoid of its own will and clothed in God's will is very pleasing to God. She is like a steed galloping off, rushing most speedily from grace to grace and virtue to virtue, having nothing to stop her race; for she has cut herself off from every disordered appetite and desire for her own will. For these appetites and desires are the attachments that halt the race forward of spiritual persons.

All that relates to the Pilgrimage [crusade] continues to make progress, and God's honor grows every day. Constantly strengthen yourselves in virtue and prepare the ships of your soul as our time is coming.[12] Please encourage Francesca and send her blessings on my behalf and that of Jesus Christ. And tell her to be diligent so that when I return, I will find that she has grown in virtue. I send comfort and blessings to all my sons and daughters in Christ.

The ambassador of the queen of Cyprus came today and reported on various matters before proceeding to see the Holy Father, Christ on earth,[13] to discuss the crusade. The Holy Father has also sent envoys to Genova to request that they be ready for the Pilgrimage.[14]

May our loving Savior give you his eternal blessing!
Remain in the tender love of God!
Tender Jesus, Jesus love!

CATHERINE OF SIENA

LETTER 125

To monna Nera, prioress of the Saint Dominic *mantellate*[15]
when Catherine was at Rocca d'Agnolino
September–October 1377 (Noffke)

Introduction

Catherine states that the purpose of her letter is to exhort the prioress of the Siena *mantellate*—Catherine's penitential group—to be a good shepherdess to her sheep. Even though the prioress of the Siena *mantellate* was someone with greater official authority than Catherine and certainly much older than she, Catherine minces no words in telling this woman that she must guard against self-centeredness, or she will not be able to offer authentic guidance and form her "sheep" into persons who practice virtue. Catherine also offers practical wisdom for the effective spiritual direction of others, offering a spirituality for this ministry.

This letter provides another instance of the detailed authority Catherine assumed over persons older and with greater authority than she, showing the confidence in her own wisdom that reveals her experience of God's guidance of her own life.

❊ ❊ ❊

To the name of Jesus Christ and tender Mary.

Dearest mother in loving Christ Jesus. I, Catherine, servant and slave of the servants of Jesus Christ, write to you in his precious blood, with desire to see you act as did the Good Shepherd who gave his life for his sheep. Dearest mother, you should occupy yourself in attending to the honor of God and the salvation of the sheep that He has placed in your hands. Avoid negligence, as in that case you would be scolded by God. Instead, diligently attend to [your sheep], letting go of all selfish self-love and concern for the opinions of others. Keep in mind, dearest mother, that the superior who acts with selfish self-love will fear to admonish others. If he[16] does admonish them, he does so following creaturely wisdom; when he doesn't like their behaviors, he often admonishes them irrespective of the truth and according to his own point of view. This would be unjust rather than just and is not the way to proceed, for God leads his servants through diverse paths and ways. And so, those under us should not be admonished according to our views but according to their faults. We should limit ourselves to seeing that they desire to follow Christ crucified. We should gently lift our deepest desire and motivation [*affetto*] toward God's honor and open the eye of understanding[17] with regard to those in our care, so that each is cared for according to their need. There should be one approach toward the less perfect and another toward the more perfect. It is important to understand the needs of each, while always admonishing their faults when you see these, making sure that nothing keeps you from such admonition. I trust in God's unlimited love that you will carry this out.

Open the eye of understanding and contemplate the love [*affetto*] of the spotless Lamb, bound and nailed to the cross; you will then grasp that this true teacher has given his life for his sheep. You will grasp with what love and affection he relates to us, tolerating and bearing with us poor sinners, always attentive to the honor of the Father and to our salvation. Our lack of gratitude, our complaints, and the malice of the evil one never prevent this Lamb—who is in love with us—from perfectly pursuing our salvation and the Father's honor. I trust, most beloved mother, that through his goodness you likewise will not be deterred due to our lack of gratitude—that of your daughters and of all our group. Nor will you be deterred due to human gossip or the malice that the evil one places in the mouths of those who say what they shouldn't in order to foil God's honor and the salvation of souls. And so, carry out all that you can, and overcome all these problems without any fear. May your understanding and will [*affetto*] never veer from the truth so that you may desire only that God be honored and that your daughters be mirrors of virtue.

CATHERINE OF SIENA

In this way God will fulfill your desire, and you will receive consolation both from within yourself and from your daughters, as joy and consolation are always experienced when we see others practice virtue. And so, for the love of Jesus Christ crucified follow this advice. I say no more.

Remain in the holy and tender love of God!
Tender Jesus! Jesus love!

LETTER 214

To Caterina dello Spedaluccio and Giovanna di Capo
November–December 1377 (Noffke)

Introduction

Giovanna, a member of the gentry, was a frequent companion on Catherine's travels and functioned as an early scribe. Catherine was particularly close friends with both Giovanna and Caterina, so in this letter she allows her feelings and authentic vulnerability (as opposed to her rhetoric about humility) to come through in a more dramatic manner than usual.

The announced purpose of the missive is to urge greater patience and humility, two critical virtues in living love. Catherine underscores the importance of transformation in order to bear suffering with patience, yet she reveals that her own patience is sorely tried. She was distraught about the sinfulness of pastors and leaders of the church, expressing this feeling in language that is extremely dramatic. "I die though I live, and I ask my Creator to take my life," crying out that despite her prayers God is not responding, and the offenses against God are too painful to bear. Further on she cries out, pained that her sins are part of the cause of so much sin against God. While we cannot with certainty interpret her experience, the dramatic rhetoric of a Latin culture and language are undoubtedly at play; at the same time, these extreme expressions may correspond to our saying "I am dying of hunger" or "I'm so mad I could kill him." Both expressions emphasize the intensity of an experience but are

Mantellate *and Close Lay Male Disciples*

not meant literally. This being said, clearly Catherine does, in her love for God and the church, feel deep pain for sin, for disordered behavior that displeases God. When she speaks of the virtue of patience in the context of this distress, she is also speaking to herself and of her experience. Patience involves bearing with suffering. Humility in this context refers to knowledge that all of us are sinful and that sinfulness—going against what is ordered in God—results in the suffering of the church and of the people of God.

As mentioned in the general introduction, Catherine acquired a reputation for compassionate but effective ministry to persons who had been leading disordered lives. This letter gives us a glimpse into this ministry as she reaches out to Andrea through Caterina and Giovanna.

❋ ❋ ❋

To the name of Jesus Christ crucified and tender Mary.

Dearest daughters in Christ, loving Jesus. I, Catherine, servant and slave of the servants of Jesus Christ, write to you in his precious blood, with desire to see you grounded in true patience and deep humility so that you are able to follow the loving and spotless Lamb; for without patience and humility you would not be able to follow him.

The time has come, my daughters, to unequivocally show—yes or no—if we are virtuous and if we are children [of the Lamb]! It is important that patiently and with true humility we bear with persecutions, false accusations, and gossip, avoiding scandal, impatience, and conflicts rooted in pride. Keep in mind the wisdom you have been taught, that you should find in the cross the food for the honor of God and the salvation of souls; you should act upon this with true, holy patience.

Oh my beloved daughters! On behalf of loving First Truth, I invite you to forgo the slumber of negligence and selfish self-love, instead offering humble, continuous prayers and vigils. Do so out of true knowledge of yourselves. For the world perishes due to the many sins and affronts against the beloved Spouse of

Christ.[18] Let's, then, give honor to God and toil on behalf of our fellow human beings.

Oh my! May neither you nor the other servants of God prevent you from enduring with tears and laments,[19] for there is no other way to forebear God's anger, which we can see coming toward us. Alas unfortunate me! I believe, my daughters, that I am that wretched person, the cause of so many ills because of my lack of gratitude and the other faults I have committed against my creator.[20]

Oh my! Oh my! Who is this God that is being offended by his creatures? He is ultimate and eternal Goodness, who out of love created persons in his image and likeness. After we fell into sin, he created us anew into a state of grace through the blood of the spotless, loving Lamb, his only Son. And who are those thoughtless, mercenary persons who offend this Creator? It is we who do not exist for ourselves because made by God, and we who on our own [without God] are filled with wretchedness. It can seem that we only seek to offend God or one another in contempt for our Creator.

With our sinful eyes we observe as the blood[21] is persecuted in God's holy Church; even as this blood has given us life. Our hearts should burst with concerned and pained desire; it would be better to let life flow out of us, to die rather than to see such offense against God. I die though I live, and I ask my Creator to take my life, but he does not heed me! I would prefer to die than to live and see so much destruction among Christian peoples! We must take up the weapons of holy prayer, for I see no other remedy. The time for the persecution of God's people has come, so it is important that they go into the cave[22] of knowledge of God and self, begging his mercy through the merits of the blood of his Son. My daughters, I say no more, for if I were to continue speaking as I feel, I would never rest until God takes me from this life.

I now address you, Andrea.[23] The crown of glory is never received by those who start out, but by those who persevere unto death. My daughter, you have begun to place your hands on the plow of virtue, leaving behind the sickness of mortal sin.

Mantellate *and Close Lay Male Disciples*

It is important that you persevere in order to harvest the fruit of your efforts. Those efforts are made by your soul seeking to block your youth from speeding toward the evil one. Oh, my daughter, have you not considered that you were part of evil, slumbering in the rot of sin? And that God, having mercy on so much wretchedness, rescued you from this fate in both body and soul? You should not disregard this or lack in gratitude, for you would risk the evil one catching you and returning more strongly than before bringing [with him] seven companions.[24] When you keep in mind[25] [God's mercy] and show gratitude, you will be strong in the battles against the Evil one, against the world and against the flesh that tempts you, and you will persevere in virtue.

My daughter, if you wish to avoid these temptations, grab on to the holy cross with your body, engaging in vigils, in prayer and fasting. Let your desire bathe in the blood of Christ crucified so that you might gain the life of grace and accomplish God's will; and you will also fulfill my desire which is that you be a true servant of Christ crucified. I pray that you leave childhood behind and become the spouse of Christ, who has restored you through his blood. Nevertheless, if you would prefer the world [marriage], you must wait until it can be arranged in such a way that it can be for your good and God's honor.

Be submissive and obedient unto death, and follow the wishes of Caterina and Giovanna, for I know they will advise you and guide you only according to God's honor and the well-being of your soul and body. Not following this advice will be of little benefit to you and I would be much displeased. I trust that through God's goodness you will choose what will give him honor, as well as benefit you, and this will bring me great consolation.

And you, Caterina and Giovanna, may you work unto death toward God's honor and her salvation.

Beloved daughters, it is a time of struggles, yet these should bring us consolation through Christ crucified. I say no more.

Remain in the holy, tender love of God!

Tender Jesus! Jesus love!

CATHERINE OF SIENA

LETTER 49

To monna Alessa
October or November 1377 (Noffke); after Spring 1374 (ISIME)

Introduction

Alessa dei Saracini, a fellow *mantellata* and a member of Siena's gentry, became an early friend and remained one of Catherine's most significant friends. She was a companion on many of Catherine's travels and was instrumental in teaching Catherine to read and perhaps the basics of writing, as well as being an early scribe. After her father's death, Catherine and her mother spent time in the home of Alessa and her family.

This letter has at its center Catherine's wisdom about discretion or discernment as right ordered measure, wisdom developed more at length in Letter 213. See also the introduction to that letter for further discussion of this wisdom which has to do with living according to the right ordered measure. God, however, must be loved without measure, while moderation in the love of friends and neighbors is most important for a spiritual journey. In the light of living an ordered life, Catherine gives practical advice about living day to day, emphasizing the importance of time for silence and solitude. This letter features Catherine's creative metaphor of two cells in one which was developed in the general introduction.

❦ ❦ ❦

To the name of Jesus Christ crucified and tender Mary.

Dearest daughter in Christ, loving Jesus. I, your unworthy, inadequate mother,[26] desire that you reach that perfection to which God chose you. It seems to me that in order to reach this perfection, it is important to move forward both with and without moderation.

We must carry out all our actions with and without moderation. We must love God without moderation, that is, in loving him we should not be measured or restrained nor follow any rule; our love should be immeasurable. [At the same time], in order to come to love perfectly, you must order your life.[27] First, avoid pointless chatter, and instead engage in conversation only as required by charity; love a lot and chatter little.

When spending time with those you love with a spiritual love, engage in conversation with moderation. If you don't do this, be aware that you could inadvertently limit the immeasurable love you should have for God by directing your love to a finite person, putting her between you and God and thus loving this person without moderation. This would hamper your perfection, which involves loving persons spiritually, with ordered love. Be a vessel that you fill at the fountain and drink it there; that is, receive love from God, who is the fountain of living water. If you don't constantly drink this living water from him, your vessel would become empty. You will know that you are not drinking from God to the full, when you are distressed because of those whom you love; maybe due to a conversation, or because you were deprived of support you usually receive, or some other situation. If you experience sorrow about anything like this or something else (other than sorrow about offending God), take it is a sign that your love is still imperfect and that you are drinking from sources other than the fountain [of living water].

How do we make the imperfect perfect? In this way: You must correct and discipline the movements of your heart based on true knowledge of self; this includes feeling repugnance and sorrow for your imperfection, that is, recognizing you are so wicked that you offer human persons the love that you should give completely to God—which means you are loving persons without measure and God in a measured manner. And of course, love for God should be without measure and the love of persons must be measured by God's measure and not based on consolations whether temporal or spiritual. Therefore, make sure that you love everything in God and that you vehemently correct all disordered desires [*affetto*].

My daughter, create two rooms. One is your physical cell,[28] [where you should spend time] so that you don't go here and there, except as required by love or particular need or obedience to the prioress. The other room you create spiritually and always carry with you. This is the cell of the true knowledge of yourself, where you find knowledge of God's goodness within you. [These two forms of knowledge] give you two cells in one; when you dwell in one of these it is important for you to dwell in the other at the same time so that the soul does not become arrogant and muddled [spiritually disoriented]. If you dwell [only] in knowledge of yourself, you would become muddled, and if you dwell only in knowledge of God, you would become proud. So the two forms of knowledge should season each other and form a whole. In this way you will reach perfection. In knowledge of yourself you will attain repugnance for your self-centered sensuality; having acquired such distaste you will be able to sit on the chair of conscience, becoming a judge who can reason and declare due justice on your faults, not permitting them to take hold.

From this knowledge emerges the strand of humility. Humility never seeks notoriety and does not become scandalized by anything; it is patient, endures all sorrow and loss of consolation, and every offense with joy no matter the cause. Humiliations are experienced as a blessing,[29] great persecutions as a relief. The person rejoices in all, accepting them as punishments for the perverse logic of her self-centered sensuality which always rebels against God. As well these experiences mold her to Christ crucified, who is the doctrine about truth and the path to it.

Through the knowledge of God, you will find the fire of divine love. Where can you delight in this love? On the cross of the spotless Lamb, seeking his honor and the salvation of souls through constant, humble prayer. And there resides our whole perfection. There are other paths, but this is the main way through which we receive so much light that we become unable to commit faults even in minor ways. And so, my daughter, take delight in the humiliations of Christ.

Be on guard regarding what's expressed with the tongue so that it doesn't end up expressing whatever emerges from the [self-centered part of the] heart. Rather, the tongue should drain that which emerges from the heart with repugnance and dislike for self [one's self-centered desires and motivations]. Make yourself the least of the least, being pliable to all others through humility and patience. You should not make excuses for yourself but say, *mea culpa*.[30] In this way you will conquer the vice within you and also within the person you address; the virtue of humility accomplishes this.

You should order your time when keeping vigil at night since you owe your body sleep, and in the morning take time in church for loving prayer. Avoid chatting at these times. Do not turn back from this and all [recommended] practices except in case of need or obedience or the call to charity. After mealtimes, spend time alone to recollect yourself, then engage in some manual labor according to need. At vespers, don't do much; what the holy Spirit calls you to do is enough. Then return to care diligently for your aged mother and provide her with all she needs; may this be your duty until I return. Make sure you fulfill my desire. I say no more.

Remain in the tender love of God.

Tender Jesus! Jesus love!

LETTER 213

To Daniella of Orvieto, clothed in the habit of Saint Dominic
October 1378 (Noffke)

Introduction

This is one of Catherine's longest letters, sent to Daniella, a *mantellata* from Orvieto and devoted follower. It contains Catherine's most complete teaching about discernment. Until the late Middle Ages there were two traditions of discernment. One was that of *discretio spirituum*, discernment of spirits, the tradition that informs most wisdom on discernment today. The other was the tradition of *discretio*, the *virtue* of discernment that orders other virtues guiding the person to recognize what she owes and to whom. While Catherine used the language and constructs from the *discretio* tradition, she went beyond these constructs in her intuitive fashion. In general, for Catherine, discernment is the direct fruit of love, where love is the result of transformation through knowledge of God and self. This dual knowledge results in the transformation of desire, and transformed desire makes possible discernment, in that what is desired by a transformed heart will likely be congruent with God's will. Discernment is also intimately tied to Catherine's teaching about the three powers of the soul,[31] since it is the light of understanding that illuminates that which is congruent with God's love. As the person becomes more and more transformed in her capacity for love and truth as a result of her knowledge of God and self, she "sees" more and more in a manner congruent with God's love and truth. As well, discernment is a fruit of continuous prayer, that is, the capacity to be present to God. In short, Catherine's teaching about discernment is tied to all her foundational concepts about transformation.[32]

In terms of Catherine's metaphors, I highlight that of the tree of love, where discernment is one of its fruits.

❊ ❊ ❊

To the name of Jesus Christ crucified and tender Mary.

Dearest sister and daughter in Christ loving Jesus. I, Catherine, servant of Jesus Christ, write to you in his precious blood, with desire to see you living the holy virtue of discernment, which we need if we want salvation.

Why is this virtue so necessary? Because this virtue is fruit of the knowledge of God and self, the home in which it is rooted. She [discernment] is an offspring born of love. What exactly is discernment and what does it accomplish? Discernment is a light and, as I said, it is knowledge of God and self. The principal result of this virtue is that with discerning light the person is able to see what she owes and to whom and is then able to act immediately and with perfect discernment regarding what she has understood, thus giving God glory and honoring his name. All acts moved by motivation and desire from the core of self united to God [*affetto* of the soul][33] and illuminated by the light of discernment are ordered, and so God is given due honor because the acts are the fruit of discernment.

The discerning person does not act as an undiscerning thief who wishes to accrue honor for herself, seeking her own renown and pleasure; an undiscerning thief makes no effort to avoid offending God and harming her fellow human beings. If the root of the *affetto* of the soul is corrupted through lack of discernment, then all acts toward self and others are corrupted. How is this manifested? Whether these persons are religious or lay, and regardless of their state in life, the person burdens them and makes demands on them without discernment. If she advises or corrects others, she does so without discretion, burdening others as she burdens herself. The discerning person acts in the opposite manner; she is able to recognize her own need and that of others. Once she has rendered what she owes to God for his honor, she acts according to what she owes to herself, which is loathing of vice and of her self-centered sensuality, together with love of virtue—loving virtue for its own sake.

By means of the same light [of discernment] through which she gives herself her due, she gives her fellow human beings their due. Yes, I said, she renders what is due to herself and to others. She gives to her fellow human beings what they are owed, which is goodness, loving in them virtue and hating vice, and loving them because created by our supreme eternal Father. To him she renders the delight of love depending on how much she is filled with such love. So the primary effect that discernment accomplishes in the person is to shine a light that discloses what she owes and to whom and enables her to carry out what she discerns.

These are the three main branches that grow from the glorious offspring of discernment,[34] which grows out of the tree of love. These branches bear an infinite quantity of fruit, all of which are soft and exceedingly sweet. When the person picks the fruits with the hand of free will and eats them with the mouth of holy and fervent desire, they nourish the soul and produce growth in the life of grace. If led by the light of discernment, the person will benefit from these fruits irrespective of her state in life; she benefits according to her reality.

Those who live as laypersons and have this light pick the fruit of obedience to God's commandments and of distaste for that which is worldly; they are able to mentally take off their worldly clothing. If they have children, they pick the fruit of nurturing them in the fear of God. If they are lords, they pick the fruit of justice tempered with discernment, rendering to each [person under them] his due; with firm justice they reward those who act rightly and punish those who have committed offenses. A lord also picks the fruit of reason so that he does not deviate from the way of justice due to false praise or servile fear.[35] Those subject to a lord pick the fruit of obedience and respect toward their lord and avoid choices and situations that would offend him. If he [the lord] were not guided by the light, he would be unable to avoid such offenses.[36]

Those who are religious or prelates [religious superiors] pick the sweet, delectable fruit of following the rule of their order, bearing and putting up with one another's faults, putting up with embarrassments and being disliked; they accept bearing on their backs the yoke of obedience. The prelate picks hunger for the honor of God and the salvation of souls; he lives an exemplary life and casts the hook of doctrine.[37] But it would take too long to describe the many ways that all categories of persons are able to pick these fruits. There are not enough words with which to do this.

Now, dearest daughter, let's examine this in particular detail, though when describing the particular we also describe the general. What guiding norms does the virtue of discernment offer the person? It seems to me this virtue offers norms for both the body and spirit to all those who wish to pursue spiritual lives, guiding each according to their rank and state in life. But let's now speak about us in particular. We have already described the most important values that the virtue of discernment instills in the person, which is to render honor to God, to offer goodness to our fellow human beings, and to develop in ourselves loathing of vice and self-centered sensuality. The virtue of discernment orders the way in which we render love to others so that we would not risk the well-being of our soul for others; we would not offend God in order to aid our fellow human beings; no, with discernment, we avoid sin. On the other hand, with the light of discernment the person is willing to endure suffering and torments in order to save a soul—or as many souls as she can—from the snares of the evil one. She is willing to forgo material well-being in order to rescue and save her fellow human beings. This is how love acts when guided by the light of discernment; this light guides a discerning expression of love toward others. Those not guided by discernment act in the opposite manner. They do not care if they offend God, they risk the well-being of their soul to please and serve others without discernment. For instance, they give false testimony, they spend time with others in wicked and dishonorable places, and there are many other undiscerning behaviors depending on circumstances. The pride and willfulness of selfish self-love, and the blindness of not knowing God and self, are the causes of the lack of discernment just described.

Once the person's love toward others has been ordered through [the virtue of] discernment, this virtue preserves and fosters growth in love which is also continuous, humble, and faithful prayer.[38] As well, this virtue [of discernment] covers the person with the mantle of desire [*affetto*] for virtue so that the person will not be caught up by lukewarmness, negligence, or selfish self-love, either bodily or spiritually. Discernment fosters this love of virtue so that the person's will, moved by her deepest ordered motivation [*affetto*], will not be directed toward anything that could lead her astray.

Discernment also orders and regulates the body. How? I'll tell you. The soul disposed to desire God is grounded in the principles we have already described; since she is, however, housed in the body, it is important that this light [of discernment] should also illuminate the body as it is the instrument through which virtue grows or should grow. Ordering [of the body through discernment] unfolds in this way: discernment keeps the body away from the delights and amusements of the world; it distances the person from worldly conversations, directing them instead toward conversations with God's servants. Further, discernment removes the person from dissolute places and keeps her in places that are conducive to devotion. Discernment orders all parts of the body, so that all are modest and temperate. Thus, the eye should not stray but place its regard on heaven and earth. The tongue should avoid vain and idle conversations and instead should confess sin and should be ordered to announce the word of God for the good of others. The ears should avoid words that flatter and titillate and should turn away from criticisms and words that can lead astray; instead, the ears should be attentive to the word of God and voluntarily listen and pay attention to the needs of one's fellow human beings. In this same manner, discernment orders the way in which hands touch and act; the way in which feet walk. [Such ordering of the body through discernment] prevents the perverse tendency of the flesh to cause disorder in the spiritual core of the person; that is, to cause disorder to the bodily instruments of the soul. Discernment orders our body, steeping it in vigils, fasts, and other exercises aimed at keeping our body in check.

   Be careful, though, that all the above be done through the benevolent light of discernment, rather than without discernment. How does she recognize [that she is acting with discernment]? Because she does not place her principal desire [*affetto*] on a particular form of penance, and to keep from doing so, the light of discernment keeps her covered with the mantel of love and desire [*affetto*] for virtue. Penance should be an instrument, used for particular needs at particular times. So, if the body should strongly resist the spirit, then bring out the discipline and the hairshirt,[39] fast, engage in multiple genuflections and long vigils; in other words, apply strong measures to discipline the body. However, if the body is weak or ill, then discernment would guide you to act differently. So, not only should you not fast, but you should eat meat. And if eating twice a day is not enough, then eat four times a day! If such an ill person cannot stand up, then she should lie in bed; if someone cannot kneel, she should sit down or lie down depending on her need. Discernment accomplishes this sorting out, for penance is an instrument and not something to which we should be attached. Do you know why? So the person can serve God with something that isn't finite, something that cannot be taken away, namely, that which is infinite; that is, desire for God, which is infinite because it is united to God's own infinite desire. Virtue is also infinite for it cannot be taken away by the evil one, or another person, or illness—unless we consent. In illness we practice the virtue of patience; in the battles against the evil one and in facing difficulties from others we practice the virtues of fortitude and patience and enduring perseverance. And so, through adversity, God allows these and other virtues to be tested and strengthened; these [virtues] are never lost unless we acquiesce.

We should be grounded in this [discernment and virtue] and not in penance, which is finite. The soul cannot be grounded in two pillars; one or the other must crumble to the ground; one is a foundational pillar, the other an accessory. If I make physical penance my pillar, I will be building the city of my soul on sand; it will be toppled by the mildest wind, and I will be unable to build anything there. However, if I build on the pillar of virtue, grounded on the living rock, Christ, loving Jesus, then even the largest building will be solid and even the strongest wind cannot topple it. For this reason and other problems that could ensue, penance should only be used as a means to an end [not an end in itself].

I have experienced many penitents who were not patient, or obedient, or humble as they labored on denying[40] the body but not their will. This is due to lack of discernment. Do you know why this comes about? All their consolation and feelings of comfort [*affetto*] are derived from doing penance their way and not accepting other wisdom; in this way they foster their self-will. And so long as they are acting according to their own will, they experience consolation and happiness, and they can think they are filled with God, as if they had accomplished what was right. They are unaware that they are deluded, that they are becoming presumptuous, judgmental, and self-referential. That is, they begin to make the judgement that whoever does not follow their way is imperfect and on the way to damnation. Lacking in discernment, they want to evaluate everyone with the same measure, the one they use on themselves. Their self-will becomes harder than a diamond should someone try to dissuade them or break their will or need them to change. Yet, when they come up against this disordered will in times of trials or temptation or when they receive offenses, they become weaker than straw. Lack of discernment could lead one to believe that penance can control anger, impatience and other behaviors related to vices, but this is not true.

This glorious light [of discernment] lets you see that you can pull out all roots of vice and eradicate it from your soul through love of virtue and keeping death before your consciousness; through loathing and despising your sinful self and reproaching your faults. It lets you see who God is whom you have offended and who you are who offend God. On the other hand, penance can cut [the plant of vice] but leaves the root which can easily sprout again, while, as I said, the light of discernment tears out the roots. Once the roots have been removed [by discernment], vice can no longer grow in this soil unless self-will—grounded in free will—persists in planting vice.

If the body of a person suffers illness and for that reason she lets go of her asceticism, she quickly experiences tiredness, distress, and loses all joy; it will seem to her she is lost and damned. She is unable to find the consolation in prayer that she had experienced when practicing penance. Where has this consolation disappeared? In her self-will. For her practice was rooted in this will, so when she is unable to carry out what her self-will determined, she lapses into sadness and suffering. Where has your[41] hope in God's kingdom gone now that you are distressed and almost in despair? It has disappeared in attachment for penance arising in your disordered depth [*affetto*], through which you expected to obtain salvation. Since you can no longer practice penance, you feel as though you will be deprived of salvation. These [distortions] are the fruit of lack of discernment. If instead she benefitted from the light of discernment, she would see in a discerning manner that the only thing that can distance her from God is being deprived of virtue; for she has eternal life through virtue mediated by the blood of Christ.

Therefore, as I have already said, we should rise above all imperfection, placing our love, attachment [*affetto*] and desire in virtue. Words could never describe the delight and joy to be found in virtue. A person living in virtue cannot be made to suffer by others, her hope in heaven cannot be taken from her; for she has let go of her self-will regarding both worldly and spiritual matters. Rather than being grounded in penance, or in her own consolation, or in revelations, her deepest desire and motivation [*affetto*] are rooted in love of virtue and in willingness to suffer for Christ crucified. Such a person is patient and faithful; her hope is in God and not in herself or her actions. She is humble and obedient, able to trust in others and not in herself; she does not assume she is always right. She extends her arms on God's mercy,[42] thus keeping at bay doubts and a troubled mind. When going through darkness and struggles, she reaches out to the light of faith with true, deep humility. When she experiences joy, she can go within herself [to connect with God] so that she does not lapse into vain pleasures. She is strong and can persevere because she has died to the selfish self-love that made her weak and fickle.

In the light of discernment, every moment can be the right one and every place the right place. If it's her time to practice penance, it is time for joy and consolation if penance is an instrument [not an end in itself]. If she must leave penance aside due to obedience or to need, she rejoices because she never leaves behind her love [*affetto*] for virtue—her principal foundation—nor can it be taken from her. Through the light [of discernment] she has learned to deny her self-will with great persistence and tenacity. She is able to pray anywhere because she carries with her the home where God dwells through grace, and where we pray. [This home] is the house of our soul, where holy, continuous desire always prays. This desire rises as the light of understanding shines upon itself [our inner self] and upon the precious fire of love.[43] This love is evidenced in the blood,[44] shed out of overabundance of love and is contained in the vessel of our soul. You must pay attention and seek to know this love and drown yourself in the blood and allow yourself to burn in its fire, so that your selfish self-will is consumed.[45] One must not settle for just saying the right number of Our Fathers.

In this way our prayer will be continuous and faithful; for in the fire of his [Christ's] love we will learn how powerful he is to bless us with all that we ask for. He is ultimate wisdom who knows how to discern and give what is needed. He is our most merciful, holy Father who wishes to bless us with much more than we desire and with those blessings we need for our salvation, blessings that we don't know we should pray for. Faithful continuous prayer is humble, so through this prayer the person knows that *she-is-not* and she knows her faults. It is through such [continuous] prayer that we acquire virtue and preserve in love [*affetto*] or virtue. What is the foundation of so much blessing? It is discernment, offspring of charity, as I have described. And it is all the goodness she acquires within herself, which she pours out upon others.

For the love and teaching[46] she has received, and the foundation built within, she demonstrates through the example of her life and her doctrine, and she pours it out onto others, instructing those who need it or those who ask for it. When someone commits a fault, she comforts them by helping them avoid despair. Through charity she takes on the illness of others [empathizes], offering the needed medicine and encouraging them to have hope in the blood of the Crucified. These and an infinite number of blessings are offered to others through the virtue of discernment. This, my dearest and most beloved daughter and sister in Christ loving Jesus, is why she [the virtue of discernment] is so necessary and useful, and why I call upon you—and upon myself—to live according to the virtue of discernment, which I must confess I have not followed in the past with the perfection with which I should.

You have not suffered as I have from having been and still being imperfect, for I have lacked strictness in my life due to my flaws. You are someone who wanted to wrestle into submission the youth of your body so that it would not rebel against your soul; for this you have taken an extreme path that does not follow the measured way of discernment. This extreme approach shows the fruit of lack of discernment as you are led to choices based on your selfish self-will. Now that you have let go of this accustomed path, it seems the evil one would like to lead you astray, moving you to believe you are damned. This is a major offense against God, for which I am very sorry. So, I want you and I beseech you to make love of virtue [*affetto*] your foundation, in the light of true discernment, as I have been explaining. Die to your selfish self-will, and as I say, rely on others and not on yourself. If your body suffers from weakness or illness, eat every day all that you need to restore your health. When illness and weakness disappear, follow an ordered life in a measured manner. Do not allow the small benefit from engaging in penance to prevent the greater good; do not clothe yourself in your preferred desire for or attachment to penance [*affetto*] for you could find yourself deceived. I want you to take the proven path of virtue, which is the genuine path. When engaged in this path, crushing and destroying our selfish self-love, we are able to guide others. We can accomplish this if we possess the virtue of discernment, otherwise we cannot do so. This is why I say want to see you clothed in the holy virtue of discernment. I say no more.

Forgive me if I have presumed to say too much; what drives me is love and desire for your perfection and salvation for the honor of God.

Remain in his holy, tender love.

Tender Jesus! Jesus love!

CATHERINE OF SIENA

LETTER 186

To Neri di Landoccio
October 1379 (Noffke)

Introduction

Neri is introduced in Letter 99 above. In this short letter sent eight years later, Catherine offers an impassioned exhortation to this close, loved disciple, desiring him to be able to taste, as she has, the depth of God's transforming love. Writing only six months before her death to one of her most beloved disciples, Catherine emphasizes her central anthropological belief: we are created in the image and likeness of God, out of love and for love. The three powers of the soul, reflections of the Trinity in human persons, are bestowed by God in order to know God and relate to God. That Catherine emphasizes these teachings to this particularly dear person and at this point in her life is a witness to the significance of these beliefs for her own life. For she fundamentally experienced herself as created out of love and for love.

Another facet of this letter is that it highlights receptivity to God's gift of love and how we can choose to nurture that receptivity.

❉ ❉ ❉

To the name of Christ crucified and tender Mary.

Dearest, very beloved son in Christ tender Jesus. I, Catherine, slave of the servants of Jesus Christ, write to you in his precious blood, with desire to see you open the vessel of your heart and soul to receive whatever the divine Goodness wishes to give you through prayer.

Why do I wish you to open yourself, to dispose yourself to receive [God's blessings]? Because otherwise you would not be able to welcome what is offered. God, for his part, is always ready to give, so the soul must constantly dispose herself to receive. How do we open up, that is, become receptive? With the readiness given to us by God, which we received when created in his image and likeness. At that time, we were given a receptive vessel; and we received light, that is, memory, a vessel that holds; and we received understanding through the light of faith in holy baptism; and we received the will, which is ready and able to love, for the will can't live without love.[47]

With our existence, we received from God the readiness to love since we were created for love. And yet, with our free will, we must stand in God's presence with our being given to us by God out of love; and with love receive love. I mean receive the general love that God gives to all reasoning creatures, as well as the particular gifts and graces that the soul senses in her interior, are given to her. And so, we invite God to pour out upon us the fire and endless depth of his unfathomable love. This love is poured out together with supernatural light, fullness of grace and with an adornment of virtues; and this love cleanses the face of the soul with the precious blood of the humble, spotless Lamb.

With hunger for God's honor and the salvation of souls she runs to the table of crucified desire, and there eats this very abundant, sweet, soft fruit that bursts and destroys selfish sensuality. In this way the will remains dead to all self-centered love or appetite. This is the way to ready oneself, as faithful spouse of Truth, to die and give one's life a thousand times—if that were possible—for this Truth. Dearest, most beloved son, this is the fullness of time to offer your life; you will be ready to give your life in this way when you acquire the readiness-receptivity I have been describing. I say no more.

Remain in the holy and tender love of God.

Tender Jesus! Jesus love!

3

FRIARS AND MONKS

LETTER 41

To Friar Tommaso da la Fonte of the Order of Preachers when he was at their hospice in Saint Quirico
Maybe 1368 but before 1374 (Noffke); after 1374 (Volpato)

Introduction

Tommaso dalla Fonte was Catherine's cousin who grew up in Catherine's home as an older brother because he was orphaned due to the plague. From her letters we know that Catherine loved Tommaso very specially. After he entered the Dominicans—who pastored the church Catherine attended—he played a major role in her formation, and eventually became her spiritual director and confessor.

This is one of the few letters in which Catherine writes about herself and her spiritual well-being and makes this the topic of the beginning of her letter instead of stating what she wants for her correspondent. When she gets to the exhortation, we note a tone that is much gentler and less authoritative than in most of her letters. Instead of starting with "I want," she says, "I beg you to fulfill my desire." Unremarkably, her desire is for Tommaso's continued transformation.

Her love for Tommaso is also seen at the end of the letter when she tries to understand his motivations and empathize with him. Even though Catherine missed Tommaso and wanted him to return to Siena, she let go of this desire if his spiritual well-being required that he delay his return; this offers an example of Catherine's care for the good of the other, or the love about which she preached.

Friars and Monks

Note another of Catherine's creative metaphors to illustrate the significance of spending time in the inner cell. In this case the cell is a well where one finds both soil (our sinfulness and need for God) and water (God as living water).

❈ ❈ ❈

To the name of Jesus Christ Crucified.

Caterina, Alessa and all your other daughters[1] send greetings to you most dear and beloved Father of our souls in Christ Jesus; we desire to see you healthy in body and soul, as would be pleasing to God. I, Catherine, useless servant in Jesus Christ and most unworthy of all your daughters, know why I have not had enough desire for God's honor and why I have poorly kept in mind the requests he has made many times that I die to my selfish self-will; I have not submitted my will with due reverence as much as I should and could, to the yoke of holy obedience. Ah my poor soul! it has not raced with a brave heart to embrace the cross of my most dear and loving spouse, Christ crucified; instead, I have been impolite and negligent, remaining seated. I am sorry about this and come before you and God conscious of my fault; and I piously beg you to absolve me; and bless me and the others as well.[2]

Now I beg you, dearest father, to fulfill my desire to see you united to God and transformed into his likeness;[3] something that cannot happen unless we are united to God's will. *Oh benevolent, eternal Will, you have taught us how to find what you desire!* And if we should ask our beloved, most cherished young man and most merciful father,[4] he would answer the following, "Most beloved children, if you wish to find and experience the reward of living in my will, always dwell in the cell of your soul." This cell is a well that contains both soil and water—where the soil can be understood to be our moral weakness, that *we-are-not*;[5] when we recognize *we-are-not*, we also realize that our being comes from God. *Oh ineffable, passionate Love! I can see that the soil has been found and the living water reached.* That is, the genuine knowledge of God's benevolent and true will, which desires nothing more than that we be made holy.

Let us then enter into the depth of this well; for if we dwell there, we will inevitably come to know ourselves and God's goodness. As we learn that *we-are-not,* we grow in humility so that we enter meekly into that open heart that warms and consumes and which is also like a window that never closes yet through which one cannot leave. As we open the eye of free will[6] that God has given us, we are able to see and learn that God's will is directed toward our sanctification and nothing else. *Love, benevolent love, open, open up our memory to receive and keep before us so much goodness received from God; and open our understanding, because in understanding we love.*[7] In loving we pass and have passed through the door, Christ crucified, and we are transformed and made one through the benevolence of the mother of love.[8] Christ said to his disciples, "I came to dwell among you." This is my desire, to see you in this dwelling, becoming transformed; and not just you, but all other persons. I beg you to remain attached and nailed to the cross.

You sent a message that you visited the body of Saint Agnes and placed our needs before her and before her sisters;[9] this gives me much consolation. You say that you have no desire to return and that you don't know why, for which I can imagine two reasons. One is that when a soul is closely united to God and transformed in him, she forgets herself and others; the other is that instead of becoming discouraged you found a place to be with yourself.[10] It is a consolation to me if these reasons apply to you, and then I would want nothing more from you. Even though I have at times believed and still believe that time [of separation from Tommaso] passes due to my weakness and ignorance, I believe God's goodness may want to punish and correct my iniquity, which he does out of special love so that I may know myself.

It seems to me you may intend to travel elsewhere, which I don't think you should do; however, may God's will and yours be done. May God help you make the best decision; may your choices be for God's honor and the salvation of your soul. Blessed be Jesus Christ crucified!

Friars and Monks

I ask that you pray for our Caterina; Alessa strongly requests that you pray for her and that you bless her in the name of Christ crucified. And do pray to God for Giovanna pazza.[11]

Catherine, servant and slave ransomed through the blood of the Son of God.[12]

Forgive me if I have presumed too much in what I write. May the fire of God's love engulf you.

Tender Jesus! Tender Jesus! Jesus, Tender Jesus!

LETTERS 127 AND 146

127 to Friars Bartolomeo Dominici and Tommaso d'Antonio
146 to Friar Bartolomeo Dominici

Introduction to Letters 127 and 146

Bartolomeo was a Dominican friar close in age to Catherine who became a close friend; he accompanied her on many of her trips and was occasionally her confessor. Tommaso d'Antonio da Siena, known as Caffarini, was another Dominican friar who was a friend, early disciple, and occasional confessor. The latter was also one of the main promoters of the cause for Catherine's canonization.

These two letters to close friends with whom Catherine spent a great deal of time offer rare examples of friendly sharing about new experiences and insights rather than the usual content, instructing others and telling them how to behave. We learn about Catherine's profound day-to-day experiences of God, experiences that reflect intuitions gained through union with God. This information balances more commonly known accounts about Catherine's piety, namely, her visions and extreme asceticism. In Letter 127 she speaks about "returning from the depth of my soul," an allusion to insight gained in an experience of union with God where she senses deeply the disparity between God's love for us and our love for God. She also communicates an insight she had while meditating on the Holy Week story about Jesus entering Jerusalem on a donkey. In Letter 146, particularly striking is her remark about discovering a new ineffable insight into the pervasiveness of God's love, while contemplating the sea (at the port of Pisa).

❧ ❧ ❧

127 to Friars Bartolomeo Dominici and Tommaso d'Antonio of the Order of Preachers When They Were in Pisa
March 1374 (Noffke, Volpato, ISIME)

To the name of Christ crucified.

With reverence for the most loving sacrament,[13] I write to you dearest and very loved fathers and brothers in the most abundant, most loving blood. Your very dear father and your brothers[14] send you manifold greetings, sending you strength and blessings in that most passionate love that holds Jesus bound and nailed to the cross.

Oh fire! Oh abyss of love! You are a fire that always burns but does not destroy; you are filled with joy, gladness, and gentleness. All sorrow feels sweet, all heavy burdens seem light to the heart struck by this lightning. Oh, tender love that fattens[15] *and tends to our soul!* I've said this fire burned without destroying, but now I tell you that it burns and destroys in that it melts from the soul all faults, all ignorance, all lukewarmness. For love is not lazy; it accomplishes great things.

I, Catherine, useless servant, die of desire, returning from the depth of my soul where I experienced pain and weeping upon recognizing and tasting our ignorance and lukewarmness in not offering love to God, when with so much love he bestows so many graces upon us. And so, dearest brothers, don't be thankless and ungrateful, for the fountain of devotion within us could easily dry up. Oh, you who are lukewarm and negligent, awake from your perverse sleep! Let's go forth to greet the King who comes to us in humility and docility! Ah, we who are proud! Let's gaze upon the master of humility who comes seated on a donkey! For our savior explained[16] that one reason—among a number of others—for his arrival on a donkey was to show us what our humanity had come to due to sin, and to show us how to manage the "donkey" in our humanity. Frankly, there is no difference between us and an animal: for due to sin our capacity to reason becomes animal-like.[17]

Oh, ancient Truth![18] *You taught us telling us,* "I want you to climb onto this donkey, and taking hold of yourselves, be humble and docile."[19] *What foot should we use to climb onto the donkey, dearest love?* That of loathing for lukewarmness and love of virtue. Let's not say more, for I would have too much to say and I can't go on! But my sons and brothers let's consider the following. The channel is open and flowing, that is, the most loving channel of the heart, soul, and body of Jesus Christ. So, seeing that we must acquire provisions for the boat of our soul, we do so in this loving channel. There we will experience that we flow with such depth of desire and motivation [*affetto*], that we will easily fill our soul; and yet I tell you, don't delay in placing your eye at the open window,[20] for ultimate Truth has set before us ways and times to accomplish great deeds for him. And so, I urge you, grow in holy desire promptly and effectively; don't be satisfied with small goals, for He wants them to be great.

Let me also tell you that the pope sent his vicar, the one who renounced as archbishop for love of virtue and who was the spiritual director of that countess who died in Rome.[21] He came to see me on behalf of the holy Father, asking me for special prayers for him and holy Church; and as a gesture, he sent me a holy indulgence. Rejoice and be glad that the holy Father has started to open his eyes [pay attention] to the honor of God and holy Church.

A young man will come to you and give you this letter. Offer him what he asks, for I witness to the fact that he has a holy desire to go to the Holy Sepulcher. He is traveling to see the holy Father to obtain permission for himself and for several others (religious and lay). I wrote a letter to the holy Father, urging him with prayers that for love of the most benevolent blood he should give these permissions, so that we may give up our bodies to necessary torments.[22] Please pray to ultimate, eternal Truth, that if it is for the best, he should grant this mercy as well to you and me; so that all of us, as a blessed brigade,[23] may give our life for him. I am certain that if this is for the best, he will grant it. I say no more.

Alessa sends effusive greetings with desire to see you again and find you once more [living] in [God's] most passionate love; she is very surprised that you have never written. May God lead us into that place where we will see each other and our God face to face. Negligent Alessa would love to conceal herself in this letter to be able to see you. Monna Giovanna sends manifold blessings asking that you raise her before God.

Jesus, Jesus, Jesus, Jesus!

I, Catherine, useless servant of Jesus Christ, offer you profuse blessings and strength. Caterina Marta asks that you pray for her.[24] Our greetings to friar Tommasso[25] and your prior and all the others.

146 to Friar Bartolomeo Dominici of the Order of Preachers When He Was Scripture Professor in Florence
Summer 1375 (Noffke); First three months 1375 (Volpato); Spring 1375 (ISIME)

To the name of Jesus Christ who was crucified for us.

With reverence for the most loving sacrament,[26] I write to you, very loved, dearest father and son in Christ Jesus. I, Catherine servant and slave of the servants of Jesus Christ, write to you wishing you strength in the precious blood of the Son of God, and with desire to see you smoldering in (his) most passionate love, submerged in it, and consumed by it, knowing that the person smoldered and consumed in true love does not focus on self. I want you to accomplish this.

Through such passionate love, I invite you to enter into a peaceful, deep sea. I have discovered something new here—not that the sea is new—but I have a new feeling in my soul when contemplating the words, "God is love." As the mirror reflects a person's face, or the sun reflects light onto the earth, "God is love" mirrors in my soul that everything is pure love, that all is made only of love, which is why he says, "I am God-love."

Friars and Monks

From this experience is born in me an insight into the immeasurable mystery of the Word incarnate, which due to the power of love was given to us with such humility that it derails my pride. It [the above experience] teaches us to pay more attention to the Word's ardent *affetto* [divine love] bestowed upon us, than to his actions. And it teaches us to act as someone who loves such that when a friend arrives with a gift, he doesn't look at his hands to see what gift he brought, but rather opens the eye of love and looks into the heart and deepest desire and motivation [*affetto*] of his friend.[27] He [God] wants us to act in this way; that is, when the eternal and most loving goodness of God fills our souls—an encounter filled with immeasurable benefits—we should immediately open our memory to receive what understanding grasps through divine love. The will[28] then arises with most passionate desire and contemplates and receives the heart of good loving Jesus, totally poured out. In this way you will find yourself immersed in the gift of the blood of the Son of God and clothed in its fire, and you will be free of all sorrow and hardship. Such an experience eased the pain of the holy disciples when they had to leave Mary and one another (which they were willing to suffer in order to spread the Word of God). So, Run! Run! Run!

I can't answer your question about Benincasa, as I am not in Siena. Please thank messer Nicolaio for the charity offered to them. Profuse greetings from Alessa, and from me, plain Cecca.[29]

May God always dwell in your soul. Amen. Jesus! Jesus! Catherine, servant of the servants of God.[30]

LETTER 134

To Bartolomeo and Jacomo, hermits in the Campo Santo[31] in Pisa
January—May 1376 (Noffke)

Introduction

The cemetery in Pisa was special in that it contained soil said to have been brought from Mt. Calvary where Christ died. In medieval

Italian cities it was customary for persons to live as hermits in or near cemeteries, living ascetical lives without belonging to particular religious orders. Most likely Catherine had met Bartolomeo and Jacomo on her visit to Pisa and writes to them as part of her campaign to invite persons to join the crusade, this cause so dear to her heart. She exhorts these hermits to a fullness and depth of union with God that would motivate them to give their life for Christ.

The letter has lyrical passages and intriguing metaphors regarding immersion in God's love, highlighting that the experience of this love lies within us, thus urging a life with space for silence and solitude. God answers the question about what he loves most saying, "look within yourselves." Catherine speaks of entering the *soul* of Christ to experience God as triune, that is, the passionate love of the Father, the wisdom of the Son, and the strength of the Holy Spirit. One becomes immersed in the blood, or the life of Christ, through union with God as Christ crucified. Consuming the blood of Christ by uniting oneself to the cross is compared to an eagle eating while flying high, where flying high refers to climbing on the cross to be fully united to Jesus. Having climbed on the cross, eating at the cross is yet another metaphor, one frequently used by Catherine to refer to taking in Christ's life when united to him in suffering and in the self-emptying of detachment.

The letter includes some of Catherine's unique rhetoric, such as highlighting the significance of seeking justice by telling us that even the animals should seek punishment for injustice!

❋ ❋ ❋

To the name of Jesus Christ and tender Mary.

My beloved and very dear brothers in Christ tender Jesus. I, Catherine, servant and slave of the servants of Jesus Christ, write to you in his precious blood, with desire to see you open up your body and allow it to bleed to death for the tender name of Jesus.[32]

Oh how joyful would be our soul if we received such great mercy that we would offer to Christ that which he gave for us with such passionate love![33] *Oh fire that burns but does not consume, yet consumes all that lives within the soul that does not correspond to God's will!* This was the true heat that cooked the spotless Lamb on the wood of the most holy cross. Oh hardened, unjust hearts! How could you keep from being dissolved by such heat! I certainly am not surprised if—with knowledge and awareness of the blood—the saints raced to spread this blood, for they were not blinded by selfish self-love but were saturated in the knowledge of God's goodness and in the fire of his passionate love; like Lorenzo who could speak to the tyrant while standing on the grate from which emerged an overwhelming fire. *So, Lorenzo, is the fire not hot enough?*[34] He would answer, "No, for the fire within is so hot that it puts out the outer fire."

So, dearest sons in Christ Jesus, don't allow your deepest motivation and attachments [*affetti*] and desires to give out before the final day of your life! Don't fall asleep! Wake up! I see no other way of staying awake than with continuous anger.[35] For from anger arises hunger for justice, so much so that one would even want the animals to seek punishment for injustice.[36] Having arrived at the desire to engage in self-retribution,[37] the soul is purged in the loving fire where God's will is fashioned within her, and where ultimate Goodness is known; this [experience] enlarges one's deepest motivation and desire [*affetto*] and one's heart, as the soul finds herself immersed in the realization of the abyss of love that God has for her. Then the eye of understanding is opened to know, memory is made free to hold in consciousness, and the will expands to love that which he loves.[38]

The soul speaks, she calls out, "Oh loving God! What do you love most?" Our loving God answers, "Look within yourself and you will find what I love." So, my most dear sons, look within yourselves. You will find and see within you that same goodness and ineffable love that God is, and with that same love he loves all persons. And so, the soul that is in love rises up and busies herself to love that which God loves most, that is, our beloved brothers [our fellow human beings]. And the person rises up with such desire and filled with so much love, that he would willingly give his life for the salvation of others, to restore them to the life of grace;[39] in this way he becomes someone who savors and eats souls.

Such persons behave like the eagle who, as it flies upward, always looks at the circle of the sun, and only after that looks down toward earth; and having captured the food to nourish itself, it eats while flying high. Human persons should act in this way. That is, they look up on high, where is found the sun of divine love, then look down toward earth, that is, toward the humanity of the Word, the incarnate son of God. Seeing the Word in the humanity that emerged from Mary's loving womb, the person recognizes the food on this table and there she eats.[40] She doesn't just remain on earth where she has eaten of Christ's humanity, but she also rises high with the food in her mouth. Having risen she enters into the soul of the Son of God which burns and blazes with love, and there she finds that this affectionate love is a fire that comes forth from the power of the Father through which the Father, out of passionate love, bequeathed upon us the wisdom of his Son and the power and strength of the Holy Spirit. And this love was of such magnitude and fruit of such union that only this union—no nails or [wood of the cross]—would be necessary to hold the Word on the cross. And this union was such that nothing could separate that divine nature from human nature—not death or anything else. So this is where[41] I want you to eat this loving food.

And if you then said to me, "With what wings would I fly?" With the wings of anger and love; with the feathers of the suffering of torments, scorn, and crucified accusations like those of Christ crucified. Don't seek to know or consider knowing anything other than him. May he be your glory, your refreshment and all your repose. Nourish yourself and graze[42] on the blood. May God attend to your desires. I say no more.

Remain in the holy, tender love of God.

Gentle Jesus! Jesus love!

Friars and Monks

LETTER 36

To certain novices of the order of Saint Mary of Monte Oliveto
April 1376 (Noffke)

Introduction

Most likely the novices addressed were from Siena and sent to this monastery by Catherine, revealing her active spiritual guidance of Sienese young men. It is unclear, however, if the novices were at the home monastery of Monte Oliveto near Siena or at a foundation near Bologna.[43]

This letter reveals Catherine's spirituality of obedience, based on theology articulated by Thomas Aquinas and common in monastic life, which held that obedience to God is a way of imitating Jesus in his obedience to the Father; it was due to such obedience that we were saved through Jesus becoming incarnate and giving his life for us. Therefore, obedience should be a goal of any Christian disciple. Aquinas taught that in religious life—seen as a higher road to holiness—obedience pertaining to the rule is sufficient for salvation. Willingness to obey beyond the basic requirements of the rule evidences a life of greater perfection.[44] Given these beliefs, Catherine elaborated a spirituality of obedience that was an expression of her central goal of the spiritual life, namely, transformation away from self-centeredness toward living out of love and for love—that is, for the good of the other (and self), and therefore, following God's will.

This letter elucidates several of Catherine's metaphors. She speaks of the inner cell as the side of Christ, a powerful variation of her focus on time in the cell. She describes the person as a bulwark [a medieval wall made of stones that protected the city] where the mortar that protects the person's soul, or core integrity, is the blood of Christ. Living in close relationship to God allows God to be the mason who creates the buttressed wall that encloses and protects us; closeness to God in Jesus fills us with mortar/blood/love that transforms us. And being in a boat is here a metaphor for a place that facilitates transformation and makes the spiritual journey safer.

The mining metaphor is less common. The lode, that is, the virtue of humility, is the foundation for recognition of our need for God; this recognition opens us to "mining" or development of our transformed selves through love.

❊ ❊ ❊

To the name of Jesus Christ crucified and tender Mary.

My dearest sons in Christ tender Jesus. I, Catherine, servant and slave of the servants of Jesus Christ write to you in his precious blood with desire to see you sons who will be obedient unto death, learning from the spotless Lamb who was obedient to the Father even to the shameful death on the cross.

Keep in mind that he is the way and the rule that you and all should observe. I want you to keep this way and rule before your mind's eye. Look and see how just and how obedient is the Word. He does not spurn the heavy burden he has to bear, placed upon him by the Father; no, he runs toward it with great desire. He demonstrated this during the supper of Holy Thursday when he said, "With desire I have wanted to eat this Passover with you before my death."

It was his intention to accomplish the Passover of fulfilling the Father's will, carrying out the mission[45] given him by the Father. When he saw that the time had come when ultimately he must offer to the Father the sacrifice of his body for us, he rejoiced and exulted and with gladness said, "With desire I have wanted it."[46] The Passover about which he spoke was that of offering himself as food and sacrificing his body in obedience to the Father. He had celebrated other Passovers with his disciples many times, but never *this* Passover. *Oh immeasurable, most loving and most passionate love, you do not heed your sufferings or your shameful death, for if you did, you would not move toward [your passion] with so much joy nor would you call this a Passover!* My sons, consider that this tender Lamb is like a true eagle that does not look at the earth—his humanity—but fixes his eye on the disk of the sun, that is, the eternal Father. He recognizes within himself that

Friars and Monks

the Father's will is that we be saved through him. For this salvation cannot be accomplished due to the sin of our first father, Adam. It requires a mediator so that this will of God [our salvation] can be achieved. The Word recognized he had been chosen [as mediator] and was given humanity as his Bride. The Father tasked the Word, under obedience, to offer his blood as intermediary, so that his [the Father's] will for our salvation would be accomplished through the blood [of the Word]. This is the loving Passover chosen by the spotless Lamb. And with great *affetto* [love] and desire he fulfilled the will of the Father for us, carrying out the mission given to him.

Oh boundless, tender love, you have united humans with their Creator and molded them to him; you have acted as one would when building with stones, fitting each stone to the other; and so that the wind cannot topple them, he places living mortar [the blood] mixed with water. You, incarnate Word, through your union with human nature, have cemented the stone of humanity by attaching humanity to their Creator through your blood, mixing in the divine essence as living mortar. You have thus made provision for times of contrary winds that bring battles and temptation; for times of many sufferings and of torments that assail us to afflict our soul due to the evil one or to other persons or to one's own flesh. I recognize, first Truth, that due to the blood that holds us together, the wall is so strong that no contrary wind can topple it. And so, my most tender Love, we humans have abundant cause to love you alone and to have no fear of any deceptions that should assail us.

And so I ask you, my dear sons in Christ tender Jesus, never fear but trust in the blood of Christ crucified. Never fear; neither due to inner urges and dissolute fantasies, nor due to fear that you will not persevere, nor due to fear of the struggles that might arise as you keep obedience to your order, nor due to anything else that might occur; never fear. Preserve a good, holy will that governs the bulwark;[47] it [the will] can choose to tear the wall down with the pickaxe of free will or to conserve it, according to what is pleasing to the Lord of good will. So I don't want you to ever fear again; may all servile fear be torn from you. Instead, say what dear Paul said; he who was so in love and who responded to the lukewarmness of his heart and the delusions of the evil one, uttering, "Oh my soul, endure today! For Christ crucified I can do anything, for he is within me strengthening me through desire and love" [Phil 4:13]. Please love, love, love! Become drunk with the blood of the tender Lamb who has made strong the buttressed wall of your soul, delivering it from enslavement to the dominion of the evil one; he gave you your soul free and in command of herself so that no one can take away her authority without her will; he [the Lamb] has given this to everyone.

For I see that divine providence has placed you on a boat that is a true, holy religious order, so that you will not flounder in the stormy sea of this dangerous life. This boat is maneuvered by the yoke of true, holy obedience. Keep in mind how immense is the grace God has bestowed on you, knowing the weakness of your arms. For whoever lives in the world must row in this sea with his own arms, while those that are in religious orders row with someone else's arms. If he is obedient, he doesn't have to account for himself; rather, the religious order is responsible so long as he has been obedient to his superior. I will be assured that you are following the sacrificed Lamb if you are obedient. For I have already told you that I want you to learn from good, tender Jesus who was obedient unto death. He fulfilled the will of the Father carrying out his mission in obedience. God wants you to do the same; he wants you to accomplish his will by observing the rule of your order, holding this rule up as a mirror. It is better to choose death than to violate obedience to your superior. Should the case ever arise that your superior orders you to do something not in God—and may God in his mercy prevent this—you should not, nor would I want you to ever obey in such a case. For we must never obey a person if their commands go against the Creator. In every other circumstance you should always obey.

Do not focus on consolation, whether spiritual or temporal. I tell you this because sometimes the evil one can lead us astray in the guise of greater virtue or piety to desire particular places

Friars and Monks

and times by telling ourselves, "In such a time and place I experience in my soul more consolation and peace." Yet this may go against what is expected under obedience. In this case, I want you to follow what has been assigned under obedience rather than to pursue your consolation. Be aware that this is a hidden deceit that all God's servants experience, that is, under the guise of serving God more fully, they do a disservice to God.

Notice that the will is that faculty that can both offer service and disservice. As a religious, the evil one will not entice you with obviously disordered matters, for you have left what is worldly behind. He will entice you with spiritual matters, making you think, "If I stay in such and such a place rather than another, I feel I am more at peace and I am more filled with God's love." And in order to obtain this [the preferred place], the person resists obeying. And even if he agrees to carry out [the order], he will do so with unhappiness so that wanting peace, he loses his peace. It is better, then, to let go of one's will and not focus on oneself. Only attend to carrying out God's will and that of your holy order and to follow the orders of your superior. I am sure you are eagle chicks who will learn from the real eagle.

When God allows any distress or persecution, those worldly persons that separate themselves from the will of their Creator say [to themselves], "I don't want this, not so much because it would be distressing, but because it could cause me to be separated from God." In this they are deceived, for their motivation is false self-centered sensuality; that is, deluded by the evil one, they fear the distress more than the offense. It is important, then, to drown out our will. Laypersons should obediently follow the commandments and religious should observe the commandments and the counsels, as promised to their holy order.

Come, then, my sons! Be obedient unto death following the true, real virtues! Keep in mind that you will be humble to the extent that you will be obedient. Obedience emerges from the lode[48] of humility and from humility emerges obedience; and both come forth from the channel of most passionate love. The channel of love emerges from the side of Christ crucified: I want you to go there and connect to that channel, which I propose to you as a place to visit and as a room to live in. Know that the religious who stays outside his cell will die as will a fish out of water. For this reason, I propose to you the cell of the side of Christ where you will find knowledge of self and knowledge of his goodness. So, get up with a strong desire that is on fire! Go! Enter and stay in that loving room, and then there will be no person, nor evil one that can take grace away from you nor keep you from arriving at your destination, there seeing and tasting God. I say no more. So, stay obedient unto death, following the Lamb, who is the rule and the way!

Bathe in the blood of Christ crucified! Hide in the wounds of Christ crucified!

Remain, etc. And love, love one another!

Tender Jesus! Jesus love! Mary!

LETTER 51

To Friar Felice da Massa of the Order of St. Augustine
September–December 1377 (Noffke)

Introduction

Felice was one of the Augustinian hermits[49] who lived in the monastery of Lecceto in the rural area outside of Siena; he was one of the monks who became Catherine's friends and advisors, contributing to her increased knowledge of ecclesiastical matters and theology. He was also one of those who accompanied Catherine when she went to Avignon, France, to see Pope Gregory XI. This letter is one of many in which Catherine assumes the authority of offering spiritual guidance to someone who was undoubtedly her senior in age, education, and experience. It reflects her confidence in God's guidance to live out an atypical role.

This letter is a very complete essay on Catherine's wisdom about knowledge of God and knowledge of self as the core dynamics of the journey of transformation. It includes a lengthy description about

Friars and Monks

the importance of one of the powers of the soul, and it elucidates the significance of understanding through a particularly detailed explanation of her metaphor, "the eye of the soul." One of the manuscripts indicates that Catherine was in ecstasy while she wrote the letter; if she was not literally in this state, she was probably dictating after a period of deep contemplation.

The letter presents several of Catherine's creative metaphors that prompt the imagination to better internalize her exhortation. Some of these include fattening one's soul (that is, nourishing it with the food of love), the danger of arrogance as "stinking fruit," while humility is "water" that extinguishes arrogance, and also a wet nurse. Catherine exhorts Felice to "eat" souls at the table of the Lamb. The table of the Lamb is the cross, so eating souls refers to working for their salvation through willingness to imitate Jesus's giving of self.

❋ ❋ ❋

To the name of Jesus Christ crucified and tender Mary.

Dearest son in Christ loving Jesus. I, Catherine, servant and slave of the servants of Jesus Christ, write to you in his precious blood with desire to see you rooted in true, perfect humility, for the humble person patiently bears all burdens required by love of truth. Because humility is the wet nurse and source of food for love, there can be no humility without charity. He who smolders within the furnace of love is not negligent; rather, he is perfect in his readiness to act, for charity is never idle; it always acts.

One can have neither love nor the humility that consumes negligence and destroys pride without the light and unless the eye[50]—illuminated by this light—has one object in sight; this is so because even if the eye is able to see and is illuminated by the light, but is not open, the capacity to see would be of no use.

The true eye of our soul is understanding that possesses the light of most holy faith; this is the case so long as the cloth of selfish self-love has not covered it up. When selfish self-love has been removed, the eye [of understanding] remains clear and can see; it is then important that your will, empowered by your deepest [ordered] motivation [*affetto*], rise up[51] and desire to love its benefactor [God, Creator]. Then, experiencing that the eye of understanding is moved by *affetto*, it opens promptly and focuses on its object, Christ crucified, in whom—especially in his blood—he recognizes the abyss of Christ's immeasurable love.

Where should the person gaze and where should he place this object [Christ]? In the house of self-knowledge. In this knowledge he recognizes his inadequacy and wretchedness, for with the eye of understanding he has seen his faults and that *he-is-not*, and he has recognized this as truth. For truth exists when the person knows himself and understands the goodness of God within him.

If the person knows only himself, or if he should want to know God without knowing himself, his knowledge would not be founded on truth; nor would the person receive the benefit that he should garner from knowledge of self. He would lose rather than gain, for from self-knowledge alone he would only garner spiritual troubles and anxiety, which would dry up the soul; and if he continued in this state without other alternatives, he would become despairing. And should he want to know God without knowing himself, he would reap the stinking fruit of considerable arrogance, which nurtures pride; and arrogance and pride feed on each other. It is important, then, that the light [of understanding] gaze upon truth, seasoning knowledge of self with knowledge of God, and knowledge of God with knowledge of self.

With this knowledge, that is, the dual knowledge of God and self, the soul does not become arrogant, nor does she[52] despair; rather, from this [dual] knowledge she acquires the fruit of life. From knowledge of herself she garners the fruit of true humility from which, [in turn], germinates dislike and loathing for our sins and for the perverse law that is always ready to contradict the Spirit. From such loathing is birthed the offspring of patience, which is the marrow of charity. And from knowledge of God's great goodness—which she finds within herself—she receives the fruit of submersion in the abyss of God's charity and love of her fellow human beings.

Friars and Monks

When with the light the person sees and learns that with the love he has for his Creator he cannot be useful to him, then immediately upon realizing this he serves his neighbor in the ways he cannot benefit God directly. Realizing how much God loves his creatures, he does this for love of God; for it is a requirement of love that one loves all that is loved by the beloved. So, my dearest son, with this light [of understanding] we will acquire the virtues of humility and charity, and with true and holy patience we will endure and bear the faults of our fellow human beings. With perfect capacity for prompt, effective action acquired in the fire of divine love, we will extinguish negligence; and arrogance will be extinguished with the water of humility. We will acquire hunger for God's honor and we will savor and eat souls[53] at the table of the humble, spotless Lamb. There is no other way. And since I have concluded that it would be important for us to stay on this path, on this road of true humility, I said and say now that I desire to see you rooted in true, perfect humility. This is how I want you to act without distress or a troubled spirit.

At this time, I again want us to take up living faith, firm hope, and ready obedience; this is the path I want for you so that you fatten your soul and so it does not dry up due to troubled thoughts or an unmotivated, wondering mind. Rather, with perfect readiness you should arise from the slumber of negligence, taking up the virtues you see in your brothers and preserve such virtues in your heart.

May the truth always give you joy and be on the tip of your tongue. May you announce it in love to each as needed, and especially to those persons that you love with special love and do so kindly; and place the faults of others on yourself. And if in the past you have not done this with due care, correct your approach in the future. I don't want you to get distressed over any of this. Do not worry about me, for the waves of a rough sea are all handled with humility, fraternal charity, and holy patience. I say no more.

Remain in the holy and tender love of God.

Tender Jesus! Jesus love!

CATHERINE OF SIENA

LETTER 326

To Friars William of England and Antonio da Nizza, in Lecceto[54] near Siena
December 1378 (Dated manuscript)

Introduction

William Flete was an English Augustinian hermit—therefore here named "of England"—who studied in Cambridge but soon felt a vocation to a contemplative life and went to an Augustinian hermitage near Siena. Catherine was introduced to William early in her post-1374 ministry and he became a friend and mentor. He is almost certainly one of the learned persons from whom Catherine informally learned theology, both in person and through correspondence. In 1378, after Urban VI was elected pope, Catherine joined in advocating for the Council of the Wise, where the pope called for select hermits and members of religious orders to intercede for the pope and for some of them to go to Rome to offer him wise counsel. This letter is Catherine's call to William to join this Council and go to Rome.

I have translated the apparently inconsistent language she used as I believe it was intentional. She admonishes in general terms that "one" should leave one's peace and quiet for the good of the church and says, "I want to verify if *we* authentically have a love for the reform of holy Church." I interpret this pronoun use to be a way of softening her "order" to William, since it is otherwise clear that all her admonitions are directed at him. This becomes evident when at the end of the letter she states that failure to respond would be against God's will. In fact, William did not go to Rome.

This letter is an interesting example of two aspects of Catherine's spirituality. While she genuinely believed she was a sinner and needed God, she also developed a confidence that she could know God's will in a way that brooked no opposition, and that led her to reproach some of her best friends and mentors—such as William and even Raymond—for not correctly perceiving God's will. Yet, Catherine's absolute perspective could be questioned, raising important questions about a spirituality of discernment.[55] This letter also shows Catherine's unquestioning commitment to the pope's authority, whom she considered Christ's representative on earth, no matter how sinful he might be. She was not alone in this belief in the church of fourteenth-century Italy.

❊ ❊ ❊

To the name of Jesus Christ and tender Mary

Dearest sons in Christ, tender Jesus. I, Catherine, slave and servant of Jesus Christ, write to you in his precious blood with desire to see you surrender yourselves so thoroughly that you do not seek peace or silence apart from Christ crucified, and that you seek to grow in hunger for the salvation of souls and the reform of holy Church at the table of the cross. The church is in such need today, that in order to come to her rescue, one must leave the woods and abandon oneself.

Knowing that one can assist her, one should not stay put saying, "I would lose my peace." For God in his grace provided holy Church with a good and just shepherd [the pope] who rejoices in the servants of God whom he wishes to join him; and he expects to be able to expose and eradicate vice and plant virtue without fear of others. Since he acts as a just and courageous man, we must come to his aid.

I want to verify if we authentically have a love for the reform of holy Church; for if this is the case you will follow God's will and that of his vicar [the pope]. You will come out of the woods and come here to join the field of battle. For if you do not do this you will have alienated yourself from the will of God.

And so I beg you, for the love of Christ crucified, to respond to the request sent to you by the holy Father and come soon, without delay. And don't worry about not having your woods, for here there are also forests and woods. Come on, dearest sons! Don't stay asleep! It's time to be as in a vigil.[56] I say no more.

Remain, etc.
Tender Jesus! Jesus love!
Rome, the 15th day of December, 1378.

CATHERINE OF SIENA

LETTER 33

To the Abbot of Monte Oliveto wishing to place back in his hands a friar who had left his religious order
September or October, 1378 (Noffke); between winter and spring 1379 or 1380 (ISIME)

Introduction

Catherine was close to the Benedictines of Monte Oliveto, near Siena, and corresponded with their abbot, who may have contributed to her own spiritual and theological formation. This letter shows the spiritual authority Catherine took upon herself, without any apparent hesitation offering advice to this abbot who was older, more educated, and with a clear authority role in the church. She presumed to proffer not just spiritual advice but also how to handle one of his monks. This authority assumed by Catherine reveals the depth of her conviction that God was guiding her. Indeed, she assumes her authority will be accepted by the abbot as she recommends that he take back a monk who had left for another monastery and now wanted to return.[57] The monk had repented of leaving Monte Oliveto and sought Catherine's intercession to be accepted again.

This letter is a detailed exhortation to grow in imitation of the sort of love God offered us through Jesus's complete giving of his life. Catherine concludes by pointing out that a religious leader, such as an abbot, who has responsibility for the precious vocations of monks, must be as perfect as possible in imitating Jesus's love. This is congruent with Catherine's wisdom that all church leaders, beginning with the pope, have a particular responsibility to lead exemplary lives of transformation.

This letter addresses a frequent theme, namely, that of the illumination of understanding—the power of the soul—with the light of faith. Illuminating understanding and will [*affetto*], this light puts before consciousness that which should be loved. In terms of metaphors, Catherine speaks about "the food of souls." Thus souls, persons-as-food, offer sustenance for the "work" of love. Working spiritually for the salvation and transformation of others indicates

Friars and Monks

hunger for souls or consuming the food of souls. Food is a multivalent metaphor as it is also the sustenance God gives us through his love shown by Jesus on the cross.

※ ※ ※

To the name of Jesus Christ crucified and tender Mary

Dearest father in Christ tender Jesus. I, Catherine, slave and servant of Jesus Christ, write to you in his precious blood with desire to see you living perfect love. Such love does not seek its own benefit; it is free, not enslaved to selfish self-love. This love is generous, it expands the heart through God's love and love of neighbor; it knows how to tolerate and bear with the faults of others for love of the Creator. It is compassionate and not cruel, because it has eliminated that which makes persons cruel, namely, selfish self-love; and so, with charity and great compassion it welcomes its neighbor for God's sake. Love[58] is benevolent, peaceful, never hateful; it seeks that which is holy and just, avoiding injustice and living according to these values so the bright light[59] of justice shines in her breast.

When love praises, it does not deceive. If it reprimands, it does so without hatred or anger; it loves all as her own children, praising or reprimanding them, depending on what is needed. Love is a mother who in her soul conceives the virtues as offspring that she bears to benefit her fellow human beings for the honor of God. Her wet nurse is authentic, deep humility. What food does this wet nurse offer? The food of light[60] and knowledge of self. Through the light the person recognizes her inadequacy and weakness due to selfish sensuality, cause of all wretchedness. Because of this self-knowledge her soul is humble, with hatred for such wretchedness;[61] through this self-knowledge she feeds the fire of divine love leading to knowledge of God's ineffable love dwelling within her. This divine goodness is the beginning and end of all her knowledge.

Filled with this light and knowledge of self, she takes delight in the food that God loves most, that is, God's creature, created by him in his image and likeness. God so loved his creatures that he bestowed on them the Word, his Son, to placate his anger[62] and redeem his creatures from the long war to which they fell victim due to the sin of Adam; and the Word would wash the creature's face with his blood to cleanse it of the filth that covered it due to sin. The Word was our peace and the mediator between us and God, taking upon himself the blows required for justice to be accomplished. He was our physician, as glorious Paul explained; when humans were prostrate due to sickness, the great physician came into the world to heal our infirmities. He is our sustenance, as he gave himself up to be our food. This tender, loving Word ran toward the table of the holy cross to bring about—in obedience—the Father's will for his creatures. And on the table of the cross he consumed the food of souls, putting up with suffering, torments, shame, injustice, and culminating with the painful death on the cross, where he offered his body so that it bled from many places.

All of this manifests God's love for us. So, whoever lives in this love takes delight in and loves the food of souls such that he no longer wishes to consume this tender food in any other way than that in which our loving, tender, Word-Christ, sweet, good Jesus,[63] consumed it.[64] If Jesus was able to endure and we want to emulate this endurance, we will share in suffering hunger, thirst, vulnerability, injustices, insults, and scorn; we will share in suffering temptations from our neighbor and from the evil one. Jesus bore with our lack of gratitude and did not withdraw his offer of salvation; and so in this respect and all else, the soul that lives out of love conforms herself as much as possible to Jesus, desiring to follow in his footsteps. She [the soul] wants to welcome and does welcome with generosity and under the wings of mercy anyone who has offended her. For she recognizes that God's goodness has offered her the same merciful welcome.

How tender is this mother, who is love! Is there any virtue that she does not encompass? No. She is not shrouded in darkness, for her guide is the light of most holy faith, which is the pupil of the eye of understanding. Understanding guided by the light of faith steers the will moved by motivation and desire arising from one's core [*affetto*] toward that which should be loved, placing before *affetto* the love God has for her and the teaching of Christ crucified. And so the will [*affetto*], seeing with the light that she[65] is loved, is compelled to love and to show that she truly loves her Creator following the doctrine of truth.[66] It is good to rise from the slumber of negligence and ignorance, and to diligently seek this mother through the blood of Christ crucified, for the blood represents this tender, loving fire. Through this path, and no other, we will acquire the life of grace. For these reasons, I said to you that I wished to see you grounded in true, perfect charity, which every person capable of reason should have within her; this is necessary in order to savor God in eternal life.

Those who are responsible for and obliged to direct and govern other souls are required even more to live in this fashion; it is particularly urgent because the responsibility is so great that if they were deprived of love, they would be unable to bear this yoke without offending God. The superior's charity cannot be lukewarm or imperfect; it must be perfect, filled with the greatest warmth of love and with desire for the salvation of his charges. The superior must know, with light and discernment, how to give to each according to his capacity to receive; he must be able to correct with love; he must be able to make himself one with [empathize with] their vulnerabilities, praising and correcting in mercy and justice. He should seek the lost sheep, and once he is found he should place him on his shoulders—bearing his weight—and he should rejoice and celebrate that the sheep has returned to the fold.

I invite you to live this joy, dearest father, with your sheep who spent so much time in the communities of other sheep; I mean brother Pietro, who is currently a monk at San Lorenzo. It seems that he is humbled and ready to receive the rod of justice. He wants to return to his sheepfold and to be obedient to you and your religious order; he is ready to bow his head and walk according to the requirements of holy obedience.

He realizes he is in danger outside of his order and recognizes his fault, and so is willing to come to you, ready to take the

crumbs that fall from the table. I beg you to open to him the arms of mercy and to receive him with love, as a father receives his child. Please be a good shepherd who, if needed, offers his life for his sheep. I say no more.
Remain in the holy, etc.
Tender Jesus! Jesus love!

LETTER 154

To Brother Francesco Tedaldi[67] of Florence, Carthusian monk from the island of Gorgona
December1378–January 1379 (Noffke)[68]

Introduction

Francesco was a new member of the monastery of the Gorgona Carthusians whose abbot was one of Catherine's correspondents and supporters. One would expect, then, the abbot and other wise members of this order of hermits to counsel the new monk. Yet in this letter Catherine writes to offer him one of her masterful summaries of her wisdom regarding the spiritual journey. Remarkably she focuses on the inner cell, which one would expect to be a central spiritual focus of someone with a vocation to be a hermit. That Catherine is writing to Francesco about such a central aspect of his new vocation suggests she was involved in inspiring or advising him to join this religious order, and it shows the spiritual authority Catherine assumed. To grasp Catherine's inner authority, imagine that his young laywoman was counseling an educated man joining a religious community where the abbot at times advises Catherine.

This letter offers an overall view of Catherine's wisdom with an extensive description of the importance of spending time in the cell, here the house of self-knowledge. Though the Carthusians have individual hermitages and are pledged to a life of silence and solitude, Catherine underscores the importance of the inner experience that should be the fruit of such silence and solitude. In other words, for Catherine it is not enough that someone has joined an order that involves living as a hermit if they are not fully committed to the process of knowledge of God and self, which is an interior process. This letter is a fine and extended elaboration about this teaching.

This letter is also one of the few places where Catherine discusses types of prayer or stages of prayer. She describes continuous prayer, vocal prayer, and mental prayer.

❊ ❊ ❊

To the name of Jesus Christ crucified and tender Mary.

Dearest and most beloved son in Christ, loving Jesus. I, Catherine, slave of the servants of Jesus Christ, write to you in his precious blood, with desire to see you dwell in the house of self-knowledge. Through self-knowledge you will acquire all virtues; without this knowledge, you would live without purpose and vulnerable to all forms of evil.

Should you say to me, "How can I enter into this house? And how can I remain inside?" I will answer. You know that without the light [of understanding] anywhere we would go, we would be in darkness, a darkness that would harm us. And in this darkness one would be unable to learn about what one needs to go on the way [to the house].

We are all wayfarers and pilgrims, placed on the path of the teaching of Christ crucified. Some walk along according to the commandments and the way of ordinary charity, others according to the counsels and the way of perfect charity (of course never forgetting the commandments).[69] No one can walk along these paths without the light, for without it he would be unable to recognize where he should pause and rest in order to discern who harms him and who aids him. This [resting] place is the house of holy self-knowledge. The soul[70] following the path of the teaching of Christ crucified is able to recognize this house with the light of most holy faith, and if she wants to follow the crucified will immediately enter within herself.

In this house he will find the main enemy who wants to do him harm; this enemy is his own [self-centered] sensuality, when covered with the cape of selfish self-love. This enemy has two main comrades and many vassals around him. One of the comrades—worldly realities with their vanity and gratifications—befriends the sensual appetite when its desires are disordered. The other comrade is the evil one, perpetrator of deceit and a multiplicity of false ideas and grievances, all attractive to selfish self-will, which deliberately takes pleasure in these, no matter the form in which they are presented by the evil one. These principal enemies have many vassals, all ready to harm the soul, unless, through the light, she discerns a way to stop this.

So, it is reason that calls forth the light of faith and enters the house, gaining control of sensuality, having recognized that sensuality, accompanied by false enemies, wants and seeks only her death. She [reason][71] recognizes this through the light and acts with vigor in order to destroy it; she brings out the knife of hatred of sensuality and love of true, real virtues and with this knife she destroys the enemy. Once this enemy is destroyed, all others are defeated, and no others can cause harm unless she allows them. With this same light of faith, she recognizes who has protected and saved her from death or raised her from death and brought her to life; it is the fire of divine love. For out of love God bestowed the virtues and empowered the soul so that with the strength of reason she could climb unto the chair of conscience; from there, with the wisdom imparted by the Word, she [the soul] would be able to declare the death sentence of sensuality. The will,[72] which shares in the mercy of the holy Spirit and the loving will of God, takes the aforementioned knife with the hand of free will to impart the death blow.

Seeing that God is her cure, rescuer and protector, the soul grows in the house of the knowledge of self, which is filled with the light of truth, and an infinite, indescribable, and unfathomable fire that burns and consumes whatever is against reason that lives in the house. In this furnace of God's love and love of neighbor, this fire burns out the moisture of both spiritual and worldly self-centered love, so that the soul's affection seeks nothing other than Christ crucified. The soul thus wants to follow Christ on the path of suffering, according to God's way and not her own. Being free, free, she allows herself to be guided by God's tender will, and so her enemies cannot harm her, even though they are allowed by our just Lord to knock on the door; he allows this so that the person might become more attentive and not fall asleep in the bed of negligence but remain prudently vigilant. As well, such knocking on the door allows the strength of the house to be tested, so that if it is not strong enough, she recognizes it must be strengthened. Further, the light will allow recognition of what and who makes the house strong and enduring; with such recognition she can firmly hold onto the sources of strength.

What will make us strong and steadfast? It is continuous humble prayer made in the house of self-knowledge and knowledge of God's presence there. If such prayer were made outside of this house, the soul would benefit little, for the foundation of this prayer is humility, which is acquired in the house. This prayer is clothed in the fire of divine love, which is acquired by knowing God, as the light reveals to the soul that she is loved by God beyond measure. This love was demonstrated and proved in the first creation where she [the soul] sees how she was created out of love in the image and likeness of God; in the second creation the soul sees herself created anew through the grace of the blood of the immaculate Lamb. These [two creations] are the two principal graces that ground all other temporal and spiritual graces, both specific and general. And so with this light [of understanding] she clothes herself in fire.[73]

Bit-by-bit follow the tears, for when the eye encounters the heart's ache, it wants to offer it an outlet. It weeps as green wood, which, when set on fire, exudes moisture due to the intense heat. This is also what happens to the soul that experiences the fire of divine love; as her desire and deepest motivation [*affetto*] burn in the fire, the eye weeps, able to express only a small part of what she experiences within. The weeping pours forth due to the many emotions felt within, which come from the capacity for love at the core of self [*affetto* of the soul]. As you know, I explain this in the tract on tears,[74] so I say no more here.

CATHERINE OF SIENA

I come back very briefly to prayer. I say briefly because you already have details. We can think about prayer in three ways. One is continuous prayer,[75] to which all persons bestowed with reason are obligated. This prayer is true holy desire rooted in the love of God and one's neighbor; so that all our acts—toward self or neighbor—are carried out for God's honor. Such desire prays always; that is, deepest desire, united to God's love [*affetto* of love], prays continuously to our Creator—at all times, wherever one is and in all that one does.

What is the fruit received from such prayer? A peaceful calm within one's soul that comes from a will submitted to and congruent with reason and dismayed by nothing. Such a person has no difficulty bearing the yoke of obedience, when tasked—depending on need—with the burden of manual labor or of serving his brother. He no longer becomes bored, nor distressed, and is not deceived by the soul's desire for the physical cell, its consolation and peace. Neither is he deceived when he wants to literally pray yet is called to do something else. I mean, he is not fooled by this desire [to pray], becoming distressed and anxious [if called to] the odor of obedience with true humility and embraces the fire of love of neighbor. This is the prayer to which the glorious apostle Paul calls us when he says that we should pray without ceasing, for without such prayer, no other prayer will be life-giving for us. Whoever would leave such unceasing prayer to obtain peace will lose that peace.

Another form of prayer is vocal prayer, such as recitation of the Divine Office or other prayers a person may want to recite in order to lead up to mental prayer. Such vocal prayer aimed at attaining mental prayer achieves this goal when the person perseveres, stretching his mind to be attentive, receptive of and focused on God's love rather than on the sound of the words he recites. With prudence he allows this experience to unfold, so that as soon as he notices grace visiting his mind, he stops saying words—except if he is reciting the Divine Office, which he is obligated to say.

And in this way, he arrives at the third form of prayer, which is mental prayer where the mind and desire have moved beyond self to meditation on the *affetto* of God's love and of one's own *affetto*;[76] in which meditation he finds the doctrine of truth, savoring the milk of divine tenderness that flows from the breasts of love of the crucified, sacrificed Christ; and only finds pleasure in being with him on the cross. With this experience he reaches and receives the grace of the unitive state, where the soul attains such a state of union that she no longer focuses on herself for her own sake, but only on herself and on her neighbor for God's sake; she focuses on God because of his infinite goodness, recognizing how much he is worthy of being loved and served. She loves him beyond anything and urgently runs away from any evil desire.

She [the soul] delights in spending time in the room and bridal bed of her Bridegroom, where God reveals himself and where she becomes aware of the many mansions that exist in the home of the eternal king. She is then able to respect and to rejoice in the differences that exist among God's sons and daughters, and so in all things she is able to make judgments according to God's will and not that of human persons. She is freed from false judgments; she does not judge or become dismayed by God's actions, nor those of her neighbor. The taste of eternal life and the joy experienced by such a soul is a gift of God's infinite mercy. Even if I wanted to, I couldn't describe this experience with either the spoken or written word!

So now you know what allows us to stay firmly put in the house of self-knowledge; and you know who leads us there and how to find it. As I've said, the light guides us to this house that we find through the doctrine of Christ crucified; and prayer turns the lock and keeps us inside; this is the truth.

And so, very dear, beloved son, in order to fulfill the vow of obedience—since you have recently entered religious life—always remain in the house of self-knowledge; otherwise you will be unable to keep this vow. This is why I said that I wanted to see you in this house of self-knowledge.

Once all enemies are chased away and our main enemy, self-centered will, is dead, the house is then filled and decorated with the virtues. Be attentive to these [the virtues], for it would be of no use to empty the house without filling it. I want you to be constantly aware of self-knowledge and the fire and goodness of God's love within you. This [inner knowledge] is the cell that I want you to carry with you wherever you go on the island and during all that you do. So don't abandon this cell in the choir, in the refectory, in the gathering of the community, or during your prayer exercises; no matter what you have to do, firmly embrace this cell.[77] And during your official time of prayer, I want you always to raise your understanding to ponder the *affetto* of God's love; do this rather than attending to whatever graces or gifts you think you are receiving from God, so that your love is pure and not a mercenary love.[78] I want you to visit your actual, physical cell when obedience allows; prefer to be happy in this cell even when experiencing inner strife, rather than seeking peace outside your cell. For the evil one uses his wiles against those living in solitude to make them feel distressed about spending time in their physical cell; he stirs up darkness, struggles, and distress when in the cell so that they will fear the cell as if time [alone] there were the cause of all this distress.

For these reasons I do not want you to look back but to remain constant, to persevere. Do not be idle; use your time for prayer, for holy reading and manual labor, keep your memory always full of God, so that your soul is not caught off guard by boredom. I want you to weigh God's will with regard to everything; and, as I explained above, to guard against displeasure with and gossip against your brothers. As well I want obedience always to shine forth from you, not in part or in a half-hearted manner, but fully, so that you do not resist any expectation of your Order or your superior. In this way you become an example of the observances and customs of your Order, making sure that you heed these unto death. So, regard your self-centered will as evil and hold it in contempt; destroy it and mortify your body according to the guidelines of your Order. I want you to make the effort to lovingly carry out the customs and follow the guidelines that are difficult and perhaps at one time seemed unbearable due to your weakness or the delusions of the evil one. Struggle with and endure through all this and everything else in order to follow the Word of Christ, who tells us that the reign of God belongs to those who strenuously push themselves. I want your memory[79] to be filled and remain full of the blood of Christ crucified, of the graces of God and the awareness of death, so that you may grow in love, in holy fear and in hunger for time.[80] I want you to contemplate all this with the eye of understanding and the light of holy faith, so that your will can speedily race forth without attachment or disordered love for what is not in God.

When the evil one—blatantly or underhandedly—or your weak flesh provokes you to rebel or to struggle spiritually, I want you to share this with your superior, no matter what the issue. Open your heart to him if he is available, and if not, speak with whomever you feel most comfortable with and who you think is most suited to help you. Also, I want you to be careful regarding your anger, paying attention that your irritation not reach your tongue, so that you do not utter reproachful words that might cause scandal or disturbance. Instead turn any reproach or loathing toward yourself. All I have just mentioned is required of you by God and by the life of perfection you have chosen. I, your unworthy, inadequate mother, cause of harm rather than good,[81] want to see these qualities in your soul.

I beg you and press you in the name of Christ crucified, the tender good Jesus, that you take care to observe all the above advice until your death, so that you may be my pride and may receive the crown of blessedness for your enduring perseverance, which is such only when crowned. I say no more.

Do act, then, in such a way that I will not have to weep for you or complain to God about you. Give my greetings to the prior and all the brethren. All the family[82] sends greetings and I send warm greetings to Barduccio.

Remain in the tender love of God.

Tender Jesus! Jesus love!

CATHERINE OF SIENA

RAYMOND OF CAPUA

LETTER 219

To Friar Raymond of Capua of the Order of Preachers, to
Master Giovanni Terzo and Brother Felice of the Order of Hermits of
St. Augustine, and to other companions with them in
Vignone [Avignon]
Early April 1376 (Noffke and Volpato)

Introduction

Raymond of Capua was the Dominican friar assigned as director to Catherine in 1374. He became not only her mentor and confessor, but also a unique best friend.[83] Giovanni Tantucci or Terzo[84] and Felice were hermits living in a monastery near Siena. Giovanni, who was a theologian, was especially close to Catherine and undoubtedly was one of the priests through whom she grew in spiritual and theological knowledge. In Catherine's testamentary letter to Raymond, she asks him and Giovanni to decide how to handle her writings, indicating they were her two most trusted friends and advisors.

These three men had gone ahead to Avignon to prepare the visit with Gregory XI that Catherine would also attend. She writes to encourage them by sharing a very reassuring vision she experienced. It is one of the few detailed accounts of Catherine's mystical experience described directly by her. While feeling wrapped up in God's presence she had a vision and inwardly heard God's words regarding the church and the church's purification and restoration. She received insight into the mystery regarding the redemption of the church even through its current difficulties and the sinfulness of its prelates and pastors. As well, she saw that both Christians and unbelievers entered the side of Christ, implying both were welcomed into his heart and therefore to the grace of salvation. This would be a revolutionary revelation in Catherine's day. Also, Catherine reported to these most trusted spiritual companions and friends that through this vision God called her to be a mediator for the church and the unbelievers.

Friars and Monks

❆ ❆ ❆

To the Name of Jesus Christ crucified and tender Mary.

My dearest sons in Christ Jesus. I, your inadequate mother, have wanted with anxious desire to see your hearts, desire, and will [*affetto*] nailed to the cross, and to see you united and bound with the rope that bound and grafted God onto human persons and persons onto God.

This is the manner in which I want to see your hearts, desire, and will [*affetto*], grafted onto loving Jesus, the incarnate Word, so that neither the evil one nor any creature can ever separate you. I have no doubts that if you are bound by loving Jesus and passionately motivated by him, all the demons of hell with all their evil cannot separate you from such a loving union. I want to make sure you never stop adding wood to the fire of holy desire, since it is so necessary and offers such strength. I mean the wood of knowledge of yourselves; this is the wood that feeds the fire of divine love, a love acquired through knowledge of the immeasurable love of God. In this way the person is also united with her neighbor, and the more she feeds the fire with the right substance, that is, the wood of self-knowledge, the more the warmth of love of Christ and neighbor increases.

So do remain hidden within the knowledge of yourselves, do not leave this space, so that Malatasca[85] cannot catch you in deceptions and conversations against one another. Such behaviors would take away the union of love. I want you to, and I order you, to be submissive to one another, bearing with one another's faults, and learning from loving First Truth who chose to be the least of all, humbly bearing all our defects and iniquities. I want you to act in this same manner, my dearest sons. Love one another, love one another, love one another!

Rejoice and sing praises! Summer is coming;[86] I see it because on the first of April during the night, God disclosed his secrets in an exceptional way, revealing his extraordinary works, and leaving me feeling as though my soul were not in my body. And I experienced a fullness that no words can describe. [God] laid out step by step the mystery about the persecution that holy Church is currently experiencing, and how it will be renewed and exalted in the future. The current situation is allowed in order to return the church to her former state. So argued First Truth using a few words from the Gospels, namely, "He [God] requires scandal to come into the world," adding, "but woe be to him through whom scandal comes about" (Matt 18:7; Luke 17:1). It's as though he were saying, "I permit this time of persecution in order to remove my spouse's thorns, for she sorely lacks pruning. Yet I do not allow the evil plots of men. Do you know what I will do? I will act as I did while in the world. I made a whip out of rope and chased out those who engaged in commerce in God's house; for I didn't want his house to become a den of thieves. So I am telling you, that is what I am doing now; I am making some persons into a whip with which I chase out the greedy, avaricious, and depraved merchants[87] who are puffed up with pride, and who buy and sell the grace and gifts of the Holy Spirit." And so, with the whip of persecution I chase them out; that is, through persecutions and misfortunes I eliminate their disordered and dishonest income.

As the fire of holy desire increased in me, I gazed and saw both Christians and unbelievers enter the side of Christ crucified; and out of desire and my deepest *affetto* of love I passed among them and entered with them into Christ loving Jesus. I was accompanied by my father Saint Dominic, by John the Unique[88] and all my children.[89] And then he [Christ] placed the cross on my shoulder and the olive branch in my hands as if he were saying to me—wanting this from me—that I carry this cross from one people to the other; and he said to me, "Tell them, I announce a great joy!" (Luke 2:10). And then, together with those who truly know the divine essence,[90] my soul became full to bursting, drenched in the divine essence through union and the deepest movement of desire and *affetto* of love. And my soul felt such love, that I could no longer sense my previous distress at seeing the offenses to God and I could even say, Oh happy and providential fault![91]

Friars and Monks

At this, loving Jesus smiled and said, "So, providential sin is nothing? Do you know what St. Gregory meant when he said, 'happy and providential fault'? What aspect is providential and happy according to St. Gregory?" I answered as he inspired me and said, "I see clearly, my loving Lord, and know well that sin is not worthy of being blessed nor is it providential in itself; it is the fruit that comes forth from sin [that is providential and blessed]. This is what I think Gregory said, I mean that due to Adam's sin, God gave us the Word, his only-begotten Son, and the Word poured out his blood so that in giving his life he restored our life with love like a blazing fire. And so, sin is providential not as sin, but as the fruit and gift we received because of that sin." And so, out of the offenses of wicked Christians who persecute the church arise the light and fragrance of virtue in his bride[92] and she is exalted. This [restoration] is due to such love, that there couldn't be any comparison between the offense committed and the boundless benevolence and goodness shown by God toward his spouse.

I sang praises and rejoiced and felt enveloped in such certainty about the future[93] that I felt I could taste it and possess it. I could say with Simeon, "Master, you are now dismissing your servant in peace according to your word" (Luke 2:29). So many mysteries were to be carried out that no words can describe them, nor can the heart conceive them, nor the eyes see them. What tongue would be capable of describing the extraordinary realities of God? Not mine, poor wretched me; and so I am led to be silent and give myself only to seeking God's honor, the salvation of souls and the renovation and exaltation of holy Church. And I wish, through the grace of the Holy Spirit, to persevere until I die.

With great love and compassion, I invited and will invite our Christ on Earth,[94] and you, father, and all my dear children to share this desire. I have asked for and obtained your petition. Be joyful! Be joyful and sing praises! *Oh tender God of love, please speedily fulfill the desires of your servants!* I say no more; I have said nothing.[95] I am struggling because I'm dying of desire; so have compassion on me and pray the divine Goodness and Christ on earth that my desire will soon come to pass.

Remain in the holy and tender love of God.

Drown yourselves in the blood of Christ crucified, finding ever more strength in it; do not relent for any reason. Rejoice, rejoice in loving difficulties! Love, love, love one another!

Tender Jesus! Jesus love!

LETTER 267

To Friar Raymond of Capua of the Order of Preachers
Oct 1377 (Noffke)

Introduction

Raymond of Capua was one of the people dearest to Catherine. Since holiness was one of her most cherished values, she passionately wanted Raymond to be holy, so she always took the opportunity to exhort him to more and more transformation, which she does in this letter. In telling Raymond—albeit in the third person—that she knows about his inner trials, she reveals her capacity to intuit in prayer the spiritual reality of those close to her.

Most of the letter, though, is devoted to her concern for the reform of the church. In this letter she gave Raymond firm instructions to be given in her name to Gregory XI. Raymond should challenge the pope about the lack of order and holiness in his life. The pope must be reprimanded for his lack of action and poor governance. The firmness and lack of self-consciousness about which Catherine asks Raymond to exhort the pope (and does so herself in other letters) reveals her conviction about the truth and spiritual authority with which she communicates.

Catherine refers to ways in which the pope is unhappy with her and to ways in which Raymond is persecuted, perhaps because of her. At the time of this letter, the pope was engaged in peace negotiations with Florence, which had left the Papal League. Florence had just turned down the latest papal offer of peace and rebelled against

Friars and Monks

the papal interdict against the celebration of the sacraments. It appears the pope believed Raymond and Catherine had not done enough to advocate for the pope's terms, and this was the cause of his anger at them. At the same time, the Sienese governing elite were distrustful of Raymond (and Catherine along with him) for support of the Papal League, against whom the Sienese had also rebelled.[96]

Though rhetorical expressions of humility were common, and Catherine uses them repeatedly, this letter goes beyond these. Catherine seems to express genuine concern that she has somehow failed in her vocation of obedience to the pope. She was unable to see as valid the concerns of the city-states regarding the pope's actions, including the interdict that banned the sacraments. This inability on Catherine's part raises important questions regarding a spirituality of discernment.[97]

Finally, this epistle reflects Catherine's belief in martyrdom and in the value of the crusade for the well-being of the church. She felt martyrdom was the ultimate proof of love for God in giving one's life for the church. Her allusions to "unto death" refer to this belief.

❊ ❊ ❊

To the name of Jesus Christ crucified and tender Mary.

Dearest, most beloved father in Christ tender Jesus. I, Catherine, servant and slave of the servants of Jesus Christ, write to you in his precious blood, with desire to see you a true combatant against the temptations and insidious suggestions of the evil one, and against the malice and persecution of others, and against your selfish self-love. For if the person does not cut off this enemy, selfish self-love, through virtue and holy hatred, he will never be able to stand firm in the battles that he faces every day.

Because selfish self-love makes us weak, it is necessary to avoid it through the strength of the virtues that we will acquire in the ineffable love God revealed through the blood of his only begotten Son. This love, which is part of divine love, gives us life and light. The light allows us to know the truth about how much we need him for our salvation and in order to acquire the great perfection of being able to endure unto death with patience, fortitude, and steadfastness. From such fortitude—acquired through the light that reveals the truth—we acquire the life of holy grace.

Become drunk, then, with the blood of the spotless Lamb. Be a faithful, not an unfaithful servant of your Creator. Have no doubts and don't turn back due to any battle or oppression that should assail you; rather, persevere in faith until death, for you know well that perseverance will yield the fruit of your efforts.

I heard from a servant of God[98]—who holds you in continuous prayer before God—that you have gone through great trials, and that darkness and oppression have filled your mind due to the guiles and deceits of the evil one. He wants to make you see what is wrong as right, and what is right as wrong. And he does this to prevent you from moving forward, and so that you do not arrive at your destination. Take comfort, though, for God has provided for you and will continue to do so; his providence will not fail you. Make sure that in all needs you appeal to Mary, that you embrace the cross, and that you never allow yourself to become spiritually confused, and that in the stormy seas you sail in the boat of divine mercy.

I know that you have received persecutions and expressions of displeasure and indignation from the vicar of Christ [the pope], from other religious, from laypersons, and even from the mystical body of Christ. Whether you have endured these because of yourself or because of me, don't struggle, but hold on with patience, and run off immediately into your cell and engage in holy reflections, focusing on knowledge of yourself. Consider that God made you worthy of enduring [hardships] for love of truth and worthy to be persecuted because of him; consider this with true humility, recognizing that you merit the suffering and not its fruit. Do everything you have to do with prudence, always placing God before you. Whatever you have to do or say, do it and say it having consulted God in holy prayer. In this practice you will find the physician of mercy, the Holy Spirit, who will infuse you with the light of wisdom that will make you discern and choose that which will be for his honor. This is the doctrine [teaching] given to you by tender, first Truth, with immeasurable love, in order to care for your needs.

Dearest father, if the situation arises that you find yourself before his Holiness, the vicar of Christ, our most fine, most holy father, humbly greet him in my name. Tell him I failed his Holiness due to my great laxness and negligence toward God, and due to my disobedience against my Creator, who had invited me to cry out with yearning desire[99] and with prayer before him, and to be by his vicar with my word and presence. I have been at great fault in many ways that, I believe, have caused him and the church to be victims of many persecutions. So if he complains about me, he is right and has the right to punish me for my faults. Do tell him that to the extent it is in my power, I will make every effort to correct my faults and to be more fully obedient to him.

And so I hope that the divine Goodness will turn the eye of his mercy toward the Bride of Christ and his vicar; and will do so also toward me, freeing me from my faults and negligence. With regard to his Bride, I hope he will offer her the relief of peace and renovation bestowing strong support; for only with a great deal of struggle can one remove the thorns of the many faults that choke the garden of holy Church. With regard to the pope, I hope he will bless him with grace when he chooses to act as a brave man without turning back due to whatever struggles or persecution he suffers from his wicked children.[100] With endurance and perseverance he [the pope] should not disdain any struggle, but he should throw himself as a lamb among the wolves, full of desire and hunger for the honor of God and the salvation of souls, leaving aside attention to temporal matters, instead attending to those that are spiritual. If he acts in this way—as divine Goodness has requested—the lamb will overcome the wolves and the wolves will become sheep. In this way they will see the glory and praise of God's name, for the good and the benefit of holy Church and for peace. There is no other way to accomplish this. For this is not accomplished with war but rather through peace and kindness, and through that holy spiritual correction that a father must impart to the child that commits a fault.

Oh, dear, dear me, most holy father![101] *You should have done this the first day you came to your city!*[102] *I am hoping in God's goodness and counting on your Holiness to now accomplish what should have been done and in this way recover both spiritually and temporally. This is what God asked you to do; as you know, you were told that you should try to achieve the reformation of holy Church by trying to punish faults and naming virtuous pastors. [You were also told] that you should establish peace with your wicked children in the best way possible and in the way most pleasing to God so that you would be free to protect [the Holy Sepulcher and therefore the Church] raising the standard of the holy cross over the unbelievers.*[103] I believe the reasons are several for so much failure, damage, and irreverence in holy Church and the failures and irreverence of her pastors. There is negligence and failure to do all that can be done—without cruelty or through war but with peace and kindness—always meting out punishment to those who have committed a fault. And doing so not to the extent deserved, but according to the extent to which the ill [sinful] person is able to bear. And I fear that if we do not take care of what wasn't done before, well, I hope our sins will not merit worse incidents—which we see coming—and which can cost us much more than losing temporal possessions!

I, wretched person, am a cause of all these evils and sufferings due to my lack of virtue and my great disobedience. Most holy father,[104] please, in the light of reason and truth, soften your unhappiness with me; I mean your unhappiness, not your punishment. If you abandon me, to whom would I have recourse? Who would help me? In whom would I find refuge if you send me away? My persecutors pursue me and I find refuge in you and in other children and servants of God. If you should abandon me due to displeasure and annoyance, I would hide in the wounds of Christ crucified, whose vicar you are. He will receive me because he does not want the death of the sinner.

Having been received by him, you can't send me away. We will be in your city to courageously fight for the Bride of Christ with the arms of virtue.[105] I want to finish my life in Christ, with sweat, tears, and sighs, and I want to give my blood and the marrow of my bones. And if everyone should send me away, I will not take heed; I will rest on the chest of the dear Bride with tears and with much endurance. *Most holy father, forgive all my negligence and the offenses I have committed against God and against you. May it be the truth, eternal Truth, that will forgive me and set me free. I humbly ask for your blessing.*

And you, dearest father, [Raymond], I ask you to go before his Holiness as soon as possible with a courageous heart, without any timidity or servile fear. Before doing so, spend time in the cell in humble and holy prayer before Mary and the holy cross; and do so with true knowledge of yourself, with living faith and the will to persevere. And then go with confidence and carry out—unto death—whatever is possible for the honor of God and the salvation of souls. And tell him [the pope] as the Spirit guides you, what I have written to you in this letter. I say no more.

Remain in the tender, holy love of God.

Gentle Jesus! Jesus love!

LETTER 272 (POSTSCRIPT)

To Friar Raymond of Capua of the Order of Preachers
October 1377 (Noffke)

Introduction

Letter 272 is a very long letter including the themes and framework that became part of *The Dialogue*. Because its content is available in that work, the body of the letter will not be translated, but the postscript is included as it is Catherine's account about learning to write, a spiritual experience of great significance in her life and one of the few of her exceptional experiences that is described directly by her.[106]

CATHERINE OF SIENA

❃ ❃ ❃

Postscript

This and another letter I sent you I wrote by myself while I was in Isola della Rocca. I did so with sighs and many tears,[107] so that while seeing, my eye didn't see. Yet I was full of awe for myself, for God's goodness, and for his providence with which he abundantly blessed me. Knowing how deprived I was of consolation (due to my inadequacy),[108] God, with the mercy he shows his creatures capable of reason, provided for me and offered me a form of relief by giving me the ability to write. He did this so that I would have a way of handling what was in my heart after coming down from the heights, so that my heart wouldn't burst! Since he didn't yet want to take me from this life filled with troubles, he formed the ability [to write] in my mind in a marvelous way. That is, in the way a master teaches a child, offering him a model, so that as soon as you left me, I began to learn with the glorious evangelist and Thomas Aquinas.[109]

Forgive me for writing too much, for the hands and tongue follow the heart [which has been bursting].

LETTER 373

To Master[110] Raymond of Capua of the Order of Preachers in a letter of February 15, 1380, in which she predicts her death; she then died on the 29th of April 1380.
February 15, 1380

Introduction

This is Catherine's last letter to Raymond of Capua, her friend and mentor. According to Noffke's dating, this is also Catherine's final letter. It is related to Letter 371, which was most likely written within a few days of Letter 373 and may have been appended to this letter as it does not have an addressee.

Friars and Monks

At the time she wrote this letter, Catherine was in the last weeks of her life—she died two months later—weakened by fasting, by whatever medical conditions had resulted from her severe asceticism, and perhaps by illness that was not identified in the fourteenth century. Indeed, some of the troubling experiences she describes here could have had a physical cause. Be that as it may, she suffered spiritual experiences, both positive and negative, that she wanted to report to Raymond; she wanted to inform him that she was struggling with uncertainty regarding how much longer God expected her to live and what He expected of her. Sensing the end of her life, Catherine leaves Raymond her last wishes regarding him, her "family," and how her Book (*The Dialogue*) and her writings were to be handled.

Catherine suffered particularly strongly due to the historical situation at the time of her death. Urban VI, an Italian, was elected less than two years before Catherine's death. A large contingent of the electing cardinals reversed this election four months later, choosing a new pope, the Frenchman Clement VII—thus starting the Western Schism—with a pope in Rome and another in Avignon. Catherine was absolutely certain Urban was "Christ on earth" and Clement the "anti-Christ." Her references in this letter to the revolts of the Romans and to her desire that all people recognize and honor Urban are allusions to this conflict. For although Urban remained in Rome and Clement had to return to Avignon, conflict regarding who had authority continued to roil Rome and some parts of Italy even at the time of Catherine's death in 1380. Such a division in the papacy caused Catherine severe suffering, and as this letter attests, she devoted her prayers and offered her final physical and spiritual sufferings for a solution to these conflicts.

❃ ❃ ❃

To the name of Jesus Christ crucified and tender Mary.

Most beloved and tender father in Christ, tender Jesus. I, Catherine, slave of the servants of Jesus Christ, write to you in his precious blood with desire to see you as a pillar rooted again in the garden of holy Church and as faithful spouse of the truth—as you should be. When this happens, I can consider my soul as blessed.

I don't want you to turn back due to any hardship or persecution; I want you to exult in adversity, for in bearing it, we show our love and perseverance, and we give glory to God's name; we would not give glory in any other way. Now is the time, dearest father, to surrender all of yourself and not to be focused at all on self. This was the way of the glorious laborers[111] who with so much love and desire were ready to give their lives; they watered the garden [of holy Church] with continuous, humble prayer and with endurance until death.

Make sure I don't see you acting cautiously, as if your shadow scared you; rather, be a courageous warrior. And never abandon the yoke of obedience placed upon you by the supreme pontiff. In your [religious] Order also carry out whatever you recognize is for the honor of God. God's great goodness asks this of us and placed us here for this. Just look at how much need there is in holy Church and how she has been left completely alone.[112]

This is what Truth explained, as I wrote to you in another letter. And as the Bride [the church] has remained alone, so has her bridegroom [the pope]. Oh, my beloved father! I will not keep from you the great mysteries[113] of God, but I will tell you about them in as brief a manner as possible, to the extent that my fragile tongue can express itself and offer a narrative. I will also tell you what I want you to do. Don't receive what I tell you with sorrow, for I don't know what the divine goodness will do with me, whether he will have me stay here or call me to him. Father, father and most loved son! God has worked amazing mysteries from the time of [the feast of] the circumcision[114] until now; they are so amazing that it would be impossible to express them.

But let me leave aside that time and get back to Sexagesima Sunday,[115] the Sunday when those mysteries occurred that I am about to describe; I don't think I had ever experienced anything similar. The sorrow in my heart was so great that my tunic was torn where I was able to hold on to it, as I moved around the chapel as someone in agony; and if someone had held me, they

Friars and Monks

would have taken my life. When Monday evening came around, I felt compelled to write to Christ on earth [the pope] and the three cardinals.[116] I asked for help to go into the study, and after I wrote to Christ on earth, I was unable to write further because of the intense pain in my body.

After a bit, the terror from the devils started such that I was horrified, as they acted almost in a rage against me, as if I—worm that I am—were the reason that the power that they held for a long time within the church was taken from them. My terror and physical pain were so great that I wanted to escape from the study to go into the chapel, feeling as though the study were the reason for my suffering.

I got up and since I could not walk, I leaned on my son Barduccio.[117] I was suddenly thrown to the ground and felt as though my soul had left my body, not in the same way as when I felt my soul leave me and I experienced being with the blessed, enjoying with them ultimate blessedness and goodness. No, this time I felt as though the experience involved just me. I felt that I was not in my body; I saw my body as though it belonged to another. And as my soul realized the suffering of my companion [Barduccio], I wanted to see if I could carry out some movement with my body, so I could tell him, "Son, don't be afraid;" but I realized that neither my tongue nor any other part of my body could move; my body acted as someone separated from life.

So, I let my body be as it was, while my understanding was focused on the abyss of the Trinity, my memory was filled with awareness of the need of holy Church and of all the Christian faithful. I cried for them, and with firmness I begged for divine help. I offered my desire, pleading in union with the blood of the Lamb and the sufferings he bore.[118] As soon as I offered this plea, I felt he would not deny my petition. I then pleaded for all of you, praying that he fulfill in you his will and my desires for you. I then begged that I would be spared eternal damnation; I remained in this state for a long time, so much so that the "family"[119] were grieving as though I had died. And as I pleaded, the terror from the evil ones had left me.

I then experienced in my soul the presence of the humble Lamb, saying, "Do not doubt. I will fulfill your desires and those of my other servants. I want you to know I am a good master. I am like a potter who forms and reforms his vessels according to his preferences. I know how to craft and recraft my vessels; in this way I take the vessel of your body and replant it in the garden of holy Church, in a different way as in the past." And as Truth pursued me with very enticing words and manners (which I omit), my body started to breathe a little, and my soul returned to her vessel. I was filled with wonder, yet so much sorrow remained in my heart that I still feel it. And all delight, all soothing and all [spiritual] nourishment were taken from me.

I was then carried upstairs, where the room seemed full of evil spirits, which started a new battle with me, the most terrible such battle I had ever experienced; they wanted to make me believe and see that it was not I who was in my body but practically an evil spirit. With loving tenderness I called upon divine help—without ceasing to fight—and said, "My God, listen to my cry for help! Lord make haste to help me! You have allowed me to be alone in this battle, without the sustenance of my spiritual father [the father of my soul][120]; I am deprived of him due to my lack of gratitude."[121] I spent two nights and days amid these storms; it's true, nevertheless, that my mind and desire were not harmed, they were always fixed on their object; however, my body seemed to have totally deteriorated.

Then on the feast of the Purification of Mary, I wanted to participate in Mass, and then all the mysteries came back. God showed me [the church's] great need; and it later became clear that Rome was about to revolt amid arguments full of moral weakness and irreverence. However, God anointed their hearts, so I think there will be a good outcome. God then assigned me the task of offering as a sacrifice, during all of Lent, the desires of the "family," and all celebrations [of Mass] should be for this cause, that is, for holy Church. I was to attend Mass every morning at dawn, which you know is impossible for me to do; yet all is possible when obeying him.

Friars and Monks

This desire became so strong within me that it filled my memory. My understanding saw nothing else, and my will could desire nothing else. This does not mean that I am rejecting all that is of this world. I continue to hold conversations with true citizens [the blessed in heaven]; and though my soul cannot, nor does it want to rejoice with their joy, it does embrace the hunger[122] that they have and had as pilgrims and wanderers in this life. In these and other ways I can't describe, my life is consumed and poured out for this beloved bride [the church]. This is the way in which my life is poured out, while that of the glorious martyrs [is poured out] in their blood.

I pray to the divine Goodness to let me see the redemption of his people. When it's time for Terce,[123] I get up from Mass, and then you would see a dead person going to St. Peter's. I go there to work again in the boat of holy Church.[124] I stay there until Vespers though I would want to stay there day and night until I see these people stopped and in a peaceful relationship with their father [the pope].[125] My body is without food, and without a drop of water, suffering such blessed pain and bodily torments as I've ever had to endure; my life hangs on a thread.

I don't know what the divine Goodness wants to do with me. With respect to what I can discern, I can't say I know in a felt way what he wants to do with me; however, as to my body, I feel I should allow it to be consumed in a new martyrdom for that which is beloved to my soul, that is, holy Church. Maybe later he will have me rise with him, finishing and bringing to an end my failures and my crucified [anguished] desires; or perhaps he will deal with me as at other times, encircling my body.[126] I have prayed and pray that his infinite mercy accomplish his will in me, and that he will not leave you and the others orphans, that he will always guide you along the path of Truth, with true, most perfect light. I am sure he will do this.

So now I pray and urge you, father and son given to me by tender Mary, that if you sense that God places his eye of mercy on me,[127] that you should renew your life, and dying to all selfish sensuality, you should throw yourself into the boat of holy Church. Be always cautious in your conversations. Undoubtedly you can spend little time in the physical cell, but I want you always to dwell in the cell of your heart,[128] and always carry this cell with you, for you know that so long as we are within this cell the enemy can't get to us. In this way all that you do will be directed toward God and ordered in him.

Please also allow your heart to ripen through true, holy prudence; and may your life be exemplary in the eyes of laypersons, never conforming to worldly things. And may the voluntary poverty you have always lived and your generosity toward the poor be refreshed with true and perfect humility. Don't relax this attitude no matter what status or honor God may give you, but instead walk more deeply into the valley of such humility, taking delight at the table of the holy cross; there eat the food of souls, embracing continuous prayer, this humble, faithful mother; and hold prayer vigils and celebrate [the eucharist] every day unless circumstances prevent you. Flee from unnecessary, superficial chatting; rather, be mature in your conversations and in all forms of behavior.

Reject all softness toward yourself as well as slavish fear, for our beloved church doesn't need such people; rather she needs people capable of being merciless with themselves and compassionate toward her. I beg you to dedicate yourself to all these matters.

I would like to ask that you deliver by hand my Book [*The Dialogue*] and all writings of mine that you should find, to the Master and to Friars Bartolomeo and Tommaso.[129] Together with messer Tommaso[130]—in whom I trust—please do whatever you think would be for the greater honor of God. To the extent it is possible for you, I ask that you be pastor and leader, as well as father to the "family;" sustain them in living a life that delights in love and perfect union. I don't want them to become or remain separated as sheep without a shepherd. I believe I will be able to do more for you and for them after my death than in this life. I will beg eternal Truth that all graces and gifts he has bestowed upon me [my soul] should be transferred to all of you, so that you may be as lights elevated on candleholders. And I ask you to pray that the eternal Bridegroom may allow me to

Friars and Monks

courageously complete the missions assigned to me, and that he may forgive my many sins.

I ask you to forgive all my acts of irreverence, my lack of gratitude, my disobedience, as well as any sorrow or disappointment I may have caused you or committed against you. Forgive also any lack of attentiveness to your salvation. I ask for your blessing. For the sake of Christ crucified, please pray assiduously for me, and have prayers said for me. Forgive any disappointing or painful words I've written. I don't write these to cause you distress, but because I have doubts and don't know what God will do with me; I want to have done my duty.

Don't be sad if we are separated bodily, though your being present is for me a great consolation; it is a greater consolation and joy to see the fruit you produce for holy Church. I ask you, now in a more pressing way, to act [in favor of the church] for she has never been more in need. Christ on Earth and messer Tommaso are sending you the instruments with which you can work well. No matter what persecution you should suffer, never leave the side of our lord the pope without permission. Take comfort, take comfort in Christ tender Jesus; and let go of sorrow. I say no more.

Remain in the holy, tender love of God.

Tender Jesus! Jesus love!

4
ECCLESIASTICAL AUTHORITIES

POPES

LETTER 185

To the Holy Father Gregory XI
January 1376 (Noffke); between December 20, 1375, and January 14, 1376 (Volpato)

Introduction

This is one of fourteen letters that Catherine wrote to Gregory XI, a Frenchman, who was pope between 1370 and March 1378.[1] Catherine's relationship with this pope began when he sought a woman mystic to pray for him and offer revelations or words from God regarding his policies. Birgitta of Sweden, who was fulfilling this role, had died in 1373. As medieval historians have asserted, Gregory XI was not looking for political advice or even guidance regarding his spiritual journey, but rather someone close to God to play the roles of visionary and intercessor.[2] Catherine, however, did not see her role as that of visionary to Gregory.

Instead, Catherine experienced a powerful call to work for the good of the church. As we have seen, she acted with authority and conviction trusting in her connection with God. Thus, she exhorted Gregory to pursue policies in which she believed, and which were strongly supported by Raymond of Capua and many ecclesiastical authorities in Tuscany. They believed it would benefit the church if the pope returned to Rome from Avignon, that it would be good for him to make peace with the Tuscan Republics after the papal troops had tried to enforce the power of the Papal States, and that the crusade would benefit the church as well as the crusaders and the "unbelievers" who lived in the Holy Land.[3]

This advice, however, was not Catherine's main goal in her communication with Gregory XI. Rather, his transformation was her foremost concern, one for which she offered her prayers and sufferings. Indeed, she acted like a formator, repeatedly calling Gregory to growth in his relationship with God through knowledge of God and self, for she was sure that only with a transformed heart and mind would Gregory be able to guide the church according to God's will.

With great firmness and mincing no words, in this letter, Catherine especially underscored the problem of selfish self-love and the particular way in which it was insidious in the case of the pope. Selfish self-love is like a worm that penetrates a tree and makes it rot from the inside; by contrast, a tree planted in true knowledge of self and God bears fruit, the sort of fruit the pope must bear for the good of the church. The problem with selfish self-love is the grave inability to correct others and to "cut out the sore" of corrupt and sinful pastors if the pope fears being disliked or losing power. "The greatest cruelty," she insisted, would be pacifying those who were wrong, which Catherine likened to putting a useless salve on a wound rather than cauterizing it.[4]

❋ ❋ ❋

To the name of Jesus Christ and tender Mary, Mother of the Son of God.

To you, most beloved, reverend father in Christ Jesus, your unworthy, most inadequate daughter Catherine, servant and slave of the servants of Jesus Christ, writes to you in the precious blood. I wish to see you a fruitful tree full of sweet, ripe fruit, planted in rich soil—the soil of true knowledge of self; for if not rooted in this soil the tree would become dry and would bear no fruit.

The soul that has knowledge of self acts humbly for she doesn't find anything about which to be proud. She nurtures within the sweet fruit of most passionate love as she experiences the boundless goodness of God. Knowing that *she-is-not*, she gives back all that she is to *He-Who-Is*. And such a soul is bound to love what God loves and loathe what God loathes. *Oh true, loving knowledge, you hold the knife of abhorrence;*[5] *with this abhorrence you extend the hand of holy desire to draw out and kill the contemptible worm of selfish self-love—for this worm destroys and eats away the roots of our tree, so it can't produce life-giving fruit.*

The tree's fruit dry up; it cannot remain lush, because whoever cares for self with selfish self-love is someone who has wicked pride living within, and such pride is the beginning and source of all evil; this is the case no matter what the status of the person, be they a prelate[6] or layperson. And so if he is isolated[7] and loves himself with selfish love—that is, he loves himself for his own sake and not because of God—he is capable only of evil and doing harm; all virtue is dead within him. Such a person is like a woman who bears dead children. This is truly what happens[8] to those who do not have within them lifegiving love and have not devoted themselves exclusively to the glory and praise of God's name.

I tell you that if this person is a prelate, he causes harm, and in him dies holy justice when he sees the faults and sins of those under his care but pretends not to see and does not admonish them; and acts in this way to avoid being disliked by those with whom he is in relationships for his own gratification and self-regard. And when he tries to correct them, he does so with such lukewarmness and half-heartedness that he accomplishes nothing; rather, he just coats[9] over the vice. He is always afraid of displeasing others or creating conflict, all because of selfish self-regard. Sometimes he just tries to pacify others. I tell you this is actually the greatest cruelty possible. If someone gets a sore, if only a salve is applied without cauterizing it with fire or cutting it out with a knife, the sufferer will obtain no healing; instead, the wound will putrefy [become infected], and the person may even die. Oh my, my most loving Babbo,[10] this is the reason that their followers [those of the prelates] are all corrupt, filled with wickedness and corruption. Oh my! I say this weeping! this worm [selfish self-love] is so dangerous because it not only kills the shepherd, but through him all others become ill or die. Why is such a prelate so prone to use a salve?[11] Because there is no cost to this; because using it on those who are ill does not lead to any unpleasantness or any resistance, so long as it is not done against their will. They[12] want a salve and that is what they get. Oh human wickedness! How blind is the sick person who doesn't know what he needs! Blind is also the shepherd who is a doctor but cares only about his own benefit and gratification; and for fear of being deprived of these, he does not use the knife of justice or the fire of passionate love.[13] These persons are like the blindman leading another blindman—as Christ tells us [Matt 15:14]—both end up in a ditch or in hell; that is, both the sick person and the doctor end up in hell.

Such a pastor is truly a mercenary, for he not only doesn't rescue the sheep from the wolf, but he actually eats them himself! And all this because his love is alienated from God and he does not follow loving Jesus, the true shepherd who gives his life for his sheep. And since this perverse love [selfish self-love] is dangerous in others and in oneself, it is important to flee from love like this; it does such harm to every generation. My revered father, I hope you will extinguish such love in yourself; I hope that you will not love yourself, your neighbor, or God selfishly. I hope you will love God because he is supreme eternal Goodness, worthy of love; and that you will love yourself and your neighbor for the honor and glory of the beloved name of Jesus. I want you to be that true, good shepherd, who, if he had one hundred thousand lives, would be ready to give them all for the honor of God and the salvation of human persons.

Oh my father, dear Christ on earth, follow our beloved Gregory, for what was possible for him will be possible for you; he was made of the same flesh as you, and God then was the same as today! All that is lacking is virtue and hunger for the salvation of souls. Here is how this is done, father: the focus of love should be removed from ourselves and from any person apart from God. One should no longer be concerned with friends or relatives or their material needs. Attention should only be focused on virtue and the advancement of spiritual matters. For, among other things, temporal matters go awry when you abandon care for spiritual matters.[14]

Shouldn't we want to have that glorious hunger that previous true and holy pastors had, that is, extinguishing in ourselves the fire of selfish self-love? Let's do as they did, who doused fire with fire; that is the fire of unlimited, passionate love that burnt in their hearts and minds led them to hunger for souls, to desire to consume them, finding delight in this. Oh benevolent, glorious fire so saturated with virtue that it douses the fire of selfish self-love and of disordered gratification and pleasure! Like a drop of water, these are quickly consumed in such a furnace. Should someone ask me how they came to be filled with such a fine fire and hunger, I would have to say that of ourselves we are fruitless trees. So, I looked to see how they did it and I see that they were joined to the fruitful tree of the most holy, most loving cross and were never separated from it; and there they found the slaughtered Lamb who had such a great fire of love for our salvation. Such a love that it seemed it could never be satiated, and he cried out with thirst as if he were saying, "I have greater passion, desire and thirst for your salvation than I can possibly show with my finite passion." *Oh kind, loving Jesus, may popes and pastors and all of us feel ashamed of our ignorance, pride, and gratifications, when we contemplate such magnanimity, goodness, and immeasurable love from our Creator; he revealed himself to us as a tree in our humanity full of sweet, soft fruit so that we—wild trees—could become grafted onto him.* This was the way of Gregory, who was in love, and all other good pastors who knew—through no virtue of their own—that *they-were-not*; and so, gazing upon the Word, our tree, they grafted themselves onto him, binding themselves to him and uniting themselves with him through the bond of love. For having

Ecclesiastical Authorities

gazed upon that which is beautiful and good, the eye takes delight in that which it sees. And so, having gazed and seen, they bound themselves—without regard for themselves—seeing and savoring everything in God. There was no wind or hail, no person or evil one, who could prevent them from producing familiar fruit, because they were grafted onto the marrow of the tree, our Jesus. And so, they produced fruit through the marrow of tender love, a marrow to which they were united. There is no other way; this is the way I want to see you pursue.

If up until now you have not been standing firmly in the truth, I want and I beg you to do so now with courage—in the time we have left—as a courageous man, following Christ, whose vicar you are. And father, no matter what happens in the future, do not be afraid of the stormy winds that have come your way—I mean those rotten members who have rebelled against you.[15] Do not be afraid, for divine help is at hand. Take care of spiritual matters, of finding good pastors and good vicars for your cities, for the rebellions have occurred due to bad pastors and vicars. You must solve these problems, find strength in Christ, and stop being afraid.

Get on with it! Carry out with holy efficiency those holy resolutions you had begun, namely, coming here [to Rome] and the holy and loving pilgrimage.[16] Don't delay any longer, for a lot of problems have occurred due to delays, and the evil one is working at preventing your resolutions from being carried out, for he sees these will damage him. Come on, father, no more slackness! Raise the standard of the holy cross,[17] for with the scent of the cross you will acquire peace. I beg you to invite those who have rebelled against you to make peace so that all war can be directed only against the unbelievers. I trust that God in his infinite goodness will soon send assistance. Take courage! Take courage! And come to strengthen the poor servants of God, also your children. They await you with affectionate, loving desire. Forgive me for saying so much to you; you know how it is, out of the fullness of the heart, the tongue wags. I am certain that if you will be that tree [I have described] and desire you to be, nothing will stand in your way.

I beg you, as a father, to send what you can to Lucca and Pisa—in whatever way God shows you—giving them a break to the extent possible and inviting them to remain firm and persevere. So far, I have been to Pisa and Lucca and have appealed to them as best as I am able not to join those rotten cities that have rebelled against you. They [Pisa and Lucca] are very worried because they have no support from you while the opposing side is always pressuring and menacing them to join. Up until now they have not agreed. I ask that you write to messer Piero,[18] even if briefly; do it promptly and do not delay. I say no more.

I have heard that you have named new cardinals. I believe it would be for the honor of God and better for you, that you always take care to choose virtuous men; if you choose those who are not virtuous, it will dishonor God and damage the church. Let's not be surprised, then, if God sends us scourges and afflictions, for these would be just. I ask you to do what you must with courage, and with awe of God.[19]

I have heard that you will elevate the Master [General] of our order[20] to another ecclesiastical office. If this is your intention, I pray that you choose a good and virtuous leader, for the Order needs such a person (as it is too disordered). You could discuss this with [cardinal] Nicola da Osimo and with the archbishop of Otronto; I will write to them.

Remain in the holy, tender love of God. Humbly I beg for your blessing, and forgive my audacity in writing to you.

Jesus, loving Jesus!

LETTER 252

To the Holy Father Gregory XI when he was at Corneto[21]
December 1376 or January 1377 (Noffke)

Introduction

Pope Gregory XI received this letter in Corneto, the nearest port to Rome, as he was returning from Avignon. Having been asked

Ecclesiastical Authorities

to be intercessor for the pope, Catherine feels called to advise and exhort, using both seductive expressions of filial closeness and firm exhortations with remarkable spiritual authority. Thus, Catherine addresses the pope both very formally, "most holy father," and at the same time permits herself great familiarity, calling him *babbo*, or "daddy."

This letter shows a typical pattern in Catherine's letters to Gregory XI. While there is a political theme, the bulk of the letter is an exhortation to conversion and transformation, which Catherine considered crucial to the pope's ability to be Christ on earth and spouse of the church, two attributes in which she firmly believed. For Catherine, the pope's level of transformation impacted the function of the church as the institution that mediated salvation through the dispensation of the sacraments—which she saw metaphorically as the blood of Christ—and through pastoral care.

We see the political theme briefly at the end of the letter, where Catherine urged the pope not to delay at Corneto; he should be courageous and determined and hasten his arrival in Rome. Catherine advocated for Siena, and probably nearby city states such as Pisa. She wanted these cities to return their allegiance to the Papal States, and for the pope to entice them back inviting their forgiveness. These city states had rebelled against the Papal States, joining a League formed by Florence to oppose papal policies.

Yet, the bulk of the letter is devoted to an exhortation about the importance of the virtues and how these are to be acquired and nurtured. In line with medieval spirituality, transformation involved growth in the virtues, which Catherine emphasized were the fruit of receiving and living out God's love. Indeed, the significant metaphor in this letter refers to this wisdom. She urges the pope to be grafted onto Christ, tree of love which produces the fruit of virtues. This metaphor is suggestive of the story of the vine and the branches in the Gospel of John. In other words, all of us, and most of all the pope, should be engaged in a close relationship with God, connected so closely to God that it is similar to being a tree or branch grafted onto another tree; for it is such closeness that allows the free flow of the sap of love from Jesus, the tree, to ourselves. And it is this sap of love that transforms us and makes possible the development of virtue.

CATHERINE OF SIENA

❅ ❅ ❅

To the name of Jesus Christ and tender Mary.

Most holy and most reverend father in Christ tender Jesus. Your unworthy and inadequate daughter, Catherine, places herself at your service in his precious blood, with desire to see your heart made firm and stable, and strengthened by true, holy patience. For I believe that a heart that is weak, changeable, and lacking in patience could not accomplish the substantial, important works of God.

All creatures endowed with reason who want to serve God and be clothed in virtue, must have steadfastness, fortitude, and patience; otherwise they could never hold God within their soul. So, if persons resume acquiring wealth for disordered pleasures, out of desire for refinements or just to please themselves and enjoy what is worldly; or if from impatience they revert to insults or cause distress; or if they abandoned love and desire [*affetto*] for the virtues which they had conceived in their soul desiring them with holy desire; then these persons would come to recognize that virtues are not acquired nor perfected without [being tested] by their opposite.[22] If persons evade the contradiction between virtue and its opposite, they are running away from the virtues, precisely when they need them to fight and counter the vice that is the opposite of a particular virtue. So, they must combat pride with humility; with voluntary poverty, they must combat wealth and worldly status and pleasures. Peace seeks out and ends the battle that goes on within the soul and with neighbors. Patience—for love of God's honor and love of virtue—triumphs over impatience. Persons must stoutly bear with patience, scorn, insults, torments, and injustices, as well as physical suffering and losses in order to practice loathing and displeasure for selfish self-love. They must constantly act with firmness, stability, and patience. For otherwise they could not be a servant of Christ but would become a servant and slave of self-centered sensuality; and this sensuality will do away with steadfastness and will make them feeble, possessing a small, weak heart. Persons should not act in this way; rather they should have loving First Truth as their objective, for it is he who restored us to life by bearing and tolerating our sins.

Oh most holy father, most loving Babbo! Open the eye of understanding and try to see with intelligence. If virtue is so necessary for all persons—so necessary for each person for the salvation of her soul—how much more necessary is virtue for you since you must nurture and govern the mystical body of holy Church, your bride. Steadfastness, fortitude, and patience are necessary! Keep in mind that since you have come in as a new plant into the garden of holy Church, you must prepare yourself through growth in virtue to resist the world, the flesh and the evil one, the three principal enemies that challenge us day and night; these enemies never sleep. I trust that as divine Goodness has helped you resist these enemies, he has worked in you all that is necessary to obtain from you that for which he created you; that is to give glory and honor to his name, and so that you would rejoice in his goodness, receiving the eternal vision in which is our blessedness.

Now you are Christ's vicar so you must set to work and do battle for the honor of God, the salvation of souls and the reform of holy Church. This mission includes burdens and sufferings particular to you which are added to the common struggles suffered by anyone who wishes to serve God (as I already explained). And since your burden is greater, you need a bolder and more virile heart that does not fear anything to come. For well you know, most holy father, that since you took the church as your Bride, you took upon yourself to work on her behalf, knowing you would have to deal with the many contrary winds, the many troubles and sufferings that would face you when doing battle on her behalf. And you should, as a courageous man, face these dangerous winds with fortitude, patience, and enduring perseverance; never turn back due to sufferings, consternations, or servile fear;[23] no, persevere, finding joy in the battles and storms!

May your heart rejoice that God's works have been and will be carried out well—in no other way should they ever be undertaken—amidst the troubles that have taken place and will take place. In this way we see that when the persecution of the church and the troubles suffered by the virtuous soul come to an end, peace arises, achieved through patience and perseverance, and crowned with a crown of glory. As I have stated, most holy father, this is the remedy. Which is why I said I desired to see you in possession of a steady and firm heart, strengthened with true, holy patience.

I want you to be a tree of love grafted onto the Word-love, Christ crucified, a tree whose roots are planted in deep humility for the honor of God and the salvation of your sheep. If you become a tree of love, lovingly rooted, you will find in yourself, tree of love, the fruits of patience and fortitude on the top of the tree, and in the middle perseverance with its crown. You will find peace, stillness, and consolation in suffering, as you experience being conformed [through suffering] to Christ crucified. After enduring with Christ crucified in this way, then, with joy, you will reverse involvement in many wars and turn to living in much peace.

Peace! Peace most holy father! May it please your holiness to receive your children who have offended you, their father. May your goodness overcome their pride and malice. For there is no shame in bending over to soothe the naughty child, since it would be for the greatest honor and value for God and to all in this world.[24]

Oh my, Babbo, no more wars of any kind! You can have peace and preserve your conscience! Send war to the unbelievers, where it belongs. Follow in the paths of docility and patience of the spotless Lamb, Christ tender Jesus, for you are his representative. I trust, in the name of our lord Jesus Christ, that he will accomplish this and other graces in you, and that he will accomplish your desire and mine—for I have no other desire in this life—than to see the honor of God, your peace and the reformation of holy Church. And I want to see the life of grace flourish in all creatures endowed with reason. Be reassured, for I have been led to understand that the [authorities] here are disposed to accept you as father, and especially this poor city [Siena], which has always been Your Holiness's daughter. She had been

Ecclesiastical Authorities

constrained by the need to take necessary action even if she disliked it. They [the Sienese] judged they had to act out of necessity. You can yourself seek their forgiveness toward your holiness by reeling them in with the hook of love. I beg you for the love of Christ crucified, that as soon as you can, you go on to your rightful place, that of the celebrated Peter and Paul [Rome].[25] On your part, seek to go with determination, and God, for his part, will provide you with all that you need and all that is needed for the good of your Bride [the church]. I say no more.

Forgive my presumptuousness. Be reassured and have confidence in the true servants of God, that is in their prayers, for they powerfully pray and intercede for you. I and your other children humbly beg your blessing.

Remain, etc.

Tender Jesus! Jesus love!

Carried by Tommaso Guelfaccio and sent with the Sienese ambassador.[26]

LETTER 305

To the Holy Father, Urban VI on the 18th day of September 1378
Dated letter

Introduction

This letter, written toward the end of Catherine's life, evidences her vocation to intercede for and work for the reform of the church, which she considered was led by too many prelates who lived disordered lives, more concerned with their worldly pleasures and power than with any pastoral effort.

Catherine and her trusted mentors, such as Raymond of Capua, supported the election in September 1378 of Urban VI, an Italian. She considered his election to be the one willed by God and, therefore, all opposition to Urban a violation of God's will. She was especially distraught over the plans to nullify Urban's election and elect another prelate. This letter, written on the eve of this alternative election—

resulting in the election of the Frenchman, Clement VII—refers to these historical events. Whether Catherine's judgment was correct and her absolute condemnation of all who objected to Urban VI was valid could be debated. In terms of her spirituality, however, what is significant is the depth of her concern for the reform of the church and for order in its governance. For she rightly felt that without these reforms, pastoral concerns would not be prioritized over temporal power struggles and the comfortable lifestyles of church leaders.

As we see in this letter, Catherine believed in the traditional spirituality of martyrdom, that is, in the value of giving one's live for the church as a form of intercession and in imitation of Jesus. She truly wished to give her life for this cause, a spirituality that underlies this letter as well.

In terms of metaphors, Catherine refers to the pope as the keeper of a wine cellar, where the wine is the blood of Christ. In turn, the blood of Christ is also a symbol for the grace of the sacraments. She refers to the betting stalls set up in the public squares as a metaphor for the practice of charging for the sacraments and for all forms of enrichment through pastoral care.

❊ ❊ ❊

To the name of Jesus Christ crucified and tender Mary.

Most holy and beloved father in Christ tender Jesus. I, Catherine, servant and slave of the servants of Jesus Christ, write to you in his precious blood with desire to see you rooted in the true light, having it illuminate the eye of your understanding so that you can know and see truth; and knowing truth you will love it, and loving truth, virtue will shine forth in you.

What, holy father, is the truth that we should come to know? It is eternal Truth,[27] with which we were loved before we existed. How shall we know this Truth? Through the knowledge of ourselves that leads us to recognize that God created us in his image and likeness out of the intensity [fire] of his love.

The truth is this, that God created us so that we might participate in his being and that we might enjoy his eternal, ultimate

Ecclesiastical Authorities

goodness. Who has announced and manifested this truth? The blood of the humble, spotless Lamb, whose vicar you are. You are the wine keeper who has the keys to the blood that restored us to grace. One could say persons are born anew every time they are freed from mortal sin and receive the blood in confession. In this way—as we receive the blessings, the fruit of the blood—we repeatedly learn that the truth is revealed in the blood.

Who knows this truth? The soul that has removed the cloud of selfish self-love so that the pupil of the light of most holy faith illuminates the eye of understanding.[28] With this light—through knowledge of self and of God's goodness within her—she learns the Truth. And with desire drenched [in this understanding], the soul savors the tenderness and gentleness [of God's goodness] that cancels all distress and makes every burden light. This tenderness—immersed in eternal truth— is so great that it dispels and removes every darkness, it clothes all nakedness, it feeds those who hunger, it both unites and divides. In eternal Truth the soul learns that God wants only her well-being and is thus able to immediately make an accurate discernment; that is, she recognizes that what God bestows and allows in this life is out of love, so that we may be made holy in him for our salvation and for our growth in perfection.

Having learned this from Truth, through the light, the person is able to value every struggle, criticism, insult, scorn, derision, disgrace, shame, and accusation. The person is able to bear with all these in true patience, while seeking only God's glory, the praise of his name, and the salvation of souls. And such a person suffers more because of offenses to God than wrongs committed against herself. She has patience for her own suffering but none for the insults against her Creator. Through patience, the soul shows that, having been stripped of selfish self-love, she is now clothed in the fire of divine love. Most holy father, when clothed in such charity, such ineffable love, all disappointment and bitterness that you suffer will turn into the deepest tenderness and gentleness. And the severe weight [of your responsibilities] will be made light through this love. For love recognizes that without great endurance, your hunger and that of the servants of God cannot be satisfied; I mean the hunger to see the reform of holy Church through good, honest, holy pastors.

You will receive the light, as you endure—through no fault of your own—the blows of these wicked persons[29] who want to assail your holiness with the club of heresy.[30] For the truth makes us free; and it is the truth that you were elected by the Holy Spirit and by them[31] whose vicar you are. And the darkness they have caused by lies and heresy will not triumph over the light. In fact, the more they want to create darkness, the more you will be blessed with the perfect light.

This Light [love] carries with it the knife of love of virtue and hatred of vice. This love is a bond that binds the soul to God and to love of neighbor. Oh! Most holy and tender father, this is the knife I want you to use; it is time to take this knife out of its sheath. You must loath vice in yourself, in the ministers of holy Church, and in those under your authority. I say in yourself, because in this life no one is free of sin. Love must first be directed toward oneself through love and desire [*affetto*] for virtue and then toward our neighbor; this is required to eliminate vice. For a person's heart cannot be changed, nor can she retract from her faults unless she tries to do so with God's help, thus removing the poison of vice. So, at least, most holy father, may you [and they] take distance from disordered living and impious ways and styles of life. May you discipline them according to that which divine Goodness requires of each according to their rank. Do not put up with licentiousness—I don't mean their cravings, which you could not stop even if you wished—but at least their actions, which it is possible for you to set straight. No simony, no great refinements, no trafficking in the blood;[32] for that which belongs to the poor and the church should not be used for public betting[33] in a place that should be God's temple; for these persons do not act as clerics or canons—who should be the flowers and the mirror of holiness—rather, they act as betting agents, shouting the stench of licentiousness and offering examples of wickedness.

Oh my, oh my, oh my, dear Babbo! I write this with tears, with sorrow, pain, and great disappointment. If it seems I say

Ecclesiastical Authorities

too much and I seem presumptuous, may I be forgiven before God and your holiness, for it is due to both pain and love, for no matter where I turn, I find no place to rest my head. If I turn one way—expecting that where Christ is there should be eternal life—I see that where you are who are Christ on earth, there is an abyss of much iniquity and the poison of selfish self-love. For it is this self-centered love that has led them to rebel against you, because your holiness did not tolerate that they live in such impiety. Don't give up! May the bright light[34] of holy justice shine in your breast! Have no fear for you have no reason to be afraid; may your heart be courageous! Rejoice and be glad for your joy will be full in heaven! Rejoice also in the struggles to come, for after this, after the struggles will come rest and the reformation of holy Church.

Do not slow down due to any sorrow or trouble because you see yourself abandoned by those who should be your pillars.[35] Rather, move forward even more so, strengthening yourself always through the support of the servants of God,[36] in order to see the truth through prayer and with the light of most holy faith. Always have the servants of God at your side, for in this life they will be your sustenance in dealing with struggles. So, in addition to divine assistance, seek the help of his [God's] servants for they will advise you frankly, without undue emotion and without contamination by self-centered love. It seems to me you greatly need such advice. I am sure that if you turn on the eye of understanding of truth, you will seek them [the advisors] with great alacrity, otherwise it won't happen. Plant true virtues in those under your authority; at least order them to plant good, virtuous plants in holy Church.

I was telling you—and this is the truth—that no matter where I turn, I can't find rest. It is the same everywhere as it is here, especially in our city, where in God's temple, a place of prayer, they have made a den of thieves. With so much wickedness, it is a wonder the ground doesn't swallow us up! And all because of bad pastors who have not restrained their sins either through the Word or through a good and holy life. Oh my dear shepherd! You who have been given to Christians ignorant about the tenderness of God's unfathomable love! You have such need of the light to recognize faults where faults exist and virtue where that exists, so that with discernment [*discrezione*] you give each his due.[37] I, most inadequate person, believe that without the light you could not remove the thorns and plant the virtues; this is why I said that I desire to see you rooted in true, perfect light, for in and through the light you will recognize the truth, and recognizing it, you will love it, and if you love it, you will be clothed in it [light]. With this garment [of light] sins are blocked from harming you; rather they will harm those who cause them. Embrace struggles with great strength! Bathe in the blood of Christ crucified, for you are his vicar!

I say no more, though if I followed my will, I would continue. I want no more words. I want to be in the field of battle, enduring the struggles and, together with you, fighting for the truth unto death for the glory of God's name and the reformation of holy Church.

Remain in the everlasting tender, holy love of God.

And forgive my lack of knowledge, most holy father, for despite this lack I dare to address you. Humbly I ask for your blessing.

Tender Jesus! Jesus love!

CARDINALS, BISHOPS

LETTER 181

To Missere Nicola of Osmo,[38] secretary and protonotary[39] of our Lord the pope
January 1376 (Noffke and Volpato)

Introduction

Nicola da Osimo, a cardinal, was secretary and manager of documents for Pope Gregory XI. Letters such as this one were probably prompted by Raymond of Capua, since Catherine advocates with the pope's secretary for a particular candidate as the next Master General of the Dominican order to be appointed by the pope.[40] While this task was probably the reason for Catherine's letter, she took the opportunity to exhort this highly placed prelate to transformation and a close relationship with God, using an elaborate metaphor about constructing a building. God, sometimes Jesus or the Spirit—Catherine is not consistent here—is a master stonemason or laborer. Jesus is also a foundational stone, though the stones most often represent the virtues. Jesus's blood is part of the material necessary to create the mortar that holds the stones together. We see yet again Catherine's readiness to forcefully exhort a very high ecclesiastical authority.

❈ ❈ ❈

To the name of Jesus Christ crucified and tender Mary, Mother of the Son of God.

Dearest and very beloved father in Christ Jesus, I, Catherine, servant and slave of the servants of Jesus Christ, write to you in his precious blood with desire to see you a firm rock, founded on the tender but firm rock, Jesus Christ.

You know that a building built on sand or soil will be toppled by any slight wind or rain. Similarly, our soul will be toppled by the least adversity when it is grounded in the passing realities of this dark and fleeting life, realities that pass as fleetingly as the wind or as dust blown into the wind. And it [our soul] will be toppled when we are grounded in selfish self-love, the worst leprosy and scourge that we could suffer. This leprosy destroys all virtues, extinguishing their life; for they [virtues] are deprived of their mother, which is love; they cannot live when not tied to life [love]. This is why my soul wants to see you grounded in the living rock.

My dearest father, what could be better and more spiritually caring than to own and build the house of our soul? It is a wonderful thing that we have found the rock, a master stonemason, and the needed laborer to build this house.[41] Oh! What a loving master stonemason we have in the eternal Father; he possesses all wisdom, knowledge, and infinite goodness! He is our God, *He-Who-Is*; all that has being is born of him. He is a master stonemason that knows all that we need; his sole desire is that we be made holy. And so all that he allows and sends us—temptations from the evil one, temptation or persecution from others, offenses or injustices or any other form of suffering—are permitted or sent for our good, for the purification of our sins, and to increase within us grace and perfection. Our benevolent master stonemason is so good! He knows so well what materials are needed to build what is necessary within us! Having seen that water did not work in order to mix the mortar needed to set the stones—that is, the real, benevolent virtues—he went further, giving us the blood of his only-begotten Son.

I want you to know that before the coming of the Son of God no virtue had the power to give us life, for it [life] had been lost due to sin. Oh, father, look at the immeasurable love of this master stonemason, who, seeing that the water of the holy prophets was not alive with water that would give us life, he drew from himself, giving us the Word, his only-begotten Son, who brought his [God's] power and virtue; these are the stones that need to be placed in just the right location of our home's structure. Without these stones we could have no life. And the Son is so sweet because he is united to the Father and is one with him, so that anything that is bitter becomes sweet because of his [Jesus's] sweetness. In him is found living mortar, not soil or sand.

O tender fire of love, you have given us the Holy Spirit—who is love—as master stonemason and laborer; his is the strong hand that supports the Word who is bound and nailed to the cross. The Holy Spirit has pressed this tender body, squeezing blood from it, enough blood to give us life and to set all stones in the building.[42] *Every virtue is effective and gives us life when rooted in Christ and mixed with his blood! Who would want anything more? Who would want to go wading through the moats looking for the sad, disordered pleasures of the world? May the warmth dissolve the stones of our hardened hearts!*

Ecclesiastical Authorities

So, it is the Father—how amazing!—who has made himself our master stonemason. For the master stonemason works out of the power within him; he uses memory, which retains what must be done; understanding, through which he knows [what to do]; and with the hand of the will he accomplishes the required task.[43] With his wisdom, power, and goodness, this master stonemason created and built our soul in his image and likeness. We had lost grace through sin, so he came, united himself to us, and grafted himself onto our human nature. He [the Father] gave us everything, placing his virtue [power of life] in the Son, as already described, making him also master stonemason filled with his [God's] power, that is, his immeasurable charity and love, which give life. And so the Father made his Son the [foundational] stone—Saint Paul tells us that our stone is Christ—as well as master stonemason and laborer [for the construction] of the building. Because of this love he gave his life; and so the mortar [for the building] is mixed with his blood, and we lack nothing. Let us rejoice and sing praises that we have such a tender master stonemason, laborer and [foundational] stone! He walled us in with his blood, making the wall so strong that neither the evil one nor any creature nor hail nor storm nor wind can shake the building, unless we consent.

Let memory awaken and keep in mind so many gifts; let the understanding and knowledge awaken to see his love and goodness that wants and seeks nothing but that we be made holy. He [Christ] did not empty himself out of self-importance but out of faithful love for the Father and for our salvation. When memory remembers this and understanding grasps this, then the will should not be held back—in fact, I don't see that it could be held back—from running with fervor and impassioned by love toward that which God loves; nor can the will be held back from loathing that which God loathes. Nothing can now trouble the will, nor would the will obstruct any holy resolutions; rather, it will act with patience because rooted in Christ, the living stone. I have told you: I want you to be a stone rooted on this living stone; and so, for love of Christ crucified, I beg you to continuously persevere and grow in this holy resolve. Do not back down or turn back due to adversities that may come your way. I want you to be a firm stone, rooted in the body of holy Church, always seeking God's honor and the exaltation and renovation of holy Church.

I beg you, do not allow your desire nor your efforts to slow down in pleading with the holy father both to return soon and to not delay in raising the shield with the coat of arms of faithful Christians, namely, the holy cross.[44] Do not pay attention to recent scandal.[45] [The pope] should not fear but should persevere courageously and soon carry out his good and holy intention. Even if you suffer blows from the evil one or anyone else, I beg you to remain a living stone, rooted in Christ's Bride, always proclaiming the truth, even at the cost of your life! Do not be preoccupied with yourself but always try to look for the honor of God. We have for so long suffered the dishonor of his name that now we should prepare ourselves to give our lives for the praise and glory of his name. So, father, do not be negligent, do not delay! Now, while we yet have time and time is on our side, let's make the effort for our fellow human beings and for the glory of God. I hope that through his goodness you will act accordingly. Please forgive my audacity, which is due to my love and care. I was overjoyed by the holy father's sound desire and resolution both to come here and to carry out the holy and glorious pilgrimage,[46] which has been awaited with such great desire by God's servants. I say no more here.

I heard that the holy father wants to promote the Master [General] of our order and offer him another ecclesiastical benefice. If this is so, I beg you to pray that Christ on earth [the pope] may find a good vicar, for we have a great need of this. If you were to agree, I ask that you mention master Stefano[47] who was procurator of the order when friar Raymond was at court.[48] I believe you know he is a good and strong man. I trust that if he were to lead us, through him and God's grace the order would make improvements. I have written to the holy father asking him to give us a good vicar—without suggesting a name—and asked him to listen to you and to the Archbishop of Otronto. If, father, for this purpose or any other need of the

Ecclesiastical Authorities

church, you want friar Raymond to visit you, please write to him and he will always be obedient to you. I say no more.

Remain in the holy and tender love of God.

LETTER 16

To an important prelate[49]
April 1376 (Noffke); second half 1375 (Volpato)

Introduction

Because she strongly chides this highly placed bishop or cardinal, Catherine wrote this letter anonymously, presumably to protect his reputation. She suggests to him that he suffers from self-centeredness, focusing on sensual pleasures, worldly delights, riches, and honor. He is so preoccupied with himself that he does not pay attention to his flock who is going astray. To challenge him to revise his self-centered and disordered ways, Catherine shares wisdom she felt God transmitted to her regarding God's suffering due to persons' lack of recognition and response to that love. This extended metaphor and reflection is a powerful insight into God's love. Catherine intuited that Christ suffered more due to human persons' lack of response to his love—by continuing to live in self-centered ways—than he suffered on the cross. This is presented through the metaphor of "the cross of holy desire," meaning the suffering of Jesus due to our lack of response to his offer of saving love. Catherine also intuited that the cross of holy desire began in Mary's womb, expressed through the image of Jesus being born with a cross around his neck. Further, she uses the metaphor that persons are birthed from the womb of the Father to strongly assert her theological anthropology that persons are created out of love, for love, and are held in being by love. Failure to recognize this not only leads people astray from becoming who they are meant to be, it also causes God suffering. This wisdom about God's love is meant to motivate a desire on the part of this prelate to reform his life and enter upon a path of transformation. Indeed, this letter repeats in unique ways Catherine's wisdom about transformation through the various meanings of desire and *affetto*.

❈ ❈ ❈

To the name of Jesus Christ crucified and tender Mary.

Dear Reverend Father in Christ Jesus. I, Catherine, servant and slave of the servants of Jesus Christ, write to you in his precious blood with desire to see you hunger for the food of human persons[50] for the honor of God, and learning from benevolent First Truth, who died due to the hunger and thirst he suffered for our salvation.

It seems this spotless Lamb cannot be satisfied; he cries out from the cross where he is saturated with humiliations, saying, "I thirst." Even if he suffered physical thirst, greater was the thirst he endured due to his holy desire for the salvation of souls. *Oh immeasurable, most tender love! Despite all you give of yourself, surrendering yourself to such torments, there remains in you a desire to give all of yourself, for this is the logic of love. I am not surprised, for your love was infinite and your suffering finite, and so the cross of desire was greater than the physical cross.*

I remember that good, tender Jesus revealed the following to his servant[51] after she asked about the cross of desire and the physical cross. "My tender Lord, what causes you more suffering, the pain from desire or physical pain?" With benevolence and tenderness, he answered, "I assure you, my daughter, that without doubt there can be no comparison between that which is finite and that which is infinite. You may think that physical pain was finite, but holy desire is unending and so is the cross of holy desire that I bore.[52] Don't you remember, my daughter, that once I revealed to you my birth and you saw me as a baby born with the cross around my neck? This shows you that when I, the incarnate Word, was planted in Mary's womb, I began to suffer the cross of holy desire to be obedient to my Father and bring about his will that persons should be restored to a life of grace and live out the purpose for which they were created. This cross caused me more suffering than any that I carried physically. Yet my spirit exulted with great joy, especially during Holy Thursday's Last Supper, when I was taken to my ultimate end, and said, 'with desire I have desired' [Luke 22:15],[53] which meant I desired to live the Passover of sacrificing my body to the Father. I experienced great joy and consolation because I saw before me the time when the cross of desire would be removed. I mean by this that I felt my suffering abate the closer I was to suffering physical torments and beatings, for the physical suffering would take away the pain from desire; this was the case because I could see that my deepest desire would be accomplished."[54]

She answered, saying, "Oh my loving Lord, you are telling me that the suffering of the cross of desire disappeared on the cross. How did this happen? Did you lose your desire for me?" He answered, "My beloved daughter, no, when I died on the cross, the suffering from holy desire came to an end with the end of my life; however, my desire and hunger for your salvation did not come to an end. If the unimaginable love that I have for the human race had come to an end, if it had been exhausted, you would not exist. For through love you were birthed from the womb of my Father who created you with his wisdom, and so through love you are held together for you are made of nothing else but love.

"If he withheld the love filled with the power and wisdom with which he created you, you would cease to be. I, the only begotten Son of God, have been made a channel through which he pours upon you the water of grace. I reveal the love [*affetto*] of my Father, for my love is his love; the love I have is also the Father's love, as the Father and I are one, and he reveals himself through me. I have said, 'That which I received from the Father I have revealed to you' (John 15:15). Everything is due to love."

So you see, reverend father, good, tender Jesus-Love perishes from hunger and thirst for our salvation; and therefore, I beg you, for love of Christ crucified, to place hunger for the Lamb before your heart and mind. The desire of my soul is that you should be dying of true and holy desire, that is, from the motivation emerging from your core [*affetto*] and the love that you have for the honor of God, the salvation of souls and the glory of holy Church. It is my wish that this hunger grow so strong in you that you die from it as Christ, the Son of God, died of hunger, as already mentioned. In this way you would die to all selfish self-love, to all [disordered] sensual passion; then your appetite for and the movement of your will toward the delights and pleasures of the world with all its pomp would cease. I don't doubt that if your eye of understanding focused on knowing yourself and recognized that *you-are-not*, you would realize that you were given your existence out of a deep fire of love; and therefore, your heart and deepest desires [*affetto*] could only be consumed with love. Selfish self-love would have no room to exist; you would not seek anything for self-centered reasons and benefits, but only for the honor of God. You would not seek your fellow human beings for selfish purposes, but you would love them and desire their salvation for the praise and glory of God's name, and all this because you would have learned how utterly God loves every created being.

These are the reasons that God's servants so readily love others because they see how utterly they are loved by their Creator. For loving that which is loved by the beloved is the nature of love. They [God's servants] do not love God for self-centered reasons, but because he is ultimate, eternal goodness worthy of love. Such persons are able to put their interests and life aside because they are no longer focused on themselves. They can welcome sufferings, insults, and torments; they disdain the sufferings of the world. The cross and the heartache experienced seeing the offenses and insults against God and the damnation of other persons is greater [than their own sufferings]. It is so great that their own affliction pales. They don't avoid suffering but even seek it and rejoice in it. They keep in mind loving Paul who was so in love that he gloried in suffering for Christ crucified. I want you to and beg you to follow this loving herald.

Oh dear, dear me, my unfortunate soul! [Father,] open your eye of understanding and observe the perversity of the death that has fallen over the world, especially over holy Church. Oh my! Your heart and soul should burst [with sorrow] at seeing so

Ecclesiastical Authorities

many offenses against God. Watch out, father, for the infernal wolf is carrying persons away, that is, the sheep that graze in the garden of holy Church. And there is no one to be found who will remove the sheep from the wolf's mouth. The pastors are asleep in their selfish self-love, in covetousness and filth. They are so drunk with pride that they are asleep and have lost awareness; and so the infernal wolf steals their own life of grace and that of those in their care; they just don't care; all this is due to the obstinacy of selfish self-love.

Oh, how dangerous is selfish self-love in bishops or cardinals and in those in their care! If these church officials are possessed by selfish self-love, they will not be able to correct those under their care, for self-love implies servile fear of correcting others. If these church officials could love themselves for God's sake, they would not suffer servile fear and so would be able to correct the faults of others with zeal and a courageous heart; they would not be silent and pretend not to notice. So, my dear father, I want you to be deprived of selfish self-love.

I beg you to act so that you will not be the object of First Truth's harsh reprimand, "cursed be you who were silent!" (Isa 6:5). Oh my! Please do not be silent any longer! Instead, shout at the top of your lungs! Due to silence the world is upside down, the bride of Christ[55] is pale. Her coloring is gone as the blood has been drained from her—I mean the blood of Christ poured out as a grace and not an obligation. They [the disordered church leaders] drained the blood with their pride, taking for themselves the honor that should belong to God; and they steal [the blood] engaging in simony, selling the blessings and graces that were given as gift at the price of the blood of the Son of God. Oh, dear me! I die but I cannot die! Do not slumber any longer in your negligence; take advantage of the present time to apply what you can.[56]

There may come a time when you can do more, but for now I invite you to strip your soul of all selfish self-love and instead clothe your soul with hunger for the real, true virtues, for the honor of God and the salvation of souls. Be strong in Christ Jesus who is tender love, for we will soon see the flowers bloom.[57]

Make sure that the standard of the cross is raised soon.[58] And may your heart, your deepest motivation and desire [*affetto*] never waiver no matter what difficulties you see coming. Rather, stay strong knowing that Christ crucified will be the one who accomplishes and carries out the most ardent desires of the servants of God. I say no more.

Remain, etc.

Drown yourself in the blood of Christ crucified! Place yourself on the cross with Christ crucified! Hide in the wounds of Christ crucified! Bathe in the blood of Christ crucified!

And forgive me, Father, my boldness [in writing to you]. Tender Jesus! Jesus love!

LETTER 7

To missere Pietro, cardinal of Ostia
December 1376 (Noffke)[59]

Introduction

Cardinal Pierre (Pietro) d'Estaing, a French Benedictine, was Legate[60] or official representative of the papacy to the kingdoms in the south of Italy (and later to Bologna). A close advisor to Gregory XI, he had been present at Avignon when Catherine was there. He was then involved in politically paving the way for Gregory's return to Rome. This letter shows that correspondence with such high prelates was almost certainly suggested by Raymond or other advisors, as Catherine tells us in the first paragraph that she has heard of Pietro's appointment as Legate. At the same time, it shows that Catherine's main concern was the conversion of the important Cardinal rather than persuasion regarding a particular political choice, though she does encourage the starting of the crusade.

The theme of this letter is the urgency of conversion in capacity to love, that is, to care for the good of the other so that the important mission of such a key prelate should be accomplished in accordance with God's will. In stating her wisdom on love, Catherine uses the

Ecclesiastical Authorities

significant metaphor of "binding" or tying together, playing on the title of the Cardinal, Legato (legate) of the pope—where *legare* is to bind and *legato* is bond and bound. We should be bound, that is, tied together to God and to the cross, as God has been bound—tied together—to humanity in the incarnation. This metaphor suggests that tying oneself to God—that is, union or connection to God—should never be neglected or allowed to become loose. The use of this metaphor related to the Cardinal's title shows Catherine's creativity and effort to write in images and language that would reach her particular correspondent.

❊ ❊ ❊

To the name of Jesus Christ crucified and tender Mary.

Most dear reverend Father in Christ, tender Jesus. I, Catherine, servant and slave of the servants of Jesus Christ, write to you in his precious blood with desire to see you bound with the bond of charity, now that you have been made Legate (as I have heard). This is a very special joy since you can bring much honor to God and benefit to holy Church.

Despite being made legate, without another bond (*legame*)[61] you would not be able to accomplish these goals, which is why I want you bound (*legato*) to the bond (*legame*) of love. For you know that without love we cannot mediate grace, either to ourselves or to others. Love is that holy, gentle bond that binds the soul to her Creator; love bound God to human persons and persons to God. This boundless love has tied and nailed God to man on the wood of the holy cross. This cross puts an end to dissension and unites those that have been divided; she [the cross][62] strengthens those lacking in virtue, for it gives life to all the virtues; she brings peace and eradicates war; she gifts patience, fortitude, lengthy perseverance, and all good, holy acts. She never tires; she is never separated from God's love and love of neighbor, even in the face of suffering, torments, insults, scorn, or injustice. She does not act out of eagerness for the pleasures and enjoyments of the world or for the gratification the world offers through flattery.

CATHERINE OF SIENA

Whoever possesses love lives out of unwavering perseverance because he is grounded in the living stone, Christ tender Jesus; that is, following in his footsteps, he has learned from him how to love his Creator. In him he has read the rule[63] and his doctrine [teaching], for he is the way, the truth, and the life. So whoever reads him who is the book of life is walking on the straight path. That is, he is concerned only with God's honor and the salvation of his neighbor. This is how Christ tender Jesus acted, never pulling back his outpouring of love for the honor of the Father and our salvation; never pulling back, due to suffering, torments, flattery, or due to our ingratitude. He persevered to the last until he accomplished his desire, which is also the mission placed in his hands by the Father; that is, the redemption of the human race, in this way bringing about the honor of the Father and our salvation.

I want you to continue in this bond of love learning from tender First Truth, who has set you on the life-giving path, has given you the structure for the rule and taught you the doctrine of truth. As a true child, and as servant ransomed by the blood of Christ crucified, I want you to follow in his footsteps with a courageous heart and readiness to act. Don't ever detach yourself [from the bond of love] due to suffering or pleasure and persevere until the end in carrying out this and any other work you take on for Christ crucified.

Pay attention to the iniquity and wretchedness of the world and the many faults committed that become insults to God's name. As someone hungry for the honor of God and the salvation of your neighbor, do whatever you can to counter so much iniquity. I am sure that since you are bound by the gentle bond of love, you will use your role as Legate, which you received from Christ's vicar [the pope], to carry out what I have just described. Without first being bound by the bond of love you would not be able to act in the way you should; so I pray that you try to develop this love within you. Bind yourself to Christ crucified; follow in his footsteps with true, authentic virtues; and bind yourself to your neighbor through acts of love.

Ecclesiastical Authorities

My most dear father, I want us to reflect on the following. If our soul is not stripped of all selfish self-love and of all pleasurable attachment to self and what is worldly, we will never reach this true, perfect love, this bond of love, for the two loves are opposed to each other. Selfish self-love separates you from God and neighbor, while true love binds you to God and neighbor; the latter brings death, the former life; the latter darkness, the former light; the latter war, the former peace. [Selfish self-love] shrinks your heart so you have no understanding for yourself or your neighbor, while divine love enlarges your heart, welcoming into your heart friends and enemies and all persons; for your heart has dressed itself in the love [*affetto*] of Christ and therefore acts like him.

Selfish self-love is disordered and breaks away from justice, committing injustices. It[64] is filled with servile fear that prevents it from carrying out what it should; it fears for its social status driven by fear or by flattery. It is this perverse enslavement and fear that led Pilate to cause Christ's death. [Those moved by selfish self-love] don't act justly but unjustly; they don't live justly and virtuously, with love united to God's love emerging from their deepest self [holy *affetto* of love], but unjustly, motivated by vice and wicked selfish self-love. I want this kind of love to be completely removed from you, so that you live [only] out of true, perfect love, loving God for God's sake; for he is worthy of being loved because he is ultimate, eternal goodness. You should love yourself and your neighbor for God's sake, not out of consideration for your own benefit. So, my father, Legate of our lord the pope, this is what I want: that you should be bound [*legato*] with the bond of true, most passionate love. That is what my soul so wants to see in you. I say no more.

Strengthen yourself in Christ tender Jesus, be committed and not negligent in your duties. I will know if you follow through on this, when I see your hunger for raising of the standard of the most Holy Cross.[65]

Remain in the holy, tender love of God.

Tender Jesus! Jesus love!

5

CIVIL AUTHORITIES

LETTER 149

To misser Piero Gambacorti,[1] nobleman from Pisa
End 1374 (Noffke); second half 1374 (Volpato)

Introduction

The family of Piero, an important Pisan official, had learned of Catherine's reputation for wisdom and holiness and so wanted him to invite her to their home; this letter was a response to this invitation. It shows us that even early in her more public vocation, she quickly attracted others with her gifts. Catherine took the opportunity to exhort Piero to transformation. She is most blunt with this patrician who is undoubtedly much older than she. Her focus is the transformation of desire and *affetto*, that is, the motivation rooted in the core of the self. The key metaphor in this letter is that of binding oneself to Christ, where binding implies being tied to or grafted onto. These metaphors offer a facet of the crystal that is her teaching on transformation of desire/*affetto*.

Catherine's travels as a single lay woman were scandalous to some, yet she stood firm in her trust in God's providence for her unusual missions and took her health and practical reality into consideration when making decisions about invitations she received to minister to important families. This reflection shared with Piero gives us a glimpse of Catherine's own practice of discernment.

Civil Authorities

❈ ❈ ❈

To the name of Jesus Christ crucified and tender Mary.

Venerable father in Christ tender Jesus, your unworthy daughter, Catherine, servant and slave of the servants of Jesus Christ, writes to you in the precious blood of the Son of God, with desire that your will, moved by desire and love [*affetto*], be stripped of and separated from the immoral pleasures and disordered amusements of the world; these cause the soul to break away and separate from God. The person who is bound to Christ crucified—ultimate, eternal goodness—must be cut off and separated from what is worldly. For he whose desire, motivation, and will [*affetto*] are caught up in what is worldly is cut off from Christ, since the world is in no way conformed to Christ. As First Truth stated: "No one can serve two opposite masters; for if she serves one, she will be in conflict with the other" [Luke 16:13].

Oh dearest father, this bond is so deadly! Because of it a person bound by the lethalness of sin is like a person whose hands and feet are bound and cannot move. That is, the soul's hands are bound so that she cannot carry out any actions for the sake of Christ, and she cannot move the feet of *affetto*,[2] so she is unable to move toward choices rooted in grace. Oh dear, dear me! Sin is so dangerous for the soul! It deprives a person of so much good and makes her vulnerable to so much evil! It makes her vulnerable to death, it extinguishes life; it extinguishes light and produces darkness; it takes away authority and produces enslavement; for whoever abounds in sin is a servant and slave to sin; such a person has lost authority over himself and allows himself to be taken over by rage and other faults.

What would it be like, most dear father, if we reigned over all the world but did not have authority over our vices and sins? These would then obscure the light of reason and prevent us from seeing, on the one hand, how seriously we have fallen from grace, and on the other, just how safe is the soul that binds herself to tender Jesus. A person [without authority over their sins and vices] has lost the life of grace because he has been cut off from the true source of life, just as the branch that is cut off from the vine dries up and bears no fruit; in the same way persons cut off from the true vine dry up, rot, and become vulnerable to the fire of eternal damnation.

Oh dear me, what sorrow! This is the great blindness, that neither the evil one nor any human being can bind a person to mortal sin, and yet persons can bind themselves to such sin on their own. So, wake up from the slumber of negligence and foolishness and cut off this damaging bond! This disorder happens because sin and worldliness are not compatible with Christ crucified; for the world seeks power, honor, and pleasures, while blessed Christ chose insults, torments, injustice, and finally, the shameful death on the cross. He wanted to serve and to be obedient, never violating the law or the will of the Father, always seeking his honor and our salvation. So let us follow in his footsteps.

I want us to be bound with this tender, true bond, and beg you to so bind yourself, so that you are better able to open the eye of understanding about yourself; then you will see that *you-are-not* and always the cause of wretchedness and moral weakness. Also with the true bond, a spring of holy justice with deep authentic humility will arise in you. Then you will, in justice, give God his due and yourself your due,[3] and gaze into his unfathomable love, seeing how the slain Lamb bore our sins with patience and docility. *O immeasurable love, with what patience you gave your life and give us time, waiting for your creature to correct her life!* Having through experience learned how God's goodness works within you, you will be united and bound to him through the bond of charity, which is gentle and loving beyond all else. Do not delay for time is short and the moment of death arrives when we least expect it.

I beg you, for the love of Christ crucified, that you stay focused on acting with holy and divine justice according to your state in life. This should be neither to please others nor out of hatred, but only to punish with divine justice any fault you uncover. And when you discover your own sin, reproach and punish it when you can; be attentive not to close your eyes to

Civil Authorities

your own sin, for God would certainly catch you. Please, please be as zealous as possible, filled with affectionate love. May all your endeavors be bound to Christ Jesus; this is the bond that my soul so desires for you, for without it you will not live a life of grace. I say no more.

I received your letter with affectionate love. I am aware that asking me to visit is due only to your love and goodness and that of the holy women[4] who humbly encouraged you to write to me, for I know you did not do it due to my virtue and goodness, as I am full of sin and weakness.[5] I would willingly like to fulfil your desire, but for now I have to excuse myself. On the one hand, my body does not allow this, and on the other, I see I would cause scandal.[6] However, I trust in God's goodness; if he considers this trip would be for his honor and the benefit of souls, he will make it possible for me to go in peace, rested and without more gossip. I will be ready to obey the command of First Truth, and to obey yours as well.

Remain, etc. May Christ reward you with his most loving grace!

Please greet the ladies[7] on my behalf with affectionate love and ask them to pray for me that God may make me humble and bound to my Creator. Amen. Praised be Jesus Christ crucified!

LETTER 131

To Nicolò Soderini in Florence
July 1375 Noffke; after July 1375 Volpato

Introduction

Nicolò[8] was a prominent Florentine leader of the Guelph political faction on whose side were the ecclesiastical authorities who supported Catherine. She was introduced to him when she travelled to Florence to advocate for the pope's policies, and he became a supporter and advisor regarding Florentine politics. He was one of those educated lay leaders who sought out this young lay woman for her spiritual gifts and advice regarding their own spiritual journey.

While Catherine exhorted Nicolò to make use of her standard teaching about transformation, this letter shows how she could adapt her rhetoric and metaphors to address a prominent businessman and political leader. She uses a multipronged metaphor about doing business and making profits. God gives us time and free will, she told Nicolò, with which to do business as a merchant might send his son away to be tested.

At the end, Catherine also seeks to persuade Nicolò to take part in the crusade and to enlist his friends. One could interpret Catherine's invitation to the crusade to persons such as Nicolò, who were most unlikely to respond, as an expression of her naiveté or as a combination of the latter and her powerful faith in God's power.

❆ ❆ ❆

To the name of Jesus Christ crucified.

Very reverend and most beloved brother in Jesus Christ. I, Catherine, servant and slave of the servants of Jesus Christ, bless you and wish you strength in the precious blood of the Son of God. I desire to see you—together with all your family—a true son and servant of Jesus Christ crucified. I wish to see you as a servant ransomed by the blood of the Son of God, always attentive, as a good servant, not to offend or displease his master.

I want you always to keep our Lord in mind in this manner for we are meant to serve him, he who always has his eye upon us. We should always be careful not to offend him, for he is such a dear loving lord. To aid us in this, holy fear enters our soul as a servant to her, in order to do away with all vice, sin, and actions that would be against the will of her lord. I want you to be a son of your heavenly Father, who created you in his image and likeness and has fashioned you and all creatures in the way a father does who places a treasure in the hand of his son and,

Civil Authorities

in order to make him grow up and get rich, sends him forth from his city.

This is the way our loving Father behaves. For having created the soul he gives her the gift of time and free will that she may become rich.[9] So, you see we are foreigners and pilgrims during our life. We have the option of doing business with the treasure of time and free will and thus becoming rich. Or we can drown out our free will and willpower and purchase the perverse vanities, the pleasures and disappointments, the preoccupations and delights of the world; this is the sort of merchandise that will always impoverish a person. It does not last and has no substance. It has no stability or strength; it has a deceptive appearance, being rotten inside, leaving the whiff of many sins; yet it is this deceptive appearance that leads to making the purchase.

So, dearest, most venerable brother in Christ Jesus, I don't want us, nor do I have any intention of having us spend this treasure the Father gave us through his grace and mercy on vile merchandise; the Father would justly rebuke us. As true children, we should therefore, with flawless resolve, spend this loving treasure on perfect merchandise. This merchandise—the opposite of worldly merchandise—may appear unappealing, of pale color and poor quality, yet it is filled with a treasure that multiplies and enriches us here [while on earth] through grace, then guides us into the eternal life of the Father where we will enjoy his inheritance.

Let's examine what treasure has been bought by a person who has grown rich. He bought disdain for honors, riches, luxuries, and for all solace, gratification, and pleasure from human beings. He has bought true, real virtues that may seem minor and that the world considers unimportant, but that are filled with the treasure of grace. The world may well think that choosing torments and scorn, insults, and abuse, and voluntarily choosing poverty is unimportant; yet such poverty brings down human pride and a sense of importance and elevated social status. It is [the treasure of] virtue that deflates these, making one humble. He [the person grown rich in virtue] wishes only to follow in the footsteps of the Father who has given the treasure of free will; with this treasure he has the choice of profiting from or squandering his merchandise.

Oh virtues, holy and tender treasure, you lead us everywhere in safety, by sea, by land, and in the midst of enemies; you fear nothing except that God should hide, for he is eternal security! God's security cannot be removed by hardships or by any person. Perfect patience is forged through hardships and difficulties, though no one wants to suffer these. Passionate, loving charity—always the opposite of selfish self-love—is also forged in this way. Having been flooded and taken over by the riches of charity, the heart seeks joy and gladness and all security [in God]. And then the person does not seek or look out for himself for his own sake but for God's sake, and also cares for his fellow human beings for God's sake; all this person's actions are no longer directed for his own gain but to honor the Father once this person returns home.[10]

And so, get up, let's not slumber any longer in the bed of negligence for it is time to invest one's treasure in loving merchandise; do you know which merchandise? Paying out our life for our God, bringing an end to all our sins. I refer to the fragrance of the flower that begins to open, namely, the holy pilgrimage [crusade], for our Holy Father, our Christ on earth is inquiring about the pious willingness and readiness of Christian people. He wants to know if they are willing to give their lives to reconquer the Holy Land. He says that if he finds sufficient willingness, he will offer all support and zealously use his power to further this cause. Indeed, he states this in the Bull that he sent to our Provincial, to Friar Raymond and to the minister of the Friars Minor. He asked them to promptly investigate in Tuscany and other territories the willingness [to participate in the crusade]. He wants to know in writing the level of commitment and the number [of volunteers] so that he can send resources and give the required orders. And so, I invite you to this wedding of eternal life;[11] may you set your desire alight to give blood for blood.[12] And please, invite all you can, for one does not

Civil Authorities

attend a wedding alone; and you cannot turn back. I say no more.

I thank you with affectionate love for the care you have extended to me as stated and intended in your letter. I cannot presume to reward your affection, but I pray and will continuously pray supreme, eternal Goodness to reward you. Bless your family one hundred thousand times and greet them in my name.

Remain in Holy Love.

Jesus! Jesus! Jesus!

LETTER 143

To Queen Giovanna of Naples
August 4, 1375 (dated letter)

Introduction

Giovanna of Anjou was "licentious, violent and fickle, an opportunist of the first degree."[13] She was queen of the Kingdom of Naples in the south of Italy, a separate political entity connected to France. Giovanna had sold Avignon to the pope and oscillated back and forth in her support for papal causes. Undoubtedly under the guidance of Raymond, Catherine wrote to encourage her to join the crusade and support the cause of the pope. Altogether, Catherine exchanged seven letters with her, the first three, of which this is one, encouraged Giovanna to support Gregory XI's policies, especially the crusade, and the last four, after 1378, lobbied on behalf of Urban VI and against the election of the schismatic pope, Clement VII, whom Giovanna eventually supported.

As the leader of the powerful Kingdom of Naples, Giovanna's cooperation with the crusade would have been particularly valuable, and Catherine must have been directed by Raymond to "lobby" her. What we see in this letter is Catherine's naiveté and faith at the same time. Her interpretation of Giovanna's response to a previous letter and her expectations of Giovanna were completely unrealistic. Catherine lobbied this queen through her passionate exhortation to notice how much God loved her and how much he wanted her as his spouse out of love. That this worldly woman with a rather tawdry reputation would want to be a bride of Christ, would want to become converted, and would desire to go on crusade herself and risk martyrdom seems totally unrealistic. Yet, that Catherine wrote this detailed exhortation and two others to preach her spirituality of conversion to this queen reveals the profound faith Catherine had in God's power and the authority she was convinced she had—through God's grace—to convince sinful persons to change their way of life.

❧ ❧ ❧

To the name of Christ crucified and tender Mary,

Lady, Queen, very dear and venerable mother, your unworthy Catherine, servant and slave of the servants of Jesus Christ, writes to you in the precious blood of the Son of God, with desire to see you a consecrated daughter and spouse of our loving God.

First Truth calls you "daughter," for we were created by God and borne of him. As he said, "let us make humankind in our image, according to our likeness." (Gen 1:26) And when God took on human nature, human persons became his spouses. *Oh Jesus, most tender love, as a sign that you took us as your bride, you gave us the ring of your most holy, most tender flesh at the time of your holy circumcision on the end of the eighth day!* So, venerable mother, flesh the size of a ring[14] was removed on the eighth day as a down payment that would give us absolute hope of future payment; that is the payment we received on the wood of the cross, when our spouse, the immaculate Lamb, was sacrificed and copiously lost blood from every part of himself. With this blood he cleansed the sins and impurities of his spouse, the human race. Notice that this fire of divine love gave us a ring, not of gold, but made from his pure flesh. And so, our most loving Father celebrates the betrothal, not with the flesh of an animal[15] but with his own precious body, that is, the Lamb as

Civil Authorities

food roasted[16] in the fire of charity on the wood of the beloved cross.

Given all this, I beg you, in Christ Jesus and with the greatest affection, that with fullness and depth of motivation of the will rooted in love [*affetto*], energy, and zeal, you raise your heart and soul to love and serve the dear, loving Father and spouse, that is, our God, who is ultimate and eternal Truth; he who loved us with so much tenderness without being loved in return. May no creature, no eminence, authority, or power, nor any other form of human glory—which anyway is vain and quickly gone like the wind—lead us to withdraw from such true love, love that is life and glory and blessedness for the soul. In this way we will show that we are faithful spouses.

When the soul loves only her Creator and desires nothing but him, everything she loves, she loves for him, and all her acts are carried out for his sake. She hates anything she knows to be against his will, such as vice, sin, all forms of injustice and all other faults; for holy hatred against sin leads her [the soul] to prefer death rather than break the trust of her eternal spouse. So let us, let us really be faithful, following the footsteps of Christ crucified, disdaining vice and embracing virtue, and engaging in and carrying out all important enterprises[17] for his sake.

Please know, my venerable Lady, that I was delighted, and I rejoiced when I received your letter, which filled me with great consolation for it seems to me you have a good, holy willingness to give your life and practical support for the glory of the name of Christ crucified. You could offer no greater sacrifice or love than to be willing to give your life, if necessary, for Christ crucified. Oh what great comfort it would be to see blood given for blood,[18] to see grow in you the flame of holy desire for the sake of the blood of God's Son; and to see this in you who have the title of Queen of Jerusalem.[19] You can be the motivator and leader of this holy pilgrimage [the crusade] so that the Holy Land will no longer be held by the dreadful unbelievers but rather held in an honorable fashion by Christians, and by you.

Know that the Holy Father greatly desires that the holy pilgrimage take place. And so, I would like you to carry out the good intentions placed within your soul by the Holy Spirit and say yes to the Holy Father, so that his desire may grow. Please order that this holy pilgrimage take place. May you, in particular, make the holy pilgrimage, together with all the Christians who may want to follow you; for certainly if you rise up and take the step, and you proclaim this holy resolution, you will find a large number of Christians who will want to follow you.

I beg you for love of Christ crucified to be attentive and diligent regarding the above; I will pray—my spiritual weakness permitting[20]—that God, ultimate eternal goodness, may give you the perfect light to guide this and all your endeavors, and make your desire multiply. And, alight with the fire of love, may you move beyond reigning in this miserable, fleeting life to reach the eternal city, Jerusalem, ideal of peace, where the divine mercy will make of all of us kings and lords and will reward all our efforts and all suffering endured for his most tender love.

Remain in the holy love of God.

Jesus! Jesus! Jesus!

LETTER 266

To messere Ristoro Canigiani of Florence
August–September 1378 (Noffke)

Introduction

Ristoro was a lawyer and influential Florentine politician, a member of the Guelphs, the party favored by Raymond of Capua and other ecclesiastical leaders. Responding to Catherine's charism that attracted so many to seek her spiritual guidance, he asks her about the practice of receiving communion; in other words, he seeks advice from a young lay woman—not from a monk or priest—about a sacramental practice. Ristoro is an example of the sort of important

Civil Authorities

leader to whom Catherine was introduced by Raymond of Capua or those connected to him, who then sought her wisdom and advice.

Catherine responds with a reflection on the centrality of transformation away from selfish self-love so the eye of understanding can see God's love clearly. But the most interesting and unique part of her letter is her wisdom about receiving communion. At a time when communion was received about once a year and eucharistic spirituality emphasized the lack of the recipient's worthiness, Catherine asserted that communion is food for the soul and there should be no false humility. She writes a beautiful, long explanation to show how God is always ready to give us far more than we want and places within us desires for that which he wants to give us. So, if we desire communion, we should assume it is placed in our hearts by God.

❦ ❦ ❦

To the name of Jesus Christ crucified and tender Mary.

Dearest son in Christ loving Jesus, I, Catherine, slave of the servants of Jesus Christ, write to you in his precious blood. I desire to see you free of all selfish self-love, so that you are not deprived of the light and understanding to recognize the unfathomable love that God has for you.

Since the light is that which makes it possible for us to recognize this love, and self-centered love is that which deprives us of the light, my greatest desire is that self-centered love be extinguished in you. Alas! This self-centered love is so dangerous for our salvation! It deprives the soul of grace by eliminating love for God and neighbor, when it is this love that allows us to live in grace. As I said, it [self-centered love] obscures the light because it clouds the eye of understanding,[21] and as the light is blocked out, we walk in darkness unable to recognize what we need. What is it that we need to recognize? God's great goodness and his unimaginable love for us, and that our wretchedness lies in this perverse law [self-centered love] that always contradicts the Spirit. Through this knowledge [of God's love] the soul begins to render God his due, that is, glory and honor to his name, loving him above all else, and loving one's neighbor as oneself with hunger and desire for virtue. She [the soul] renders to herself abhorrence and displeasure for vice and selfish sensuality—the cause of all vice.[22] As I've stated, the soul acquires all virtue and grace spending time in knowledge of herself illuminated by the light. Where will the soul find fullness of contrition for her sins together with the abundance of God's mercy? In the house of knowledge of self. So, let's see if we find it [contrition] there.

Let's talk about this since, according to what you wrote to me, you wish to achieve contrition for your sins; and, feeling that you had not achieved this, you stopped receiving holy communion. Let's examine if this is a reason to stop receiving it. As you know, God is immeasurably good and loved us before we came to be. He is eternal wisdom; his power and virtue are immeasurable. For all these reasons we can be sure that he knows all that we need, and he wants to give it to us and is able to do so. So, let's look at the proof that he gives us more than we ourselves know we need and more than we ask for. Did we ask God to create us in his image and likeness, as beings capable of reason—and not brute beasts? No, we didn't. Neither did we ask to be reborn to grace through the blood of the Word, the only begotten son of God; nor did we ask that he give us as food the fullness of his being—God and Man—in his flesh and blood, body and soul united in the godhead. Besides these incalculable blessings—which are so great—he bestowed upon us a great fire of love so that the most hardened heart or one made of stone, having considered each of these gifts, would dissolve their hardness and coldness. In other words, we receive infinite graces and blessings without asking for them. Since he gives so much without our asking, how much more will he fulfill our desires when we desire something that is just? As well, who prompts our desire and our requests? Only God. So, if he prompts us to ask, it is a sign that he wants to fulfill our requests by giving us what we ask for.

You may tell me, "I acknowledge he [God] is as you say; so why are there so many times when I make requests, including for contrition, and my requests do not seem to be fulfilled?" Let me answer. One possibility is that the person making the request is at fault, asking without prudence[23] and only in word and not out of deep-seated motivation rooted in God's love [*affetto*].[24] Remember that our Savior said that those who just say "Lord! Lord" will not be recognized by him [Matt 7:22–23]. It's not that he doesn't know them, but rather that due to their sins they are not recognized by his mercy.[25] Another possibility is that the person may request something that would be harmful to their salvation, thinking it would be for their good. And so, if they received their request, it would be harmful to them, and if they do not receive it, it would be a blessing. By not giving what would be harmful, God is fulfilling the request.

We always receive [a response] from God, who fortunately knows both what is hidden and what is evident, as well as our imperfections. And so, he recognizes that if he immediately offered us a grace we requested, we would act like a fly—that disgusting insect—which, having had its fill of honey, which is so sweet, will not land on something that stinks. God realizes that we often act this way. That is, we receive his graces and benefits, filling ourselves with the sweetness of his love, and then we do not pay attention to sufferings that should be accepted, and instead return to the vomit[26] from drunkenness on worldly things. So sometimes God does not give us what we want as promptly as we want in order to foster growth in desire and hunger [for him]; for God takes pleasure and delights in this desire and hunger of his creature.

Sometimes God will effectively grant a grace but without affective satisfaction. This is the way of providence, for knowing the soul, God recognizes that with the affective experience of receiving the [requested] grace, she would slacken the cord of desire or would become proud; in this case God withdraws affective satisfaction but not the grace. Others receive [the requested] grace and feel its consolation as it pleases God's loving goodness, who, as our physician, bestows his grace on those of us who are sick, giving to each according to their illness. So you see that the desire emerging from her core [*affetto*] with which the person asks God for blessings is always fulfilled.

Now let's look at that which we should pray for with prudence. In my view, first loving Truth teaches us about what we should request, when in the holy Gospels he scolds persons for their disordered petitions for the acquisition and possession of worldly riches and status. "Don't think about tomorrow, to each day its need" [Matt 6:34].[27] With this he teaches us that prudence calls attention to the fleetingness of time. And then adds, "Ask first for the reign of heaven; for God well knows all that you need, even the smallest things" [Matt 6:32–33].

What is this reign? And how do we ask for it? It is the reign of eternal life, the reign of our soul; if the soul is not regulated by reason[28] it can never enter God's kingdom. How do we ask for this [reign]? Not with words alone—we have seen that words alone are not recognized by God—but with ordered love emerging from the core of self [*affetto*] for true, real virtues.

It is virtue that asks for and possesses the reign of God, for virtue makes persons prudent. It is with prudence and maturity that a man acts for the honor of God and the salvation of his neighbors, bearing with and tolerating their faults. With prudence he orders the *affetto* of love,[29] loving God above all else and his neighbor as himself. To act in an ordered manner means the person is ready to give the life of his body for the salvation of souls, and his material possessions to save his neighbor's body; prudent love is ordered in this way. If someone is lacking in prudence they would act in a contrary manner, as do many whose love is foolish and false; so, many times, in order to save their neighbor—not their soul but their physical body—they risk their own soul giving false witness with [false] judgments and lies. Such persons squander love because it is not seasoned with prudence.

We have seen that for our good we should ask prudently for the reign of God. Now I will tell you how we should act with regard to holy communion and how we should receive it. We should be free of a foolish humility such as that of many worldly laypersons.[30] Receiving this loving sacrament, I tell you, is for our good because we are commanded to do so and because it is food for the soul, and without this food we cannot live in grace. Therefore, no attachment of our soul is so great that it should not or could not be severed in order to come to this loving sacrament; and so the person should do the best he can and that is enough.

How should we receive it [communion]? With the mouth of holy desire, and with the light of most holy faith we should gaze upon God—fully God and Man—dwelling in that host. And so, as the will ordered by love [*affetto*] follows understanding, in her deepest motivation and capacity for love [*affetto*] the person receives the host with affectionate love and with holy attention to his faults and sins; in this way he experiences contrition.[31] As well, he meditates on the generosity and unfathomable love of God for giving himself to him as food. And even though he doesn't think his contrition and disposition are as perfect as he would want, he should not avoid [taking communion]; for good will and a good disposition are sufficient.

I also tell you that it is good for you to receive [communion] as was commanded in the Old Testament,[32] when the people were asked to eat the lamb whole and not cut up, roasted and not boiled, and to do so as they were standing and with their belts tied and their staff in hand; and they were told the blood of the lamb should be placed on the door frame [Exod 12:3–11]. This is the way you should take this sacrament [of communion]: eat it roasted and not boiled; if boiled it would be halfway between the lamb and the fire, between water and soil; that is, between worldly desires, attachments, and motivations [*affetto*] and the water of self-love. It should be roasted so it is not half-cooked; we receive it roasted when we receive it with the fire of tender love. We must have around us the corded belt[33] of chastity. For it would be most unseemly to go around with [spiritual] cleanliness and purity, but with a filthy mind and body. We must remain upright, that is, our heart and mind must be upright before God [fully focused on God] and faithful to God. We must take our staff in hand, which is the wood of the holy cross, so that we carry the doctrine of Christ crucified, who is the staff on which we lean; this staff protects us from our enemies, that is, from the world, the evil one, and the flesh. And we should eat it whole and not in pieces, meaning that with the light of faith we should not pay attention only to the human dimension of this sacrament, but rather to the body and soul of Christ crucified united and blended with the godhead, that is, fully God and fully human. It would be good for us to take the blood of this lamb and place it on our forehead by which we give witness about him to all persons; we should never deny him due to any suffering or even death. And so it is good to lovingly eat this Lamb roasted in the fire of love on the wood of the cross; in this way we will be found tagged with the sign of Tau and will not be struck by the executing angel [Exod 12:23].

I have said it is not good to act like imprudent laypeople who violate the commandments of holy Church while saying, "I am not worthy." With these words they live a long time in mortal sin and without food for their soul. Oh, what foolish humility! Don't you see you are indeed not worthy? How long are you going to wait to be worthy? Don't wait for this, as you will be worthy only at the end, as at the beginning,[34] for despite all our judgments we will never be worthy. It is God who is worthy and makes us worthy through his goodness, and his goodness never lessens. How should we act? For our part we should be well disposed and observe the loving commandment. For, as I said, if we give up communion thinking we are avoiding sin, we will fall into sin.

Now I bring this to a close. I don't want such foolishness to dwell within you; I want you to dispose yourself to receive holy communion as a faithful Christian, as I have explained. The more you know yourself, the more perfectly you will accomplish this; otherwise, you will fail. For when you live out of knowledge of yourself, you will see everything honestly. Do not diminish your desire no matter what harm or sorrow or insult you may suffer; nor diminish your desire due to lack of gratitude from those you have served. Rather, with courage and true, lasting perseverance you will endure unto death. I ask you to act in this way for the love of Christ crucified. I say no more.

Civil Authorities

Remain in the holy, tender love of God. Tender Jesus! Jesus love!

LETTER 358

To master Andrea Vanni, painter, while he was captain of the citizens of Siena
September or October 1379 (Noffke, ISIME)

Introduction

Andrea di Vanni, about fifteen years older than Catherine, held various political offices in Siena, including that of captain (a sort of mayor); he was also an accomplished painter in the style of Lorenzetti. He and Catherine knew each other, and judging from the three letters she wrote to him and the fresco he painted of her—the only image of her by someone who knew her—it is assumed he followed her wisdom.

In this letter, Catherine spells out a version of her teaching on discernment as the virtue of discretion, applying it to Vanni's role as Captain (mayor) of Siena. Discretion/discernment enables persons to act with just right-order based on knowledge of God and self so that the person is able to recognize what is due to God, to others, and to self from the perspective of God's love and truth. Knowledge of love and truth occurs through the three powers of the soul, which, when ordered through such knowledge, become capable of discernment (see Letter 213 and its introduction for more on Catherine's teaching on discernment). When Catherine uses the word *justice* in this letter, she mostly means right-order, that is, rendering what is due to God, others, and self, according to the standards of God's love.[35] Thus, Andrea must walk the journey of transformation acquiring knowledge of God and self so that he makes possible ordering the three powers of the soul. This would enable him to recognize what must be done for others so that the city of Siena is governed with the justice or right-order based on God's love; this would be so because the city's highest official is capable of discernment. This letter to

Vanni is another example of Catherine's wise adaptation of her rhetoric, language, metaphors, and examples to the life situation of her correspondent.

Notice the personification of desire/*affetto* and of selfish self-love, a rhetorical move that emphasizes the significance of these dimensions of experience.

✺ ✺ ✺

To the name of Jesus Christ and tender Mary.

Dearest son in Christ tender Jesus. I, Catherine, servant and slave of Jesus Christ, write to you in his precious blood with desire to see you be a just and good official so that God is honored and your desire is accomplished. I know God in his mercy has blessed you with good desires. I don't see, though, how we can govern others if we don't first govern ourselves well.

When the person can manage himself, he is able to do this with others. He can love his fellow human beings with the same love as himself for the perfect love of God engenders perfect love of neighbor. So, with the perfect love with which a man governs himself, he governs his citizens. How does someone who reverences God bring order to himself? With what form of justice? This is his approach. With the light of reason, he orders the three powers of the soul, and with this right-order he regulates his entire life, both spiritually and physically; then he acts with right-order in every situation or role he holds and in all circumstances. He orders memory to enable presence to all of God's blessings as well as to the offenses he might have committed against ultimate Good. He orders understanding, enabling recognition of the love with which God has bestowed his grace and in order to learn the teachings of his truth. Likewise, he orders the will, enabling love for the infinite goodness of God, which he has seen and recognized with the light of understanding.

Because he has recognized that God should be loved by his children with all their heart, with all their motivation arising from their core [*affetto*], and with all their strength, when he becomes aware that disordered sensuality could seek to spoil such a fine, outstanding order, he climbs onto the chair that oversees conscience[36] in order to rule in ordered fashion. And if due to weakness or the delusions of the evil one this perfection[37]—fruit of such a holy right-order—were to be damaged or thwarted, he brings about right-order, because in his breast shines this justice. And he renders justice as one who has achieved discernment, rendering to each his due. And so, if selfish sensuality deals a deadly blow, he decapitates his own disordered self-centered will with the knife of hatred of vice and love of virtue. Then, depending on the seriousness of the offense, right-order within [the virtue of discretion] chastens disordered desire arising from her core [*affetto* of the soul], making it pay the penalty assigned by divine justice.

What is this penalty and how is it meted out? I'll tell you. Just reason wants self-centered desire, which seeks worldly status, honors, and wealth, to embrace repentance, disdaining honors, choosing what is humble, willingly abandoning riches and espousing poverty; just reason expects the person to trust in God and not in herself or in worldly status, neither of which possess stability or solidity. If disordered desire seeks the stench of immorality,[38] justice constrains and forces desire to seek and take pleasure in being chaste. If the person seeks pride, justice assigns her humility; if infidelity, faith; if greediness, the generosity of charity; if hatred and dislike of neighbor, compassion; if lack of discretion, the practice of prudence. Similarly, the virtues are the sentences and constraints that the judge sitting on the seat of conscience discerns must be imposed on the *affetto* of the soul to punish selfish sensuality and destroy motivation toward and desire [*affetto*] for vice. As I've said, this is how the self-centered will is beheaded. In this way reason remains in charge of the soul, managing right-order with the virtues. Reason is placed in charge as mistress, and self-centered sensuality as servant, so the soul renders due honor to God and the spiritual love of charity to her neighbor.

The soul should dwell in the house of knowledge of self and of God's goodness dwelling within her; and she should judge others with the same goodness with which she is judged. She should often wash from her face the stain of sin with the blood of Christ, partaking of confession;[39] she should feed her soul with the food of angels, that is, the loving sacrament of the body and blood of Christ—fully God and fully man—since all the Christian faithful are required to receive it at least once a year. Whoever wants to receive [communion] more often should do so, and no one, neither sinners nor those justified, should forgo communion. If the sinner is not prepared, he should prepare; if he is in a state of grace, he should not say out of humility, "I am not worthy of such a great mystery; when I am worthy, I will receive communion." One should not think like this, for out of his own merit he will never be worthy; and should he make himself worthy, he would surely be unworthy. He would be covering up pride with the cloak of humility. God has the honor and power to make us worthy, and so it is with God's honor (worthiness) that we should receive communion.

And we should receive communion in two ways, in actual practice and in with our heart, that is, with true, holy, consuming desire. We should have this desire not only when we receive communion, but all the time, in every place; for it is the food we should consume to provide the life of grace to our soul. All this, and the right-ordered acts already mentioned, are the outcome brought about through the three powers of the soul as these are ordered and lived out with right-ordered reason [i.e., with discretion]. So, once the person possesses this quality, he acts accordingly toward his neighbor through prayer, through his words, and through a good and holy life.

And if the person is a man charged with governing, he wants his subjects to observe the law [of right-order] that he observes himself. He sees to it that it should be observed with zeal for justice [right-order], punishing those who violate the law. And since he has punished his own selfish sensuality, which rebels against the divine law, he seeks to punish his subjects when they don't observe civil law and other statutes. This is right-ordered behavior for those who have to rule and govern. Based on the right-order of justice, he punishes more or less severely based

Civil Authorities

on reason. Such sentencing should not be contaminated nor diminished by fear of suffering or physical death, nor out of fear [of criticism] or due to flattery, neither due to taking pleasure in others or in any worldly good. Nor should honor or one's flesh be sold for gain, as is done by those who live without just order or the light of reason. He who lives with just order does not abandon his authority and power for any reason, even a just cause; he carries out his authority, to the extent he can, seeking God's honor, the salvation of his soul, and the common good for each person, straightforwardly counseling the truth and making it clear to the extent that he can.

This is how you should act to keep the city in peace and preserve justice. For it is precisely due to lack of justice [right-order] that so many troubles have occurred and are coming.

And so, I have said that I wanted to see you be a true, just authority. I desire to see justice in you and to see you manage, rule, and govern our city with the virtue of discretion. As I said, if one does not start with right-order within oneself, one is unable to have it lived out by others, no matter what one's role. I therefore invite you—and want you to—be diligent in preserving right-order within you, so that you can competently carry out the task divine Goodness has assigned you. In all the tasks you must accomplish, always have God before your eyes,[40] and act with true humility so that God may be glorified in you, etc.[41]

Remain, etc.

Tender Jesus! Jesus love!

6
KNIGHTS, MILITARY LEADERS

LETTER 374

To Messer Bartolomeo della pace[1]
November–December 1375 (Noffke); second half 1375 (Volpato); June 1375 (ISIME)

Introduction

Bartolomeo Smeducci di San Severino was a knight[2] who at first fought on the side of Gregory XI, then in 1376 on the side of Florence and Perugia against the papal forces. He is an example of someone that Catherine is unlikely to have known but whom she would have been encouraged to "lobby" for the crusade as he had a reputation as a successful knight.

The crusade was a cause dear to Catherine's heart because she saw it as an opportunity for transformation and to work for the good of the church. In line with the twelfth-century spirituality and theology of crusade, she believed that this project was a pilgrimage that mediated the salvation of those who participated in it and could serve as an opportunity for unbelievers, the Muslims, to be converted. Catherine's assertion in this letter that the unbelievers were equally saved by Christ was an innovative belief for her time and was most likely a direct fruit of the wisdom she received through the Spirit. Catherine considered martyrdom one of the most prized ideals of a spiritual journey because it would be the exemplary imitation of Jesus giving his life for us, and going on crusade was an opportunity for martyrdom. She was very disappointed that she could not pursue such a pilgrimage herself, so she exhorted others with great diligence and passion.[3]

Though writing to a worldly warrior, Catherine dedicates a large part of this letter to her wisdom about transformation, encouraging this knight to actualize his potential through connection to God's love, moving away from worldly and disordered love so God can give him strength and, thus strengthened, he can participate in the crusade. Catherine's rhetorical gifts are evident in the manner in which she uses the language of chivalry to present this wisdom in order to make it particularly persuasive. Thus, she refers to the chainmail of love, to the knives of battle that should be used to remove disordered attachments; sins are the enemy, and the soul is a bulwark or fortress. And Catherine tells Bartolomeo that turning back from a path of virtue and practicing love would be as serious as a knight fleeing from the field of battle.

❦ ❦ ❦

To the name of Jesus Christ crucified and tender Mary

Dear reverend father[4] in Christ, loving Jesus. I, Catherine, servant and slave of the servants of Jesus Christ, write to you in his precious blood with desire to see you a brave rather than a fearful knight. For slavish fear[5] saps the soul's strength, which would not please her Creator, and so it is important to be completely free of such fear.

I think no one should have reason to be fearful, for God has given us strength against all adversaries.[6] What power can the evil one have against us? He was created weak, his power lost through the death of the Son of God. What power can the flesh have when it has been rendered weak through the flagellations and thrashings endured by Christ crucified? Reflecting on this and contemplating her Creator—who is God and Man—bleeding on the wood of the holy cross, the soul will immediately put a stop to all sensuality and fleshly pleasures. What power can the world have with its pride and foolish pleasures when [Christ] has defeated the world with his deep humility, absorbing insults and disgrace? If God has so humbled himself, human pride must be subjugated. Inviting us to let go of slavish fear, our Savior said, "Rejoice that I have vanquished the world." Our enemies have been defeated, and human persons made so strong that—unless they allow it—they cannot be defeated. This loving God has given us the fortress of the will that forms the bulwark of our soul so that it cannot be captured by others or by the evil one. And so, we can be safe and let go of fear.

I want your safety to be in Christ, loving Jesus. He has clothed us in the sturdiest clothing possible, which is love covered with the chainmail of free will; you have the choice of fully buckling up this armor or of loosening it. If someone wants to remove this clothing of love, they are free to do so; and if someone wants to keep it on, they can do so as well. Think about this, dearest father, the first clothing we had was love, since we were created out of sheer love, in the image and likeness of God; and so persons cannot live without love, as they are made of nothing else but love. All that persons possess in terms both of their soul and of their body is due to God's love. Similarly, a father and mother give life to their child out of their own flesh, and through God's grace do so only out of love.

A child is inclined by nature to be beholden to the Father because of the latter's love for him. And so, if the child is a true offspring, he[7] cannot tolerate any insults to the Father.[8] (Be attentive, for if due to selfish self-love a person comes to be at odds with the Father, such blindness would lead him to act against his nature). Dear father in Christ loving Jesus, it is truly so, that it is in the nature of the soul herself to love and follow the Father, her Creator, God eternal. For realizing she has been created out of sheer love, she is drawn to him and cannot tolerate any injuries done to him.

Out of love for the Father, the soul always wants to seek retribution[9] against her sensuality, her selfish self-love, which is her mortal enemy; for whoever pursues the desires of his sensual, selfish self-love, will suffer death, an eternal death, and will

Knights, Military Leaders

crucify Christ anew. For as you know, it is only due to sin that Christ died. The soul who is in love with God, our supreme eternal Father, wants to follow her natural inclination [to love]. Being in love, she is willing to lose her life for God and seeks retribution for her own sinfulness, attacking disordered attachments caused by the evil one, the world, and the flesh. She attacks these with the knives of both love and hate, that is, hatred and distaste for sin and love for virtue; and she rejoices in that which God loves and hates what God hates. And so, following her natural inclination, the soul renders to the Father his due,[10] never again deviating from this, so long as she is not poisoned by the taint of selfish self-love, which leads to loving oneself apart from what is in God. For such selfish self-love leads to getting caught up in the pleasures, delights, and status of the world, thus making a God of one's flesh, catering to it with disordered delight and lack of boundaries. If the soul so deviates [acting out of the poison of selfish self-love], she does not avenge the enemy that destroyed her Father; rather, she destroys herself.[11]

And so, I don't want this to happen to you but want you to act according to the caring quality that God has given you. With love and free will you must bind and tighten this clothing [chainmail of love] so that neither the evil one nor any creature would be able to remove it. When you are clothed in this way and you are armed with virtue as well as the knives of both hatred and of love, you will leave aside slavish fear and you will hold the city of your soul; you will endure any blows you receive and any suffering that you might have to endure; you will not turn back; that is, you will not start down the path of virtue and then turn back to the vomit of mortal sin. I wouldn't want this. Rather I want you to persevere until the end, because that which will be crowned and worthy of glory is only perseverance, not the first steps taken. It is a great cowardice to start something and not bring it to fruition. How worthy of humiliation would be a knight that would turn his back while in the field of battle!

So, come on, dearest father! No more negligent behavior! Never again turn back or care for the foolish and silly vanities of the world whose enjoyment is as fleeting as the wind; they have no substance or stability. Don't count on the youth of your body or the honorable titles of the world. Today a person is alive, tomorrow dead; today healthy and tomorrow ill; today he is a lord and tomorrow a servant. Persons are foolish to regard what is so fleeting with disordered desire, to trust in what cannot be trusted; they wait for that which will not take place yet flee from that which they could have and hold as theirs, namely, grace, which is available in whatever measure and at whatever moment one is open to receiving it. Such grace we cannot give ourselves; it is the gift of the Holy Spirit who has endowed us with free will.

Oh infinite, benevolent charity, what moves you? Only love! Oh Jesus, most benevolent love, you walled in this soul in order to strengthen her and to relieve her of the weakness into which she fell due to sin; you mixed the mortar for this wall with your blood, since the blood unites the soul to the divine will and makes her conform to God's love and will! As water is mixed with lime to strengthen the mortar for the joints between each stone, so God has put the blood of his only Son between him and the soul. The blood is the living mortar of most intense love. It is not blood without fire or fire without blood. For the blood was sprinkled over the human race with the fire of God's love. And so, because of this wall, the soul is made so strong that no contrary wind can topple her, unless the person herself chooses to destroy the wall with the pickaxe of mortal sin.

It would be hard to find a heart so hard and stubborn that it would be unmoved by such infinite love and by the great dignity that God's grace has bestowed on persons as a gift and not out of obligation! There can be no person who, having seen and considered these truths, would not overcome selfish sensual pursuits and let go of laxness and hardness of heart, and thus receive the perfect light and knowledge of self; for she recognizes that while *she-is-not* she is filled with God's goodness, which bestows being and all grace built upon being.

May your heart and soul become fired up with love and desire through Christ, loving Jesus, so that you can return so much love, giving your life for him as he did for you. He gave his life for you, so desire to give your life for him—blood for blood. On behalf of Christ crucified, I invite you to offer your blood on behalf of his,[12] when the time comes for God's servants to reconquer that which was taken, namely, the Holy Sepulcher of Christ and the souls of the unbelievers—our brothers—who were ransomed by Christ's blood in the same way as we. Take the Holy Sepulcher from them and retrieve their souls from their infidelity and from the evil one. I urge you, do not be negligent; do not delay when you receive the invitation, that is, when the Holy Father raises the standard of the holy cross ordering the holy passage [crusade]. I don't think anyone should avoid or escape this call; he should not fear death. As I said, I want to see you a courageous and not a fearful knight. The blood will fortify you and give you courage, removing all fear.

I beg you for love of Christ crucified that you await with joy and desire the invitation to this glorious, loving wedding,[13] an espousal full of joy, benevolence, and gentle goodness. At this wedding, all sinfulness is left behind and all are freed from their faults and sins,[14] for they will be gathered at the table where the Lamb is the food and serves the food. The Father is the table upon which is all that is, except sin, which *is-not*.[15] The Word, the Son of God, has become food for us, roasted on the fire of blazing love. The Spirit is the waiter who serves that love; through the hands of the Spirit, God has given us and continues to bestow on us every grace and gift, both spiritual and temporal. He continuously bestows these gifts; you and anyone else would be foolish if you stayed away from such joy! If you cannot walk [toward God] standing straight, then do so on all fours; whatever it takes to offer some sign of love, proffering your life for love of life. In this way we pay for our sins and faults with the instrument of our body, since it is through this instrument that we have sinned. This will be the holy and loving retribution that we will impose upon ourselves, for when our selfish sensuality and our weak body are overcome, we will have conquered. Our reason and our soul will be free and sovereign, possessing God who is the highest, eternal good.

Dearest father, let us not waste more time. Follow the footsteps of Christ crucified! Bathe in the blood of Christ crucified! Hide in the wounds of Christ crucified! Place Christ crucified as the central object before the eyes of your soul, that you may remain in filial awe and love. Do not fear suffering, fear sin. I say no more.

Forgive my ignorance. May I be forgiven due to my love and desire, and because of my sorrow at seeing you stubbornly and blindly race toward the wretchedness of mortal sin.

Remain in the holy, benevolent affection of God.

Jesus, loving Jesus!

LETTER 256

To messer Friar Niccolò, prior of the Tuscan province of the Knights Hospitallers when he was in Venice to order the pilgrimage [crusade] on which they were about to embark against the unbelievers
March–April 1377 (Noffke)

Introduction

Niccolò was the prior of the Hospitallers,[16] a religious congregation of men who followed the Rule of St. Benedict and were also knights. They were founded to help preserve the Holy Land and to tend to the wounded there, hence, the name Hospitallers. Since orders of knights were being recruited to take part in Gregory XI's crusade, Niccolò had travelled to Venice to organize transport for his men.

There is no information regarding Catherine's relationship with Niccolò, so most likely he was one more person she was invited to encourage regarding the crusade. Catherine does, indeed, encourage Niccolò in his task of sending troops to the Holy Land; however, she mostly spurs him to continue a spiritual journey, engaging in the crusade pilgrimage and becoming willing to give his life as a martyr.

Knights, Military Leaders

In other words, she preaches her spirituality of crusade.[17] That she advised the prior of a military religious order shows again the authority she felt from God.

Catherine employs the language of chivalry to exhort this Hospitaller, using language and images from the life reality of her hearer, imagining life situations very unlike her own. The rhetoric of chivalry is used both to exhort to transformation and to encourage knightly feats. Niccolò should go on the crusade pilgrimage as a form of intercession, and as a way of letting God know he was willing to give his life in imitation of Christ crucified; at the same time, going on crusade would win back the Holy Land for Christians and enable the conversion of unbelievers, battle goals Catherine considered to be for the good of the church.

In this letter Catherine also shares her wisdom about the different states in life.

❆ ❆ ❆

To the name of Jesus Christ crucified and tender Mary.

My dearest son in Christ tender Jesus. I, Catherine, servant and slave of the servants of Jesus Christ, write to you in his precious blood, with desire to see you a brave knight, having taken off the clothing of selfish self-love and clothed yourself in divine love. For a knight who must fight on the battlefield must be armed with love as a weapon; love is the most powerful weapon possible. It is not enough that a man be armed with armor and breast plates; if he does not possess the weapons of love and related desire for honor and for the cause for which he is fighting, it could easily happen that as soon as he faced his enemies he would fear and turn back.

So I say to you that the soul who seeks to enter the field of battle in order to fight against vice, the evil one, and self-centered sensuality while not clothed in the armor of love of virtue, while not holding in hand the knife of loathing [of sin], and while not possessed of a holy conscience formed by divine love, will never do battle but will be defeated in advance; such a person is negligent, clothed in the armor of self-centered sensuality, and so will lie down and sleep in vice and sin. This [love of virtue] is the glorious armor that saves one from eternal death, provides light and removes darkness, and raises us from the level of an animal to that of human being. For the person who lives in vice, sin, and litter takes on the habits and characteristics of an animal;[18] like an animal he does not possess reason but acts according to his appetites. The man who becomes like an animal has lost the light of reason and allows himself to be guided by the instincts of the flesh and other disordered appetites that arise within him. All his pleasure lies in dishonesty, in eating and drinking abundantly, in experiencing pleasures and amusements, in acquiring worldly honors, even as all these things are as fleeting as the wind. Such a person is not a true knight and is unable to handle any attacks, because he has put on the armor of death and taken on the characteristics of an animal.

I don't want this to happen to you. I want you to be a true, brave human being [as opposed to an animal devoid of reason], and not just a human being but one who is growing in virtue. Having battled against vice, as I explained, you should arrive at the angelic state[19] to which you and your order are called by God. You know that the [ordinary] human state is marriage; the angelic state is that to which you and your order are called, as are other religious whom he has called to celibacy. It would not be good; in fact, it would be displeasing to God and terrible for the world, if you who are called to greater perfection, to walk toward this greater perfection, should remain as animals. For you are not only called to be human and to an angelic state, but you are called to the glorious martyrdom of giving your life for Christ crucified. It would be highly offensive to mix such a treasure with dreadful, wretched mud.[20]

Come now! Without slavish fear but with courage take up the two battles God has placed before you. The first is a general battle to which all reasoning creatures are called. For as we become able to discern vice from virtue, we are at the same time surrounded by our enemies, that is, the world, the evil one, and our own flesh and disordered sensuality, which always resist the Spirit. However, with love of virtue and loathing of vice you will defeat these enemies. To the other battle[21] you are particularly called by grace, a grace of which we are undeserving. It is important to go into that battle armed not only with body armor, but with spiritual weapons. For if you do not have the armor of love for the honor of God and the desire to conquer the city of the wretched infidel souls who do not share in the blood of the Lamb, the fruit acquired with the weapons of war would be minimal.

And so my dearest father and son, I would like you and your whole company to set before you as goal [of battle] Christ crucified, that is, his most loving, precious blood which was shed with such fire of love to free us from death and give us life. You should do this so that the goal you are seeking [through crusade] should fully and perfectly come about; and so that you might also receive the greatest benefit, that is, the fruits of grace and life, for through grace we move on to eternal life. Learn from this Lamb, sacrificed and totally given for us, who on the table of the cross did not turn his attention to distress and suffering, but took delight in the food of the Father's honor and our salvation, and ate this food on the table of the ghastly cross. As one in love with the honor of the eternal Father and the salvation of human persons, he remained steady and firm, so troubles, torments, offenses, scorn, and injustices did not derail him; nor did our lack of gratitude. He realized he was giving his life for thankless people who had no appreciation for such a great grace.

Our King acts like a true knight who perseveres in battle until the enemy is defeated. Having consumed this food, he conquered the enemy of our flesh with his flagellated flesh. He defeated pride, worldly pleasures, and status with sorrow and mortification and with true humility (God humbling himself to become human). With his wisdom he defeated the malice of the evil one. With his hand unarmed, and bound and nailed to the cross, and with the holy cross as his mount,[22] he defeated the prince of the world.

CATHERINE OF SIENA

Our knight [Jesus] was armed with the armor of Mary's flesh, and in this flesh received the wounds that restored our iniquity. For a helmet he wore the painful crown of thorns pressed into his head. For the lance at his side, he bore the wound to his side that revealed the secret of his heart, which is a knife made of light that must pierce our heart and our interior self with the deepest force of [Christ's] love [*affetto* of love]. The reed placed in his hand to mock him and the gloves for his hands and the spurs for his feet are the red wounds of the hands and feet of this kind, loving Word.[23] And who armed him in this way? Love. Who held him firm, bound and nailed to the cross? Neither the nails, nor the cross, nor the stone, nor the soil that held the cross upright; none of this was sufficient to hold the God-Man. No, it was the bond of love for the Father's honor and our salvation. The stone that raised him [made possible the planting of the cross] and held him upright [on the cross] was love for us.

Who could be the man of such evil heart that, gazing upon this captain and knight, dead yet triumphant, would not be challenged to overcome his heart's weakness and become courageous against all enemies? There is no such person. And so, I tell you to place before you as goal Christ crucified. Soak your cloak in the blood of Christ crucified; in this way you will defeat the first set of enemies—in the first battle described above—because he has already defeated them for us and liberated us, rescuing us from the perverse slavery to the evil one. And should he try to attack us, we should immediately take up the armor of the Son of God. Once your soul's vices are destroyed, you will partake of the food; that is, you will be made into someone who savors and eats the honor of God and the salvation of his fellow human beings. Though this hunger you will follow the Lamb in order to obtain this fine quarry,[24] which through love and desire [*affetto* of love] you must hold in memory.[25] No sorrow, nor death, nor any possible circumstance will lead you to turn back and let go of this prey. This battle is so glorious! He who was defeated really won and can never lose, unless he were

Knights, Military Leaders

so cowardly that he turned his back [to martyrdom]. If he perseveres, however, he will always win.

He acts as did the Son of God, who did hand-to-hand battle with death on the cross, so life [Jesus's life] defeated death. Death then defeated life as in giving the life of his body he destroyed sin which is [a form of] death. So, his death defeated death [sin], and death defeated life because death was the cause of the death of the Son of God. He accomplished such a loving feint and exchange! You have been chosen to do the same, that is, to bear the cross of desire for the honor of God and to acquire the souls of the unbelievers, which you must accomplish, dying to infidelity and with the life of the light of faith. Should you die, you have received the best part; for death will defeat death, as the blood of the martyrs gave life [salvation] to the unbelievers and the evil tyrants. If I triumph without shedding blood, I still win; that is, if God doesn't allow me to give my life,[26] triumph is no less significant; it offers glory. It would not bring glory to those who are foolish and frivolous who would go [on the crusade pilgrimage] for vain and self-centered reasons; they would accomplish little and would pay a high price for meager provisions. Indeed, they would pay the price of their life for the wretched superficiality of the world. These persons will receive their reward in this finite life, for their armor is selfish self-love, which is the garment of death. They are not men of deeds but men of the wind; and so they will fly away as leaves, possessing no solidity or stability since Christ is not their goal, nor have they taken up the arms of life.

My desire is that you and your companions should be true knights, which is why I said I wanted to see you become a courageous knight fighting in this glorious battlefield. I trust that with God's infinite and immeasurable goodness, you will fulfill his will—what has just been described that he requires of you—and which is also my will. I say no more.

Bathe in the blood of Christ crucified and hide in his most loving wounds! And take as shield the most holy cross!

Remain, etc.

Tender Jesus! Jesus love! Oh Mary!

CATHERINE OF SIENA

LETTER 347

To Count Alberigo da Barbiano, captain general of the Company of Saint George and the other knights[27]
May 6, 1379 (Dated letter)

Introduction

The context of this letter is the struggle between Urban VI, elected in April 1378 after Gregory XI's death, and Clement VII, so called antipope, elected in September of the same year. The fight for the seat of the papacy in Rome included battles between companies of knights hired by each side. For in Catherine's Italy, fighting was done frequently by companies of men who were for hire. The Company of Saint George was hired by Urban VI to take Castel Sant'Angelo, the fort near the Vatican that was held by forces representing Clement.

Catherine, who believed that whoever held the office of pope was Christ's representative on earth, was convinced that Urban VI was the true pope[28] and that anyone who did not believe this was in the wrong, indeed on the side of evil. Accordingly, she wrote several letters to try to keep certain prelates and political leaders faithful to Urban. While the Company of Saint George had taken over Castel Sant'Angelo, it was not ceded to the pope but to the Roman authorities. Thus, Catherine exhorted Captain Alberigo and his men to understand the significance of supporting Urban, not just as the person who paid them to fight well, but as Christ on earth. She wanted to make sure these knights remained faithful to the cause of Urban and that they understood that their spiritual well-being was tied to this fidelity. Notice at the end of the letter she wants *each* knight to ponder that Rome is the "garden" of Christ and the land in which faith is rooted. Catherine appears to have known that the Clementines were ready to pay victorious knights in order to fight on their side. Thus, she emphasized fidelity and pointed out that the ultimate sin of self-centeredness would lead to prioritizing earnings or booty, leading to betrayal and loss of life.

Knights, Military Leaders

We see, then, Catherine applying her core wisdom about transformation of selfish self-love, necessary to see correctly in order to act according to God's love and will. In this case this is done in the service of affecting the behavior of mercenary knights fighting for Urban VI.

❈ ❈ ❈

To the name of Jesus Christ crucified and tender Mary.

Dearest brother in Christ tender Jesus. I, Catherine, slave of the servants of Jesus Christ, write to you in his precious blood with desire to see you and all your company engage truly and faithfully in the battle for the truth that you may receive the fruit of your labors.[29] For you are all faithful to holy mother Church and to his holiness Pope Urban VI, true supreme pontiff.

What enables you to receive this fruit and what impedes it? I'll tell you. It is the light of most holy faith, for with this light we see the dignity and goodness of Him whom we serve, and so seeing we recognize the fruit; and seeing the fruit, we love it. And so, with this light [of holy faith] illuminating understanding, love is nourished and grows for the task undertaken and for him whom we serve.

Who is the Lord for whom you engaged in the field of battle? It is Christ crucified, who is ultimate and eternal Goodness; no one can fathom the importance of his rank, only he can do so. He is such a faithful lord that, wanting persons to be receptive and ready to receive the fruit of their labors—in whatever circumstances they choose—he ran as one in love to the shameful death of the most holy cross and poured out the fullness of his blood with great torment and suffering.

Ah my brother and most dear sons! You are knights who entered the field of battle to give your life for love of life and your blood for love of the blood of Christ crucified.[30] This is the time for a new form of martyrdom. You are the first to have given blood. How great is the fruit that you receive? It is eternal life, an infinite fruit. And what are these struggles in the face of this ultimate good? They are as nothing! As Saint Paul says, "The sufferings of this life are as nothing compared to the future glory set for us in the next life" (Rom 8:18). In other words, the fruit is immense! One cannot but gain in this situation, whether one lives or dies. If you die, you gain eternal life, and you will be in a secure, lastingly stable place. If you are spared, you will have sacrificed yourselves voluntarily for God, and you can keep your goods[31] in good conscience. If you gaze upon this honor with the light of most holy faith, you will all be strengthened and faithful to Christ crucified and to holy Church. For serving the church and the vicar of Christ, you serve Christ, which is why I told you that the lord you serve is Christ crucified.

Will you choose to be very strong so that any one of you will be worth many others? Then place before the eye of your understanding your faith and the blood of tender good Jesus, the humble Lamb. For you can see that this faith has been contaminated by sinful men who love themselves with selfish self-love, men who are in league with the evil one in denying the very truth that they gave us,[32] by asserting that Pope Urban VI is not the true pope. They are not telling the truth, they are liars, lying over their heads; for Urban VI is the true pope in whom are entrusted the keys of the blood.[33] Strengthen yourselves well [in this belief] in order to fight for the truth, a truth which is our faith. Don't have the least doubt, for it is truth that sets us free.

So that we might more effectively call upon divine help for this good, holy task, eternal Truth wants you to engage in it with good, holy intentions, focused on carrying out your foundational and principal task for the honor of God, that is, the defense of our faith, of the holy Church and of the vicar of Christ. See that you [Count Alberigo] and the others do this with a blameless conscience, purifying it when possible, through holy confession.

For you know that sins block good and holy actions and call the wrath of God upon us. As their leader, be the first [to be purified through confession] to act out of true holy fear of God. For otherwise, the rod of justice may reach you. And if the others

Knights, Military Leaders

don't have the time to make confession at this time, practice it mentally, through holy desire. In this way you will be faithful, and through your actions, you will show that you have seen with the light of most holy faith whom you are meant to serve, and you have recognized his authority and goodness. And you will recognize the fruit that follows after the struggle.

What keeps us from being faithful, leading us to be unfaithful to God and creatures? It is selfish self-love, which is a poison that poisons everyone; selfish self-love is a cloud that obscures the eye of our understanding, preventing us from recognizing and discerning the truth. Selfish self-love sees nothing but its own pleasure deriving such pleasure from creatures rather than from the Creator, paying attention only to the transitory things of this life that are shrouded in darkness. It [selfish self-love] seeks worldly status, amusements, and riches that flit by as does the wind.

The disordered motivation arising from one's core [*affetto*] on which such deeds have been based most likely makes persons lack loyalty and fidelity, unless they think they will benefit personally. [Such disordered *affetto*] can result in a very high risk that a man may protect himself, letting others perish when all he wants is to pillage. For understanding cannot pay attention to two concrete tasks at once, that is, both to rob and to fight. Many have lost because of this type of [self-centered] acts. Truth does not want this to happen to you. So, please bring this to the attention of those who are under your command. And I also pray that for the love of Christ crucified you go with fidelity and loyalty, with wise, frank, and mature counsel to guide you. For your knights, choose men who are faithful and courageous, with the best consciences possible. A good leader will rarely have anything other than good followers. Be attentive that no one betrays you from within or without.

And since it is hard to protect ourselves, I want you always, first thing in the morning and every evening, to offer yourself to our tender mother Mary, asking her to be your advocate and defender for the love of that tender loving Word that she carried in her womb. Ask that she protect you from all trickery and alert you to any deception, so that the latter does not cause your defeat. I am sure that if you practice the sound principles I have described, she will accept your offer [of yourself] and will graciously receive your petition as Mother of grace and mercy for us sinners.

However, if we direct the motivation from our core that moves to action—the will [*affetto*]—toward that which impairs fidelity, we would deprive ourselves of all good and would make ourselves deserving of evil. We would lose the fruit of eternal life and waste the struggles made to gain it. And so, I said I wanted to see you faithful to our holy mother Church and to Christ on earth, Pope Urban VI.

Strengthen, do strengthen yourselves in Christ tender Jesus keeping always before you the blood shed with such passionate love! Raise the standard of the most holy cross in the field of battle; keep in mind that the blood of the glorious martyrs constantly cries out in God's presence calling forth his help upon you. Keep in mind as well that this land [Rome] is the garden of blessed Christ and the foundational ground of our faith, something that should motivate each person. When we sincerely want to serve God and his holy Church, our sins will be paid off. I say no more.

Remain, etc.

You and the others should be grateful to God and to the great knight, Saint George—whose name you honor—for the blessings that you are receiving. May he defend you and be your guardian to the point of death.

Forgive me if I have said too many words. My excuse is the honor of the church and your salvation; also, my conscience, which has felt compelled by God's loving will. Let's do as did Moses; the people entered into battle while Moses prayed, and while he prayed the people were victorious. We will do the same, for our prayer will be welcome and pleasing. Please, may you and the other knights at least read this letter.

Tender Jesus! Jesus love!

7

OTHER LAYMEN AND WOMEN

LETTER 130

To Pòlito[1] of the Ubertini, in Florence
December 1376 (Noffke)[2]

Introduction

Ipòlito, a Florentine widower whom Catherine is likely to have met on one of her trips to Florence, consulted her about his vocation. He feels called to be a monk but has been held up in his decision by responsibility for a daughter and by the handling of his affairs. By this point in her life, Catherine had already become convinced that she had wisdom and discernment that should be shared in guiding others; as shown in this letter—as in many others—she discerned without doubts or hesitation that this person consulting her had a religious vocation, and she discerned where he should enter religious life, namely, at the Carthusian monastery in Gorgona.

In her exhortation about growth in transformation, Catherine cautions Ipòlito about selfish self-love that can block listening to God's will and acting upon it. She cautions him against delay in following the guidance of the Spirit and advises him to find someone who can care for his daughter and someone to tie up his affairs. Even though Catherine herself never became a nun, she considered any inspiration to religious life or priesthood a major gift of God that should be acted upon without delay, lest temptation to tarry or desist impede the guidance of the Spirit.

Children and parenthood were experienced differently in Catherine's day, so that it would have been considered normal for a widower to find a suitable person or family to finish raising a daughter. We cannot judge Catherine's advice by our standards of parenthood.

❈ ❈ ❈

To the name of Jesus Christ crucified and tender Mary.

My dearest brother in Christ tender Jesus. I, Catherine, servant and slave of the servants of Jesus Christ, write to you in his precious blood, with desire to see you possess a courageous heart, free of all passions and sensual weakness. For such weakness, which comes from selfish self-love, is at the root of all evil and hinders all holy desires.

Those caught up in selfish self-love are moved by a lukewarm heart. On the one hand, they sense God's call to see that life is short, that what is worldly is fragile and wicked; they recognize God is showing them their lack of stability and their incapacity to stand firm. As well they are shown that every effort made or small pleasure taken that is not ordered in God results in wretchedness as a chastisement. And so, the person comes to dislike what is worldly and gladly wants to leave the world, realizing that whoever leaves the world will possess it. I mean the person cares nothing for worldly status or pleasures or for pomp and ceremony, for he recognizes that all goodness will be rewarded, and he will receive a hundredfold.[3] And so he gets ready to leave everything behind. However, this desire can be impaired by the weakness of self-centeredness that remains in the soul and assails his desire, and so he begins to delay. This is not the way to act. You must destroy all selfish self-love, reflecting that you cannot count on how much time you have. If one had certainty regarding a time frame, one could say [to one-

Other Laymen and Women

self], "I will set about breaking my ties to the world, and when they are broken, then I will bind myself to Christ with the yoke of holy obedience."

My dear brother, since you are not certain to have time, throw away all sensual weakness and selfish self-love; don't spend time loosening ties [to the world] but rather cut them. With the hand of free will take hold of a double-edged knife, which is hatred and love. I mean, love of virtue and hatred and dislike of your disordered sensuality and what is worldly. You will show the world that you are a courageous man, not a lukewarm, negligent person.

Respond! Respond to God who calls through good and holy inspirations. He has set the table with a place for you; it is holy, pious, and separated from the world; and you would have a father, who is the prior of Gorgona,[4] who is really an angel, a mirror of virtue, and leads a good and holy family [the monks under him]. Don't resist holy grace, which has with such magnanimity asked to dwell in the heart of your core self from which emerges all desire and motivation [*affetto*].

According to what I understand from the letter you sent me, it seems you have had good and holy intentions but have been taking too much time, asking for two years. This is a ruse of the evil one who is disturbed by your good fortune. He makes you think you have things to do, thus troubling your peace and tranquility. It seems to me you would do well to find a home as soon as possible for your daughter, and thus remove this weight from your back; any other matters should be expedited quickly. You could leave other business you need to take care of to someone whom you know to be good and suited to work for love of God and for you. Regarding your daughter, take care of this yourself. On behalf of Christ crucified, I ask that you hasten to act; don't take your time, for time does not wait for you!

The prior of Gorgona will go to see you. Tell him your intention clearly, making a strong, firm, and true decision. If you do go to that holy and pious place—which would give life to your soul[5]—or anywhere else, if you decide to give away your possessions to the poor, give them to Gorgona, for the place needs to be furnished in order to be up to the traditions of the Carthusian order. Come now! Act courageously, for I trust in God's goodness, which, drenching you in the blood of Christ crucified, will enable you to take these actions and do all else without delay. I say no more.

In my name greet Leonardo, Niccolò Soderini, monna Antonia; and bless all the rest of the family in the name of Christ tender Jesus.

Remain, etc.

Tender Jesus, etc.

LETTER 241

To monna Giovanna di Curado,[6] when I, Stefano, was in Vignone (Avignon) with Catherine
July–August 1376 (Noffke)

Introduction

Giovanna di Corrado Maconi had sent her son, Stefano, to Catherine so that she would help him with a family feud. Like other young members of the nobility, he was highly impressed by Catherine's spirituality and became one of her followers. He eventually became one of her companions on the trip to Avignon and on other trips. He was also one of her reliable scribes—one of three for *The Dialogue*—and eventually assembled one of the largest early collections of her letters. After Catherine's death, he became a Carthusian monk.

This letter is a response to Giovanna who felt deprived of her son's presence. Catherine replied with her wisdom about spending time in the cell—connected to God and self—in order to become free of the sort of self-centeredness that leads to disordered attachment, even to members of one's family. A balanced attachment, Catherine advises, is found in relationship with God attained through the three powers of the soul. She tells Giovanna that "all of God" will be found within, a particularly powerful description about the presence of

Other Laymen and Women

God in the person. Through this advice to Giovanna, we have a good example of Catherine's teaching about the three powers of the soul.

Note an infrequent but significant metaphor, namely, that cultivating the presence of God should lead us to make our soul—our core identity—a beautiful garden.

❦ ❦ ❦

To the name of Jesus Christ crucified and tender Mary

Dearest mother in Christ tender Jesus. I, Catherine, servant and slave of the servants of Jesus Christ, write to you in his precious blood, with desire to see you make a room in the cell of knowledge of yourself, so that you may achieve perfect love. For I believe that the person who does not love her Creator cannot please him. Because he is love, he wants nothing but love.

The soul that knows herself finds this love. She comes to recognize that *she-is-not* and yet she is endowed with being through grace [free gift] and not obligation;[7] and she recognizes that all grace is rooted in such being which has been bestowed with unfathomable love. And so she learns how much she is filled with the utter fullness of God's goodness, and that there are no words to express this. When she recognizes herself so loved by God, she cannot but love. She loves God in herself and loves reason but hates that sensuality that seeks pleasure in that which is worldly, such as status or riches or finding more pleasure in others than in God, or being rooted in worldly perspectives, pleasures, or amusements. Also, some love their children, their spouse, or their parents in a disordered manner with too much self-centered love. Such love becomes a block between the soul and God and doesn't allow the person to learn the truth about genuine and supreme love.

Loving First Truth said, "Whoever does not abandon mother and father, sisters and brothers and themselves is not worthy of me."[8] God's true servants recognize and see this well, so they immediately strip their heart, their motivation and desire [*affetto*], and their soul of attachment to all persons outside of God and all the pleasures and pomp of the world. This doesn't mean they don't love others, but rather that they love them only in God, as they are loved by the Creator without measure. And since they abhor their selfish sensuality that makes them rebel against God, they also abhor this in their fellow human beings when they see that due to this selfishness, they offend ultimate eternal Goodness.

My dearest mother in Christ tender Jesus, I want you to follow this advice. I want you to love God's goodness within you and his boundless love, which you will find in the cell of self-knowledge. In this cell you will find God, who, as God, encompasses all that has being; and therefore, within yourself you will find memory,[9] which holds and is made to hold the treasure of God's blessings. There you will find understanding, which makes possible our sharing in the wisdom of the Son of God, knowing and comprehending his will and realizing that he wants only our sanctification. Understanding all this, the soul cannot be disturbed or pained by anything that may come her way as she has learned that all is imbued with God's providence and his utmost love. Now that you understand this, I beg you and I want you, in the name of the sacrificed Lamb, to assuage the upset and hurt that you felt due to Stefano's departure. Rejoice and be glad, for he will not lack an increase of grace for his soul and yours. And with God's grace you will see him soon.

I also want to tell you that in knowledge of yourself you will find the tender mercy of the Holy Spirit, the Person [of the Trinity] who is nothing but love and imparts nothing but love; and whatever he does or carries out, he does out of love. You will find in your soul [*affetto*], the capacity to love united to God's love which empowers the will, for the will is nothing more than love; desire moved by love [*affetto*] and all the will's drives are moved by nothing else but love. The will loves and hates that which the eye of understanding has seen and comprehended. And so, my dearest mother, it is true that you will find within the soul all of God, who gives tenderness, comfort and consolation that cannot be disturbed by any situation, for the soul is made with capacity to carry out the will of God. This applies so long as the soul has discarded all selfish self-love, and all that is outside of God's will.

When the latter is accomplished, the soul becomes a garden filled with the perfumed flowers of holy desire, a garden in the center of which is planted the tree of the most holy cross. On it lies the spotless Lamb who pours out his blood which washes over and irrigates this glorious garden, which produces the ripe fruit of genuine, holy virtues. If you wish to acquire patience, docility is found there, for the Lamb never complains. Deep humility is manifested in God humbling himself to become human, and [in the way] the Word was humbled in the shameful death on the cross. With regards to [the virtue] of love, the Word is love, for it is the strength of love that held him bound and nailed to the cross. The wood of the cross and the nails would not have been enough to hold the God-Man if Love had not held him. It is not a surprise, then, if she who makes a garden from her knowledge of self is strong in resisting all that is worldly. For she has been conformed to and made one with ultimate Strength. She truly begins to benefit from the down payment of eternal life already in this life; she has conquered what is worldly, because she holds it in scorn.

The devils fear coming near a soul that burns with divine love. Therefore, my dearest mother, don't slumber any more in sensual self-centeredness. Rather, with most passionate and boundless love, rise up and bathe in the blood of Christ and seclude yourself in the wounds of Christ crucified.

I say no more. I am certain that if you will spend time in the cell as I have advised, you will focus on Christ crucified and nothing else. Please ask Curado[10] to do the same.

Remain, etc.

Tender Jesus! Jesus love! Mary!

CATHERINE OF SIENA

LETTER 120

To monna Rabe di Francesco di Tato Tolomei
Fall 1377(Noffke)

Introduction

Rabe is the wife of Francesco Tolomei, and a member of one of two important families who were often rivals. Indeed, at this time, Catherine is likely staying with the Salimbeni, the rival family. Rabe is the mother of three of Catherine's followers, two *mantellate* and Matteo, a Dominican friar and one of Catherine's frequent companions.

This letter shows Catherine's authoritative advice to members of important families much older than her, revealing her certainty about her connection to God and her knowledge of God's wisdom. In this letter she chides Rabe for self-centeredness in wanting her Dominican son to leave his mission in order to comfort his sister and probably Rabe herself. The language that Catherine uses is hardly subtle. She accuses Rabe of the worst spiritual flaw from Catherine's perspective, namely, selfish self-love. Catherine does not cease to repeat that the latter is the cause of all sin and disorder, as it is diametrically opposite to the purpose for which we were created, namely, to love; and loving involves the capacity to care for the good of the other. In this case the self-centeredness lies in Rabe's desire for emotional comfort at the expense of the ministry of her Dominican son.

Before these reprimands, Catherine offers her wisdom, encouraging Rabe to transformation. She highlights the importance of growing in knowledge of God's love, together with the progression in living out of that love. This progression is presented in terms of the metaphor of "stairs" that climb the body of the crucified Christ, from the feet to the mouth. The mouth represents the kiss of peace and is a metaphor for union offered to those who have allowed their *affetto*—their deepest desire and capacity to choose—to be transformed by the blood of Christ that is the grace of salvation. So progression involves, first, conscious connection to one's deepest motivation and desire, second, conversion of this deepest part of consciousness through connection to God's love, and third, acquiring peace because one has learned to live out of this love, fruit of a union with God.[11]

❊ ❊ ❊

To the name of Jesus Christ crucified and tender Mary.

Dearest daughter in Christ, tender Jesus. I, Catherine, servant and slave of the servants of Jesus Christ, write to you in his precious blood with desire to see you die to self-centered sensuality, for otherwise you would be unable to share in the life of grace.

For this reason, with the deepest desire and motivation from your core [*affetto*], I want you to find a way to live apart from the weakness of that which is worldly. For it is not good that we who are made to enjoy a heavenly home and to be nourished on the food of virtue should instead enjoy what is worldly and nourish ourselves on selfish self-love, from which flow all vices.

We must rise up and walk up to the heights of virtue, opening the eye of understanding and gazing upon the wood of the cross where we encounter the spotless Lamb, tree of life who has made of his body a staircase.

The first stair that he taught us to climb is that of the feet and *affetto*. For as the feet carry the body, deepest desire and motivation [*affetto*][12] carry the soul. After climbing up to the feet, which are nailed and bound to the cross, your deepest motivation and desire, your capacity to love [*affetto*] will be stripped of disordered love. When you climb to the second stair, which is the open side of Christ crucified, you will encounter the secret of the heart; that is, you will learn with what immeasurable love he has bathed you in his blood. *Affetto* comes up to the first stair and is stripped; on the second stair *affetto* tastes the love found in the open heart of Christ.

Having seen the third stair and thus reaching the mouth of the Son of God, she is nourished with peace. For once the soul is clothed in the love of Christ crucified and stripped of warped selfish self-love that causes her inner conflict, she achieves patience so that every disappointment seems sweet. She can even rejoice in worldly persecutions and trials—from wherever God permits them—because she has found the peace of the mouth. The person who offers peace becomes united to whomever she offers this peace; and so the soul, clothed in virtue, tastes God with *affetto* of love and unites the mouth of holy desire to God's desire, and in God's desire she finds peace and tranquility. So you see that Christ crucified has created stairs on his body so that we might reach the heights, the heaven of eternal life, where there is life without death and light without darkness, where we feel full[13] without distress and experience hunger without pain. For as Saint Augustine tells us, the distress from fullness and the suffering from hunger are removed from those citizens who reach eternal life since that for which they hungered and desired is satisfied in the eternal vision of God.

Ignorant and inadequate is the soul that loses such goodness due to her faults and in so doing makes herself susceptible to evil. Come on, then, my dearest daughter! Don't wait for time you don't have! Rather, with great *affetto* of love rise from the willfulness of selfish self-love, which deprives you of the light of reason and leads you to love your children and what is worldly to excess; otherwise you will not reach the end for which you were created. This is why I said I wanted to see you die to selfish self-love and self-centered will; it's my judgment that these are quite alive in you.

I noticed this from the letter you wrote to me, which showed that blind love led you to leave the path ordered by God. You said Francesca was very ill so that Friar Mateio[14] should go to you no matter what, and if he didn't go, your curse would be upon him. If nothing else, you expected that he should take a farmer as companion.[15] You can't deny your foolishness and senselessness. For even if we leave aside that it is not congruent with what is in God, if we consider your proposal, we see that, even with the little wisdom given us by nature, you would not have acted in this manner. If, in order to please your daughter, you had or still have a desire that Friar Mateio should go, you would have sent a couple of friars so that one could remain here and the other return with Mateio, for you well know that one person cannot go or remain alone. But you acted foolishly out of passion, having filled your ears with gossip.[16]

All this happens to you because you have not turned your face away from what is worldly, nor have you climbed to the first stair of the feet. If you had climbed there, you would want nothing else but that your son seek God's honor and the salvation of souls.

Therefore, I want you and the others to plug your ears and bite your tongue, so that you do not listen to gossip and you do not repeat it. Don't behave in this way anymore; rather, bathe in the blood of Christ crucified; and rise above the chit chat of those who are dead and dialogue with those who are alive with true virtues. I have no more to say to you.

Comfort Francesca, etc.

Remain etc.

Jesus, etc.

LETTER 95

To certain Florentine young men adopted by don Giovanni da le[17] Celle
October 1377 (Noffke)

Introduction

Catherine advised three young men mentored by Father Giovanni dalle Celle, one of Catherine's correspondents and spiritual friends. These youths had visited Catherine when she was staying at Val d'Orcia[18] and she followed up with this letter. That these young men had the counsel of a wise mentor and yet sought out Catherine's advice, even when they had to travel from Florence to Val d'Orcia, witnesses to the reputation for wisdom and holiness she had acquired.

Catherine recommended entering religious life and urged these young men to be witnesses to God's love by being bound to a community that exemplifies love. For this to be so, they themselves need conversion in their capacity to love. Very practically she tells them not to be discouraged by lax monasteries and makes a particular recommendation. While we do not know the context, it is remarkable that this laywoman would presume to recommend a monastery to those mentored by a priest well known as a spiritual guide.

This letter offers one of Catherine's more complete teachings in one place—a significant facet—of Catherine's wisdom about the three powers of the soul. Also, two rhetorical devices are interesting here. Catherine refers to Jesus being attached to the cross through love without which the nails would not suffice to hold him, thus highlighting the power of self-emptying love. Selfish self-love, a theme in most letters, here appears as a "servant" that aids in the transformation to capacity to love, and humility is depicted as a wet nurse of love.

※ ※ ※

To the name of Jesus Christ Crucified and tender Mary.

Dearest sons in Christ, loving Jesus, I, Catherine, servant and slave of the servants of Jesus Christ, write to you in his precious blood, with desire to see you bound with the benevolent bond of charity so that nothing, not the evil one nor any creature can ever separate you from this bond. This is the loving bond that bound God to man and man to God when the divine nature became one with human nature; such was the unspeakable love that infused being into man, as God brought him forth from himself, creating him in his image and likeness (Gen1:26).

Love regulates the powers of the soul and binds these three powers together, for the soul is made of pure love. The will, desiring to love something, moves understanding to open its eye. Becoming aware that the will wants to love, the understanding—if reasonable—chooses as object to love the ineffable love of the eternal Father, who has given us the Word, his Son. As well, the understanding places before the will, as object to love, the obedience and humility of the Son, who meekly and

Other Laymen and Women

with infinite love endured pain, insults, scorn, torments, and false accusations. So, that which the eye of understanding has seen, the will pursues with ineffable love; and with a strong hand, the will places in memory this treasure it has grasped through love. And so the person becomes grateful and indebted to her Creator for the graces and gifts that he[19] has received from him. And the person realizes that whatever he has is the fruit of grace and not due to his own efforts. For *we-are-not*, yet we create that which is not, namely, sin.

Oh how horrible are deadly faults that rob us of life! When the soul understands this, she[20] clothes herself in love and perfect humility; through God's goodness, she finds and tastes love, which she recognizes within herself in the many gifts and graces that she has received and continuously receives. Through knowledge of self, she learns to recognize sin in the perverse pattern of rebellion—past and ongoing—against her Creator; because of this knowledge she develops distaste and hatred of this sinfulness. Experiencing this hatred, she finds patience, which strengthens her in order to suffer sorrow, injustice, hunger, thirst, cold, heat, temptations, and disturbances of the devil; she develops an aversion to the world and runs from it and all its pleasures. And through this experience, humility is born. Humility is the wet nurse of love and that which nourishes it; and so, she [the soul] endures with patience, because charity, unimaginable love, has found its wet nurse, humility.

Hatred of selfish self-love is the servant that with perfect patience serves her [the soul], bringing to justice the enemies of divine love and seeking retribution from them. These enemies are selfish self-love—which loves self and all other objects for self-serving reasons rather than for God's sake—also pleasures, amusements, status, honors, and riches. What does this retribution consist of? It's such a caring retribution,[21] that there are no words to describe it. From death-dealing selfish self-love she moves toward divine love, which gives life; from darkness, hatred, and distaste for virtue, she moves toward light and love of virtue. And this transformation is so strong that she would choose death rather than abandon a life of virtue. In fact, she cultivates all the ways and paths through which she can grow in virtue and preserve the virtues she has.

Since she realizes that the delights of the senses, the weakness of the body, the gossip of bad and evil laypersons is deleterious for her, she avoids these with all her heart and will and all the depth of her motivation [*affetto*]. She disciplines her body, submitting it to penance, fasting, vigils, prayers, and other ascetical practices; she especially does this when needed, particularly when the body wants to rebel against the spirit. She disciplines her will with death, that is, she annihilates selfish self-will, submitting it to God's commandments and to the counsels left to us by Christ, God's only begotten son. With these commandments and counsels, she clothes herself in the eternal loving will; and so clothed she can sail through the stormy sea with strength and truly following in the footsteps of Christ crucified.

This, then, is the loving bond with which I want you to be bound. Oh benevolent and loving bond that ties the soul to her Creator! As I said, you bound God to man and man to God when you, Eternal Father, gave us your Son, the Word, and thus united divine and human nature. Oh, my dearest sons, this was the bond of love that held the God-Man bound and nailed to the cross. If love had not held him, the wood of the cross and the nails would not have sufficed to hold him. The love that Christ had for the honor of the Father and for our salvation together with Christ's hatred and distaste for sin redeemed our iniquities—hatred together with love—for Christ assumed them [our iniquities] onto his body with suffering and torments.[22] And so the soul that is bound to Christ crucified will—for the honor of God and the salvation of her fellow human beings—eradicate her selfishness, and fight off the enemies of her soul, that is, vice and disobedience to her Creator in violating his commandments; instead, she will welcome and allow in those who are friends. These friends—made through perfect love—are true, authentic virtues. One of the soul's most important friends is true obedience, which is as much humble as obedient to God's holy commandments. The soul that falls strongly in love with

Other Laymen and Women

this obedience—which involves drowning and destroying one's self-centered will—wants to go one step further. She wishes to be bound by obedience to the counsels of Christ [religious vows], carrying the yoke of holy obedience within a religious order; do not doubt, my sons, that this is the most certain, proven way. Even though we may see unhealthy religious who do not observe the rule, the rule never becomes unhealthy, as it is founded and created by the Holy Spirit.

And so, if you feel God calling you to this form of obedience, do respond. If you are concerned about having to settle for one of those lax religious orders that is having trouble due to lack of love, my answer is this: there are many monasteries from which all problematic elements[23] have been eradicated. Therefore, if you wish to enter a religious order it would be for the greater good and honor of God that you should do so, assuming they have a good superior. I can recommend the monastery of Saint Antimo, which has an abbot who is a model of humility—he does not seek to be the most important but the least of all—and is also a model of poverty and unity, as Father Giovanni can attest. May God, through his infinite goodness, bless you with that which is for his greatest honor and your greatest good.

My sons, unite, bind yourselves to one another through love! May each of you be tolerant and bear with the faults of the other in order to be bound together in Christ, loving Jesus. Love one another, all of you, for you know this is the sign that blessed Jesus left his disciples when he said that God's children are identified by their unity through love, as they love one another with perfect charity [John 13:35]. I found great consolation in the good news I received that you are united in love. Continue to grow in this way and don't go backward, so that I can say with Saint Paul what he said to his disciples, that they were his joy, his happiness, his crown. I beg you to act so that I can continue to say this. I say no more.

Bathe in the blood of Christ crucified and be united through the bond of love!

Remain in the holy, tender love of God!

Tender Jesus, Jesus love!

CATHERINE OF SIENA

LETTER 113

To the Countess Bandecca[24] daughter of Giovanni d'Agnolino de' Salimbeni
November or December 1377 (Noffke); between January and March 1377 (ISIME)

Introduction

Bandecca was a member of the Salimbeni family, with whom Catherine was close; indeed, she spent many weeks in their castle at Rocca D'Orcia outside Siena. In Letter 112 Catherine invited Bandecca, who was then a widow, to join a monastery Catherine had organized (but not joined herself). This letter suggests Bandecca had not joined this monastery but did care to follow Catherine's teaching.[25] This missive to a noblewoman shows how much Catherine expected people of all walks of life to order their life so they could "be grounded in true, perfect love," as Catherine says in her opening sentences.

In this exhortation to Bandecca, we have an example of one of the more intricate intertwining of metaphors found in Catherine's letters. Light, a predominant metaphor, has several connotations. It is God as love that illuminates with the truth of the law of love. Light is also the light of understanding, one of the three powers of the soul. Through faith illuminating the eye of understanding, light discerns correctly what is according to God and in God and motivates desire emerging from the core of the person (*affetto*). Light highlights that knowledge of God, and what is in God is necessary to "see" clearly and correctly. Light is contrasted to darkness, that is, sin—rooted in self-centeredness—which obscures or blocks the light. Light makes possible discernment of what is life-giving versus what is death-dealing.

The tree of love and its flowers and fruit is a metaphor Catherine uses in other letters and in *The Dialogue*. We are each a tree capable of love and the flowers and fruit of the tree are metaphors for the results of transformation when our tree is rooted in the right soil, which is humility. When this is the case, we will develop virtuous lives that give praise to God, and the virtues are the flowers. The fruits are the benefits of living an ordered life. "Light" and "tree" are intertwined with the metaphor of the inner cell. That is, in order to bear fruit and to be present to the eye of understanding and allow ourselves to be illuminated by Light-Love, we must take time for silence and solitude, for knowledge of God and self.

Catherine adds the metaphor of a sponge. Made to absorb liquid, the sponge will absorb nothing unless it is immersed. Similarly, we will be unable to consciously cooperate with transforming Light/Love—despite our God-given potential for love—unless we are consciously and freely immersed in a relationship with God.

❆ ❆ ❆

To the name of Jesus Christ crucified and tender Mary.

Dearest daughter in Christ tender Jesus. I, Catherine, servant and slave of the servants of Jesus Christ, write to you in his precious blood, with desire to see you grounded in true and perfect love. This love is a wedding garment that covers our nakedness and hides our shame—that is, our sin, which incubates shame—extinguishing this sin with its warmth. Without this garment we could not enter into the everlasting life to which we are invited.

What is charity/love? It is an immeasurable, ineffable love that the soul received from her Creator to love him with all her heart, with all the motivation arising from her core [*affetto*], and with all her strength. I affirm that it is true, this love is received from the Creator. But how is it obtained? With love, for love can only be derived from love in order to be able to give love. My dearest daughter, you might say to me, "What should I do to find and obtain this love?" I'll answer you. The following is the way. All love is obtained through the light [of understanding],[26] for what cannot be seen cannot be known; without knowing one another we cannot love one another. So it is important that you acquire the light so that you may see and come to know what you should love. Because light was necessary, God took care of this need, giving us the light of understanding, which together with the pupil of most holy faith is the most important part of the soul. And I assure you, if a person offends her Creator, that doesn't mean she lives without light or love, because persons are made out of love and for love—in the image and likeness of God—and cannot live without love. At the same time, the soul cannot love without the light, for if she wants to love it is important that she be able to see.

Do you know what it means to see and love in the case of worldly persons? It means seeing in a dim, dark way, and due to this dark night they are unable to discern the truth. It [worldly love] is a death-dealing love because it destroys the soul, blocking the life of grace. Why is this [love] dark? Because it is focused on the darkness of the transitory things of this world, preferring them apart from God, focusing on the pleasure these [transitory things] offer her selfish sensuality, unable to recognize their goodness. Such pleasure and self-centered love move understanding to see and pay attention to sensual things. And then such *affetto* [desire], nurtured by the light of understanding—assuming the *affetto* just mentioned moved understanding—will destroy her by leading her to commit sin and lose the life of grace.[27] For nothing can be loved or attended to apart from God, lest it destroy us; whatever is loved must be loved in him and for him. That is, it must be discerned if things originate in his Goodness, and then they can be appreciated and loved; we can't live [well] without discerning and loving.

The love of worldly persons, which leads to death, is quite different from the life-giving love of a servant of God. For the love that is received from ultimate, eternal Love brings about the life of grace. So having the light of the eye of understanding, one must open this eye with the light of most holy faith and fix it on the unfathomable love God has for us. And so, our core self in its capacity to desire out of love [*affetto*], experiencing that it is loved, cannot but love that which understanding recognized and came to know in truth.

Oh my dearest daughter! Don't you see that we are a tree of love since we are made for love? And this tree is so well made that no one can prevent it from growing and no one can remove its fruit unless it permits it. God has assigned to this tree a gardener—free will—who can tend to the tree as it pleases [with freedom]. If the soul should not have such a gardener—the tree is the soul—she would not be free. If she were not free, she would have an excuse for sinning; but she can't have this excuse. For nothing in the world, neither what is worldly, nor the evil one, nor the weakness of the flesh, can force her [the soul] to sin unless she consents. For this tree is filled with reason, which free will can use; and it possesses the eye of understanding that knows and recognizes truth—assuming that the eye is not clouded by the fog of selfish self-love. With this light she sees where the tree should be planted. However, if she should see this without having the blessed power of understanding, the gardener could have an excuse and could say, "I was free, but I couldn't see whether I could plant my tree up high or down below." But she [the gardener] can't say this because she possesses understanding, which is able to see; and she possesses reason, a bond of rational love with which she can bind and graft her tree to the tree of life, Christ loving Jesus. Once the eye of understanding has discerned the location and the type of soil that will produce life-giving fruit, the gardener must plant her tree. My dearest daughter, if the gardener, free will, plants where she should, namely, in the soil of true humility—for it [the tree] should not be planted on the hill of pride but in the valley of humility—then the tree will produce fragrant flowers, namely, the virtues, and, most specially, it will produce the greatest flower, the glory and praise of God's name. And then all her acts and virtues will become sweet fruit and flowers perfumed with this scent [of the glory and praise of God's name]. This is the flower, my dearest daughter, which makes our virtues bloom; these blooms God wants for himself, while he wants the fruit[28] to belong to us.

From this tree God only wants the flower of glory, which is that we give glory and praise to his name. The fruit he bestows upon us, for he doesn't need this fruit—he lacks nothing. He is *He-Who-Is*; however, we, *who-are-not*, do need them [the fruit]. We are not made for ourselves but for him who has given us being and all the graces that are part of being. We are made for him but not to be useful to him.[29] Since the ultimate, eternal Goodness realizes humans don't live from flowers—from flowers we would die and from fruit we could live—he takes the flowers for himself and offers us the fruit. If an ignorant person should try to nourish herself with flowers, that is, if she gave herself the glory and praise belonging to God, she would lose the life of grace. Instead, she would earn eternal death if she should die without changing her life, which is offering glory—the flower—to God, keeping the fruit for herself. When our tree is planted in this ordered manner, [as described above], it grows so well that no creature can see where the top of the tree, that is our deepest desire and motivation [the *affetto* of the soul], is united and joined with the infinite God through *affetto* of love;[30] it can only be seen with the eye of understanding that guided the soul to this union. Oh, dearest daughter, I want to show you the field where this [fertile] soil is found so that you can make no mistake. As I have said, this soil is true humility, which is in the enclosed garden of knowledge of self.

I say this garden is enclosed, because the soul that dwells in the cell of self-knowledge dwells in an enclosed space, not one that is open. I mean, the soul does not waste time in worldly pleasures, she doesn't seek riches for herself or others, but remains in voluntary poverty; and she doesn't waste time pleasing creatures, but only pleases her Creator. When the evil one tempts her with obscene and other thoughts causing mental distress and disordered fears, she does not open herself to them, exploring them, nor does she try to sort out why she is visited with them, nor does she try to fight them; and she doesn't allow her heart to wander, whether out of confusion or boredom, nor does she abandon her spiritual exercises. Rather, she closes herself off and tightly shuts herself in the company of hope and of the light of most holy faith, together with dislike and hatred of her self-centered sensuality; she acknowledges she is not worthy of peace and quiet. In true humility she acknowledges she deserves struggles rather than benefits, that is, she believes she deserves the suffering from those times of deep inner strife. She then holds before her mind Christ crucified, finding joy in being with him on the cross. With these thoughts she chases [unwanted] thoughts away. This is the space where you find the soil of true humility.

The person's deepest desire [*affetto*] is united with that of Christ crucified when the top of the tree—as explained, the person's core capacity for love moving the will [*affetto* of the soul] that follows upon understanding—has reached its objective, that is, Christ crucified, who is the abyss and fire of love; this love is known in the Word, through whom is revealed God's love for us. The soul comes to know the Word through knowledge of herself, coming to understand that she is a reasoning creature created in the image and likeness of God and created anew in the blood of his Son. And so with love she draws love to herself. That is, with ordered love—love grown beyond sensual self-centered love—she draws to herself the consuming love of Christ crucified. For, when in love with divine love, our heart acts like a sponge that draws water into itself. Of course, even if the sponge is ready to absorb water, it will not do so if it is not placed in water. This is how I want you to imagine the readiness of our heart which is made to love and ready to love. Our heart—though made for and readied to love—will never fill with grace unless the light of understanding and the hand of free will lift it into the fire of divine love; for when united with divine love our heart will always be filled. Which is why I said that through love and with love, love is brought forth.

When the vessel of the heart is full, it waters the tree with the water of divine love for our neighbor. This love is dew and rain that water the base of the tree and the soil of humility, fattening [fertilizing] the soil and the garden of knowledge of self; the heart will then be made receptive with the seasoning of knowledge of the Goodness of God within her. You know well that if the tree is not watered with the dew and rain and warmed by the sun, it would not produce fruit, nor would any fruit ripen; in this case the tree would not be perfect but imperfect. Similarly, the soul—which is like a tree, as I said—if she were planted, but not watered with the rain of love of neighbor and the dew of knowledge of self, or if she were not warmed with the heat of the sun of divine charity, she would not produce any life-giving fruit, nor would her fruit ripen. As the tree grows it extends its branches, offering fruit to her neighbor, that is, the fruit of most holy, humble continuous prayer, and the example of a good, holy life. When she can, she also offers material support, with a liberal, generous heart, without pretenses or artifices—proposing something but not acting on it—but straightforwardly, with affectionate love. She offers her service in whatever manner she can that suits the needs of the other.

Love doesn't seek its own well-being, it does not seek itself for its own sake, but rather for God's sake, to offer him the flowers of glory and praise of his name. Love doesn't seek God for her own benefit, but for God's sake, for he is worthy in his goodness to be loved by us. Love doesn't seek out or serve her neighbors for their own sake, but only for God's sake, to give the neighbors what it cannot offer God directly; through her neighbor she serves God. For I already explained that we cannot offer God anything useful, so God wants us to offer useful service to our neighbors. In this way God puts our virtue to the test and makes it possible for us to show the love we have for him, our loving, eternal God. Such love has tasted eternal life, it has consumed and consumes all our sins and gives us perfect light and true patience. It also makes us strong and perseverant, so that we don't look back to check the plough [left behind].[31] Rather, we persevere until death, finding joy when fighting in the field of battle on behalf of Christ crucified, holding his blood in our mind's eye so that it encourages us in doing battle as true knights.

Without such love which is so useful, necessary, and desirable we would be vulnerable. Without it we would live in continuous unhappiness, we would become victims of what is deadly, our indignity would be uncovered, and on the last day we would be shamed before the whole world and universe, before angelic beings and all who dwell in everlasting life; and it is in everlasting life that there is life without death, light without darkness, and where communal love is perfect, as through *affetto* of love all share in one another's goodness. And so we should embrace this benevolent queen, this wedding garment which is love. With intense and loving desire we should be ready to do anything, even unto death, to acquire this queen, and once we have her, we should be willing to endure any suffering—no matter its source—also unto death; we should do anything possible in order to keep her and foster her growth in the garden of our soul. I see no other route or way to see you rooted in true, perfect charity, which I want for you.

I beg for love of Christ crucified that as much as possible, you work out how to develop this rootedness [in love]. For then you would not have to fear with servile fear, nor have any fear of the contrary winds from disturbances from other persons or the evil one; all these contrary winds seek to hinder our salvation. But if our tree is planted in the valley [of humility], it cannot be blown about; so be humble and docile of heart. I say no more.

Remain in the holy and tender love of God.

Tender Jesus! Jesus love!

LETTER 375

To an unknown correspondent[32]
End 1377 (Noffke)

Introduction

The recipient of this letter is unknown, but the form of address indicates he is a male layman to whom Catherine offers spiritual advice. The significance of this letter is the concise teaching about the three powers of the soul.

❈ ❈ ❈

To the name of Jesus Christ crucified and tender Mary.

Dearest son in Christ, tender Jesus. I, Catherine, servant and slave of the servants of Jesus Christ, write to you in his precious blood with desire to see your memory full of the blood of Christ, loving crucified Jesus; and to see the eye of understanding focused on the fire of divine love, which has been shown to you through this blood of Christ, loving Jesus. When this is so the will and desire-motivation [*affetto*] will be filled and satisfied with love, because the will [*affetto*][33] loves that which the understanding has seen. In this way I will be able to see the three powers of our soul gathered and brought into harmony, and the following words of our Savior will be accomplished: "When two or three are gathered in my name, I will be in their midst" [Matt 18:20]. This is indeed so. What our Savior wished to make clear is that when the three powers of the soul are gathered together, the memory is filled with the blood and the blessings of God, the eye of understanding can see and can focus on the ineffable love of God as object to love, and then the will loves.

It follows that when the three powers are gathered, then all that a person accomplishes and carries out is gathered under the name of God, for all is done for God. And so our soul rejoices, seeing that God is in her midst through grace and tender *affetto*[34] of love. And so I want you to be prompt about going to the fountain of the blood and fill the vessel of your memory with it. I say no more. I beg in the name of the love of Christ crucified, etc.

Remain in the holy, tender love of God!
Tender Jesus! Tender Jesus! Amen!

LETTER 307

To a woman in Florence to scold her for gossiping and grumbling; the twentieth day of October 1378
Dated manuscript

Introduction

A Florentine acquaintance or disciple must have referred this woman to Catherine, or she might have met her during one of her visits to Florence. Almost certainly this woman was of the higher classes, which does not deter Catherine from writing a strong exhortation against judging others.

Catherine elaborates her teaching on discernment in general and of discernment of providence in particular. The latter involves recognizing God's provident care, which includes trials that test and strengthen us and punishments intended to change our sinful behavior. Discernment involves seeing and recognizing God's will and provident care through the understanding filled with light. Through the light we know how much God loves us, and it is this knowledge that allows the interpretation of our life experience from the perspective of a God who wants our good. The light that reveals God's love allows us to recognize the goodness of our fellow human beings—this is also discernment.

As the product of the theology and piety of the Middle Ages, Catherine's wisdom also includes beliefs that may sound harsh to our contemporary ears. She believed that God allows suffering as punishment for our sins, though this punishment is corrective; and she believed that to the extent that we are punished during our lifetime we will avoid due punishment in eternal life.

✻ ✻ ✻

To the name of Jesus Christ and tender Mary.

Dear sister and daughter in Christ, tender Jesus. I, Catherine, servant and slave of the servants of Jesus Christ, write to you in his precious blood with desire to see you possessed of true, perfect light, for without light we cannot know God's truth or the truth about other people; instead, we would end up making false, inadequate judgments. Why? Because we would be deprived of the light the soul needs to be illuminated and lifted above self-centered sensuality so that she can discern and know the truth and become able to judge rightly and with great discretion.

What is this discernment that we should give and render to God, and what is the truth that we should recognize in him and in our neighbor? I'll tell you. We should recognize the following truth: that God loves us immeasurably and created us in his image and likeness out of love so that we might receive and taste his eternal goodness; this truth is not seen with the eye of the body but with the eye of understanding, which is filled with the light of faith. Who reveals to us that this is the truth? The blood of the humble, spotless Lamb, blood that was poured out with such passionate love on the wood of the most holy cross.

After the soul has seen and known this truth, she loves it; and with love she discerns that whatever God gives and permits in this life, he does so for our good, so that we might be made holy in him. The soul [who has known the truth] discerns with the light of discretion.[35] If God allows prosperity, the person recognizes this is given by her Creator because of his infinite goodness and not due to her virtue. Through this discernment the person loves her possessions with ordered attachment, loving them for God's honor and possessing them as something on loan rather than belonging to her, for her possessions are not hers. We know this because sometimes when we want to hold on to our possessions, they are taken from us, and not just our material goods, but also life and health and every other thing. They all pass away like the wind so we can't hold onto them as we would wish; rather we are able to hold on to them according to the will of him who gives them. The person enlightened by this gentle truth is able to make this discernment.

And if she suffers adversity or hardships, she accepts these with humility and with true holy patience, accepting that she merits these, while being unworthy of the fruit that follows sorrow.[36] Interiorly, with humility, she recognizes that hardships are due to her sins, because she knows that the ultimate Judge rewards all goodness and punishes all evil. She considers it a great grace—for it is so—that God bestows abundance of mercy for her faults. He sends finite punishment of toil and troubles when she deserves infinite punishment for offending infinite Goodness. In whatever way God punishes, he, eternal Truth, does so in order to correct our sins and to help us achieve great perfection; in whatever way he acts we can be certain he acts out of love, not out of displeasure.

The soul illuminated by loving truth sees and discerns all this and so receives each experience with due deference. She is correctly able to discern God's will and God's providence for her life, recognizing that providence provides for all our needs, and God's will wants nothing but our good. Since the soul has so lovingly discovered the truth in her Creator, and so lovingly discerned his mysteries [truths] to be for the good, she turns toward her neighbor with this same truth and discernment; for love of neighbor flows out of love for God.

So this is the rule followed by those who fear God. They never want to form judgments except for the good, unless they explicitly see wrong, such as mortal sin. Even this is not judged; no, out of holy compassion the soul brings this [judgment] before God. And says to herself, "Today it happened to you, and if it were not because eternal Goodness protects me, tomorrow it may happen to me." She leaves all judgment to the supreme Judge or the civil judge, who are there to render justice when it is deserved.

She does not make judgments due to hearsay, nor based on outward habits or actions, because she is well aware that in the Gospels, blessed Christ prohibits such behavior. He says, "Don't judge based on appearances!" [Matt 7:1; Luke 6:37]. She cares about the truth regarding her neighbor with the same sincere love she has for God, a love that is not focused on self. She discerns God's truth in others with holiness, recognizing goodness and letting God find what is wrong. She does not become upset by God's ways or by her neighbor. She does not diminish the charity, love, and reverence toward her Creator or other people no matter what troubles he allows—whether material loss or insults—because with holiness she has discerned that God allows these to try her deepest motivation and love [*affetto* of love] toward those who insult and harm her and to punish her for her sins. She says, "My Lord, with justice you allow all this; if I haven't insulted this person who is harming me, I must have offended you, so that you have sent her as an instrument to help me correct my faults."

I tell you, my dearest sister, such a soul will taste eternal life in this life, because she evaluates everything about God and others with the light of truth. I invite you to always find a way of acting in this way, so that you might avoid ultimate evil and accomplish ultimate good, for we will be judged in the ways in which we judge others. Let's not act like the foolish ones who act in the opposite manner. They only care to judge the intentions of others without assessing how or why they are doing this; rather they are led by their blind passion, and so judge the truth as a lie and lies as truth. Oh, how distorted is their path! Being blind they want to judge the light! They want to judge God's great mysteries in their own way and judge the way he acts in his servants' lives, and in their habits and ways of acting.

Woe be to human pride! How could it be that the human creature feels no shame at taking away the Creator's job! For the creature should be judged, not become a judge herself! But she is ignorant of this because she is deprived of the light, and so her conscience remains covered up; and so, she carelessly judges and condemns what she hears or has heard and what she has never witnessed. Deprived of charitable, spiritual love, such a person becomes upset by God and her neighbor so that she is undiscerning, and all evil flows from her. Her taste becomes distorted so that which tastes good tastes bad to her and that which is bad seems good to her. She dislikes and is displeased with the mysteries [wisdom] of God and the works of others. She is deprived of the price paid with the blood of Christ crucified. She separates herself from all good and stumbles into every evil; she becomes ungrateful and thankless for any benefits that she receives or has received. And this lack of gratitude dries up the fountain of devotion. Such a person becomes alienated from herself, distanced from God, and, in a disordered manner, she holds unto and loves the riches, pleasures, and status of the world. Such a person bears her burdens with impatience, not realizing that these are due to her sins; instead, she blames those who are blameless.

This can be seen in this world and especially in your city, where great tribulations and changes—and those to come—are due to our faults and failings.[37] But we want to place these on the shoulders of others as though we were crippled [and unable to bear these burdens]. We judge holy intentions as evil and

Other Laymen and Women

wicked, and disordered intentions—fruit of nothing other than selfish self-love—we judge as good. All this happens because a person is deprived of the light. Of course, stones can also fall on those who throw them. So don't act in this way, my dearest daughter, but keep in mind that our own faults are ours, and each owns her own. In this way we will allay God's anger, we will escape evil and many troubles, and we will receive mercy. I am sure that if you and the others can be rooted in the light—as you say you will be—you will know the truth; otherwise you won't. I have said that I wanted to see you rooted in true most perfect light; and so I beg you, for the love of Christ crucified, that you always find a way of finding it.

Please put a stop to all your passions right away and don't spend time listening to what you shouldn't. Instead, pay attention to the truth, act as a person who does not want the condemnation of her soul; and don't distress others for flighty reasons. Receive the *affetto* [affection] of those who love you tenderly. In this way you will benefit from the good and will not suffer sorrow. I am sure that if you want to use the discernment and wisdom God has given you, you will be disposed to receive that which I have written for your salvation. I say no more.

Remain, etc.

[I ask that] you and the others flee from the death of lies and false judgements; don't be lax about this. Don't wait for time you don't have in order to give up these behaviors.

Tender Jesus! Jesus love! Mary!

LETTER 13

To Marco Bindi, merchant
December 1378 (Noffke)[38]

Introduction

Marco was a Sienese merchant who at some point was also a city councilor and accompanied a group of banished Sienese citizens to Florence. He is an example of the sort of civic leader who, though much more educated than Catherine, was attracted to Catherine's holiness and wisdom and therefore sought her guidance. Marco has clearly suffered a major loss; apparently he has lost more than one family member. He appealed to Catherine for wisdom on how to bear this loss.

In a supportive letter asserting her wisdom on God's providence, Catherine advises that acquiring the virtue of patience is crucial to living through sorrow and loss so that these experiences can become a source of spiritual transformation. Patience, as virtue, means more than the contemporary noun. It means a capacity for detachment that enables recognition of the action of grace in any life experience. If patient and detached, the person can recognize and cooperate with God's grace, allowing God to transform the sorrow of the moment into an occasion of growth.

Catherine advises Marco that to acquire patience and live his losses in God, he needs particular spiritual qualities. He must turn his consciousness inward to receive the light of faith; he must let this light transform him, and he must learn through relationship with God that if God is ultimate Goodness, then all that happens to him can be transformed into good.

❊ ❊ ❊

To the name of Jesus Christ and tender Mary.

Dearest brother in Christ gentle Jesus. I, Catherine, servant and slave of the servants of Jesus Christ, write to you in his precious blood with desire to see you rooted in true holy patience; otherwise, we would be unable to please God and the fruit of our efforts would be wasted; which is why we need patience, this glorious virtue.

My dearest brother, if you said to me, "I have great burdens, and feel I don't have the strength for such patience, nor do I know how to acquire it," I would answer as follows: anyone who chooses to act with reason can possess it [patience]. Yet I acknowledge that of ourselves, we are weak and fragile due to

Other Laymen and Women

our [self-centered] sensuality, especially when we love ourselves and others too much, and when we love all material goods with self-centered sensuality. If we love all these things with a lax, self-centered love, when we lose them, our sorrow is intolerable.

However, if we so desire, with God who is our strength we can defeat our weakness with reason, with the strength of our willpower, and with the hand of free will. And God will take into account how much we constrained ourselves in order not to grieve in a disordered manner. Since God is one who receives holy desires, he will give us this gentle, true virtue [patience] so that we can bear every difficulty with true, holy patience. So you see, anyone can obtain patience, if he chooses to use human reason given him by God and not just give in to weakness. For it would be most unseemly that we, who are reasoning creatures, would behave as brutish[39] animals who cannot avail themselves of reason, since they do not possess it. Since we do possess reason, we must use it, for when we don't, we become impatient and astonished by those things God allows in our lives; we offend him with such an attitude.

How should we act, then, to obtain this patience, since I[40] can and must acquire it, for without it I offend God? We need to keep in mind and possess four main qualities. I believe that first we must have the light of faith, for through this light of holy faith we will acquire all virtue; without this light we would be walking in the darkness, just like a blind person for whom day has turned into night. This is what happens to the soul deprived of the light—that light God created out of love with a love that is bright beyond any other light. I was saying, deprived of the light, she [the soul] ends up in the night, a night of anger, where she feels that God allows the troubles that assail her out of displeasure. So you see how important it is to have the light of holy faith.

The second quality is obtained through this light [of faith]. That is, we must be convinced that it is important to have faith, and not just to believe but have certainty, that all creatures possessed of being come forth from God, with the exception of sin, which *is-not*. God did not create the sinful will that commits sin; however, everything else, fire, water, death, and anything else that exists, it all comes forth from him. Christ states this in the Gospel, namely, that no leaf falls from a tree without his providence; and even further, that all the hairs on our head are numbered, and none fall from our head without his knowledge. So if this is what he says about inanimate objects, how much more will he care for us, reasoning creatures. And so, he provides for us through his providence in all that he sends or allows to happen; all is done with mystery [the unknowable power of God] and out of love, not anger.

The third quality is recognizing and knowing as truth—with the light of faith—that God is ultimate, eternal Goodness. Therefore, he can only want our good, and it is his will that we be made holy in him; all that he sends us and allows, he does so toward this end. Should we doubt that he wants only our good, we should then focus on the blood of the immaculate Lamb, and then we would be unable to entertain any such doubts. That Christ on the cross was wounded, distraught, and afflicted with thirst shows us that the supreme, eternal Father loves us beyond measure. And so out of the love he has for us—even as we were alienated due to our sins—he gave us the Word, the only begotten Son; and the Son gave us life, rushing as someone in love toward the shameful death on the cross.

And what was the reason? His love for our salvation. So you see that the blood removes all doubt we could have that God would want our good. Anyway, how could ultimate Goodness do anything but good? He can't! How could ultimate eternal Providence act in any way other than through providence? He who loved us before we came to be and created us out of love in his image and likeness cannot act toward us in any way but out of love, nor act toward us except through providence, providing for our every need of body and soul.

He always loves us because we are his creatures and only abhors our sinfulness. And so, in this life he allows troubles and suffering to befall our body or affect other aspects of our life only according to what he considers to be our needs. And as a true doctor, he offers the medicine required for our particular illness. He does this either to punish our faults in this finite time so that

Other Laymen and Women

we might receive fewer punishments in eternal life;[41] or he does this in order to exercise in us the virtue of patience, just as he did with Job. In order to exercise Job's patience, he took away all his material possessions and all his children, and he sent him an illness that kept producing maggots. He left him his wife as a cross and irritation, for she always needled Job, scolding him and making unjust accusations. After God had tested Job's patience, he restored everything to him twofold. Job had never complained; he even said, "God has given me these things, God has taken them away. May his name be forever blessed" (Job 1:21).

Sometimes God allows misfortunes to help us know ourselves and to learn about the lack of permanency and dependability of the world. He wants us to learn that all that we possess—life, health, spouse and children, riches, status, and the pleasures of the world—is on loan, to be used, not as our own, but for God's purposes; this is how our possessions should be used. This makes it clear that anything we possesses, except God's grace, can be taken away. Grace cannot be taken from us by any creature or by the evil one, or through any trial, unless we agree. When persons recognize this reality—that is, the perfection of grace and the imperfection of embodied life and of what is worldly—they come to dislike their own weakness, and all that is worldly with all its pleasures. For due to this weakness—loving with selfish self-love—we are often cut off from grace. On the other hand, persons [who understand what I have said] come to love the virtues realizing that they are the means of remaining in grace.

So you see, God allows us suffering out of love, so that with a courageous heart we might, with holy zeal and with our heart and desire [*affetto*], become detached from what is worldly. We can then focus on seeking eternal goods and heaven, abandoning what is earthly with all its stench; for we were not made to eat soil.[42] Rather we are made to be pilgrims in this life, racing—with true, authentic virtues—toward our objective, namely, eternal life. We should not make any stops [along this race] for prosperity or pleasure that the world offers us; nor make stops due to adversity. Rather, we should courageously race without stopping either out of impatience or disordered enjoyment but should pass by everything with patience and fear of God.

Your sorrow was necessary for you. God gave you the desire to let go of many attachments and to develop your conscience as you experienced being pulled to one side by God and to the other by what is worldly. Now, out of the vast love God has for your salvation, he cut loose those attachments and is offering you a [new] path, if you are able to receive it. He has given them eternal life [the deceased family members], and he has called you through the treasure of sorrow so that you are not deprived of eternal life, and so that, henceforth, in the time you have left, you may come to know his goodness and your faults.

The fourth quality we need in order to acquire patience is this. We must recognize our faults and sins and how much, through these, we have offended God, who is infinite goodness; since he is infinite goodness, it would follow that our punishments should be infinite, and not just for big offenses but also for small ones. Indeed, we are worthy of a thousand hells since we are the wicked who have offended our Creator. [Imagine], he, our tender Creator, offended by us! We see he is infinite Goodness, while we are *we-who-are-not*, even as our very being and every grace bestowed on our being comes from him. Of our own accord we are worthless and inadequate.

Even though we deserve eternal punishment, out of his mercy, he punishes us in finite time,[43] for if in finite time we bear our sorrows with patience, punishment due [in eternal life] is discounted and we acquire merits. This is not the case with the suffering in the afterlife. If the soul is suffering in purgatory, punishment is discounted but no further merits accrue. And so it behooves us to willingly bear this small sorrow. We can consider it small due to the shortness of time; for sorrow is as extensive as time in this [earthly] life. How much time do we have in this life? It's like the point of a needle, in other words, brief. Suffering that has gone by is no longer with me, for time has gone by. Suffering to come I don't yet experience, and I don't know if I will have time to do so, since I must die but don't know

Other Laymen and Women

when. So the only time that exists is this moment in the present, nothing else.

And so we must bear [sufferings] with great joy, since all good is rewarded and all faults punished. Paul says, "There is no comparison between the sufferings of this life and the future glory received by the human soul who has been patient" [Rom 8:18]. So this is the way in which you can acquire and live the virtue of true patience. When patience is acquired out of love and with the light of holy faith, you will be rewarded with the fruits of all your efforts [to live patiently]. Acting in any other manner would lead to losing the blessings of earthly life as well as the blessings of heaven; so there is no other way. This is why I said I wanted to see you grounded in true, holy patience. I beg you to carry this out [the recommendations of this letter]. Hold in memory[44] the blood of Christ crucified, then all that is disagreeable will become sweet and all that is heavy will become light. Don't try to find times and places according to your will but be pleased with the way God provides the time and the place.

I do have compassion for what has happened to you for it seems to be very serious. Nevertheless, it has occurred through providence, in a timely manner for your salvation. I beg you to be consoled so that God's loving discipline doesn't come to nothing. I say no more, except [to suggest] you discern how to use time while you have it.

Remain in the holy, tender love of God.
Tender Jesus! Jesus love!

LETTERS 300 AND 249

To Agnesa and Francesco di Pipino

Introduction

Agnesa and Francesco were a couple from Florence who became Catherine's friends and followers and in 1378 offered Catherine hospitality during a difficult stay in Florence.[45] She wrote six letters to them as a couple, an additional seven to Agnesa, and five to Francesco. This correspondence shows her friendship with married couples and her expectation that they, too, were called, together and individually, to grow in union with God and to intercede for the good of the church through the practice of prayer and penance.

The letter to Agnesa offers significant insight into Catherine's spirituality regarding the practice of fasting and penance. Catherine had practiced extreme forms of fasting in the early years of her life, but her views were transformed, no doubt through God's action within her, for both in Letter 213 (1378) to a *mantellata* and in this letter she counsels moderation in physical penance and fasting, while emphasizing prayer. Catherine tells Agnesa that the cord around the waist used as a form of penance should be worn loosely, as Catherine would wear it. In other words, Catherine is counseling a moderate asceticism she herself practiced in 1378, a year and a half before her death.

The letter to Francesco is actually to the couple, as can be seen in the line of address. It is significant in that it speaks of the spiritual path as a pilgrimage, a concept Catherine had primarily used for the crusade. Through this metaphor, Catherine emphasizes perseverance in the face of spiritual and day-to-day difficulties that were stumbling blocks for this couple.

These letters also give us insight into the practical mediation Catherine engaged in while in Rome, obtaining indulgences for her followers.

❊ ❊ ❊

LETTER 300

To the aforementioned monna Agnesa di Francesco di Pipino
October 4, 1378 (Dated letter)

To the name of Jesus Christ and tender Mary.

Dearest daughter in Christ tender Jesus. I, Catherine, servant and slave of the servants of Jesus Christ, write to you in his pre-

Other Laymen and Women

cious blood, with desire to see you bathed and submerged in the blood of Christ crucified; so that for love of his blood you might give your own blood, and your life for love of Life.

Ah, dearest daughter, this is the time to die longing for the honor of God and the salvation of souls; [it is time] to offer humble tears and continuous prayer before God for the needs of the entire world. And therefore, I want you to bury yourself in the side of Christ crucified in order to find the best way to sacrifice yourself to God and bathe yourself in his most tender blood. I say no more.

Remain in the holy and tender love of God.

I order you not to fast except in the ways I prescribed, and don't use the discipline.[46] Rather, engage as much as you want in the prayer of holy, consuming desire or practice of other true, authentic virtues, or hold vigils [in prayer], but don't use the discipline. And for a corded belt,[47] I want you to have a small chain like the one I had, not the one you have. And wear it so loosely that you can put your finger in [between it and your body]. Be sure not to disregard this obedience [order].

Remain in the holy and tender love of God.

Please greet all my daughters, Ginevra and all the others. Blessings to Bastiano;[48] may God fill him with his most tender grace.

Tender Jesus! Jesus love!

Written on the 4th of October.

LETTER 249

To the aforementioned Francesco, a tailor
April 1379 (Noffke)

To the name of Jesus Christ crucified and tender Mary.

Dearest son and daughter in Christ tender Jesus. I, Catherine, servant and slave of the servants of Jesus Christ, write to you in his precious blood with desire to see you true pilgrims. Every person is a pilgrim in this life, for our final end is not here but in eternal life, the culmination toward which we must journey and for which we were created. And so, I want us to be under way, for the path—the teachings of Jesus crucified—has been set out, so we do not travel in darkness but are accompanied by a most perfect light. And so it is important to be the sort of a pilgrim who does not turn back either due to pleasures he may find or to hardships found on the way; nor does such a pilgrim get caught up in delays, but with perseverance walks until he comes to his final goal.

We should act in this way, my dearest son and daughter. We have started walking along this path of the teachings of the tender loving Word in order to reach the eternal Father. Certainly [on this path] are found trying sections, the difficulties of the insults and scorn of others, and the struggles with the evil one. We should not stop and sit down or turn back due to impatience; rather with courage and the light of faith we should move beyond all this. And with true humility we should bow our head to the tender will of God, who allows these dark passages for our good, so that he has more cause to repay us. As says the glorious Paul, "Blessed is he who bears with temptations, so that after he is tested, he will receive the crown of life." And elsewhere he says, "Only he who has authentically done battle will be crowned."[49]

Be glad, then, when you are on the receiving end of the troubles caused by the evil one, or by other persons, for they are in fact, crafting your crown.[50] And so, with true perseverance walk along the road of life. In this way the many pleasures, amusements, and honors that our fragile flesh might desire, or that the world promises or places before us will not be a reason to rest and indulge yourself; rather like true pilgrims, make believe you don't see these, and with fortitude continue your journey until death, and in this way, you will reach your goal. I entreat you to do as I say for the love of Jesus Christ. I say no more.

More and more days have gone by since I wrote a letter to Bartalo in which I let him know that I had acted on obtaining an indulgence of faults and punishments,[51] for him, for both of you, for monna Orsa, and several others. As it is less cumbersome, there will be a benefit [decree of indulgence] issued for all of you together; and I will send it as soon as possible. And so, rejoice in Christ, my children, and find ways to be appreciative and grateful to your Creator. I ask that you effectively deliver the letters sent with this one. And tell monna Gostanzia that I was diligent in asking for the indulgence for her and....[52]

Remain in the holy and tender love of God. All the family supports you.

Tender Jesus! Jesus Love!

8

FAMILY

LETTER 14

To three of her brothers who were in Florence
1370 to September 1373 (Noffke); end of 1372 to beginning of 1373 (Volpato)

Introduction

This short letter is one of the few written before 1373 and unique in being directed to her three oldest brothers, Benincasa, Stefano, and Bartolomeo. They inherited their father's wool business in 1368 and in 1370 moved to Florence, probably due to political trouble in Siena, where all three had formed part of a government that was now out of power. This letter was written to offer support at a difficult time for them politically and financially.

Since she was the twenty-fourth (and last) child, Catherine's brothers would have been many years older. She would not have had a close relationship with them, and the family lines of authority would have placed Catherine, the last child and a female, at the bottom of the ladder. Yet, given the vocation of evangelizer she had taken on by the time of her letter writing, she advised these older brothers with authority especially about detachment from material goods at a time when they were suffering from financial reverses and loss of social status. In line with her spirituality focused on transformation in the capacity to love, she urges them to transformation of desire and *affetto*, the motivation emerging from the core of their

Family

being. Care for their spiritual life should be reflected in a harmonious relationship as brothers.

❊ ❊ ❊

To the name of Jesus Christ Crucified and tender Mary.

Dearest brothers in Christ Jesus. I bring to mind the boundless love that our loving Savior had in giving himself up to death in order to offer us the life of grace. Seeing that we veered off the path of ordered love, and in order to restore us to union with that love, our loving Savior was willing to embrace the most insulting death he could have chosen. Oh, my! Our Savior saw us become sinful due to the emergence of disordered desires[1] harbored within us. These desires are for fleeting objects that are gone as a passing wind, objects that pass fleetingly from us or we pass fleetingly from them.

I, Catherine, unworthy and useless servant, beg you to place your hope in God; don't place your trust in this passing life. I beg you, as servants who have been ransomed, to conscientiously place your soul's desire and deepest motivation [*affetto*] in your Lord. For he has ransomed you, as St. Peter tells us, "He did not ransom you with gold or silver, but rather with his loving and precious blood" [1 Pet 1:18–19]. And I beg you, dearest brothers, that you hold dear and love this price paid for you. To show that you hold it [the precious blood shed for us] dear, you should always be persons who observe and love God's commandments.

Especially, I beg you and direct you, on behalf of Christ crucified, to follow the first and the last commandments,[2] that is, those related to love of God and union with God. I want to see you all in love with holy love and your souls filled with this love. If you wish to show me that you live such love, it is my desire to see you always united and bound by this tender bond of love. In this way neither the evil one nor any words said can separate you.

I call to mind the words uttered by Jesus Christ, that all who humble themselves shall be exalted [Matt 23:12, Luke 14:11, 18:14]. And so, Benincasa, I beg you as the eldest to be willing to be as the youngest; and you Bartolomeo, be willing to be the youngest of the young; and you Stefano, I pray that you will submit to your brothers and to God. In this manner you will gently remain in perfect love. May God give you always his perfect grace. I say no more.

Remain, etc.!

Tender Jesus! Jesus love!

LETTERS 1 AND 117

To Catherine's Mother

Introduction

Lapa, Catherine's mother, was considered a strong, persistent woman. The daughter of a poet, she bore twenty-four children and managed well the large home that included extended family and the family wool business. While Lapa at first resisted Catherine's vocation and determination not to marry and become a *mantellata*, once she was widowed, she joined the *mantellate* herself. While Catherine was in Siena, she lived with Lapa most of the time, either in the family home or those of others.

These two brief letters give us insight into Catherine's relationship with her mother. By this time, her thirtieth year, three years before her death, Catherine clearly saw herself as a spiritual guide with authority over her own mother. She exhorts Lapa with the same uncompromising and firm manner used toward correspondents she doesn't know. In the first letter she urges Lapa to knowledge of God and self and to patience—the capacity to bear with suffering—that makes possible faithful living of God's will. Significantly, Lapa was reported to be impatient. In the second letter, Catherine also exhorts her to patience but focuses on detachment, especially with regard to Catherine herself. Catherine affirms her vocation, that she felt elected

Family

by God, indeed, placed on this earth for the purpose of laboring for his honor and for the salvation of others. Her mother must learn not to interfere. She should imitate Mary, who let the apostles leave her side for the sake of their mission.

In Letter 117 we have a testament to Catherine's ministry of bringing reconciliation between important families. Actively working for peace—at the broad political level—and reconciliation among people and families was a major expression of Catherine's spirituality focused on living God's love. Here she tells us she is trying to "remedy a great scandal," though not one related to a countess. These few sentences witness to the way this daughter of a wool dyer, with no official role or title, was sought for a major role by leading Sienese families. Though Letter 117 includes Cecca[3] as a recipient, the message is directed to her mother, with a few words of greeting to Cecca at the end. Indeed, Noffke does not include Cecca as a recipient.

❊ ❊ ❊

LETTER 1

To monna Lapa
August or September 1377 (Noffke)

To the name of Jesus Christ crucified and tender Mary.

Dearest mother in our loving Jesus Christ. I, Catherine, servant and slave of the servants of Jesus Christ, write to you in his precious blood with desire to see you acquire true knowledge of yourself and of God's goodness in you. For without this true knowledge, you could not participate in the life of grace. And so, with holy devotion you should learn to know that *you-are-not*, and that your being is owed to God. As well that you owe God the many gifts and graces that you have received and all those you receive every day.

You will then be grateful and appreciative, and thus achieve holy patience, and in this way, small issues will not seem large, and large issues will seem easy to bear for Christ crucified. The knight is not considered competent unless he has been tested on the field of battle. Similarly, our soul must be tested through battle in many trials. And so, when the soul's patience is tested, she does not turn her back due to impatience, becoming scandalized by what God allows; rather she is able to rejoice and exult. And with perfect joy she can await life eternal because she has relied on the cross, receiving strength through the sufferings and humiliations of Christ crucified. In this way she can reasonably expect the eternal vision of God. For Jesus has promised that those who suffer and are persecuted in this life will be consoled and satisfied [Matt 5:6, Luke 6:21] and illuminated with the eternal vision of God, thus experiencing God's tenderness fully and without limit. And even in this life, God begins to offer consolation to those who labor in his name.

However, without knowledge of ourselves and God, we cannot attain all this goodness. And so I beg you—as strongly as I can with all that I know— to make the effort to acquire this dual knowledge so that we will not lose the fruit of our efforts. I say no more.

Remain in the holy and tender love of God.

Tender Jesus! Jesus love!

LETTER 117

To monna Lapa her mother and monna Cecca, when they were in the Monastery of Saint Agnes of Montepulciano while Catherine was at Rocca d'Agnolino
September 1377 (Noffke)

To the name of Jesus Christ crucified and tender Mary.

Dearest mother and daughter in Christ, loving Jesus. I, Catherine, servant and slave of the servants of Jesus Christ, write to you in his precious blood with desire to see you clothed in the fire of divine love, so that you may live through all suffering and torments, hunger and thirst, persecutions and abuses,

Family

scorn, harassment, and ill treatment. And may you live through all this and more with true patience, learning from the slain and consumed Lamb who with such fire of love ran to his shameful death on the cross.

And so, walk with Mary, that most tender mother, who in order that the holy disciples might seek the honor of God and the salvation of souls by following in the tracks of her loving son, accepted that the disciples leave her side, even though she loved them so deeply. And so she remained alone, a pilgrim and a guest. And the disciples, who loved her immensely, took their leave and with joy embraced all hardships for the honor of God. They travelled among tyrants and endured many persecutions. If you were to ask them, "Why are you so joyful and why are you leaving Mary?" They would answer, "because we have surrendered ourselves and we are in love with the honor of God and the salvation of souls." My dearest mother and my daughter, I want you to do as they did. Even if up to now you have not done so, I want you to burn with divine love and always to seek the honor of God and the salvation of souls. Otherwise you will endure much suffering and distress, and your pain would cause me pain. Please understand, my dearest mother, that I, your miserable daughter, have been placed on earth for no other reason [than to seek the honor of God and the salvation of souls]; my Creator has elected me for this. I know you are happy that I obey him.

And so, if you think I am staying here longer than you would wish, pray to be at peace because I cannot do otherwise.

If you knew of the situation [at Rocca d'Agnolino], I believe you would send me here yourself. Hoping I am able to do so, I am here to remedy a great scandal. It has nothing to do with the countess. Please all pray to God and the glorious virgin [Saint Agnes] for a good outcome. And you Cecca and Giustina,[4] immerse yourselves in the blood of Christ crucified, for this is the hour and time to test the virtues within your soul. May God give all of you his benevolent and eternal blessing. I say no more.

Remain in the holy and tender love of God!

Tender Jesus! Jesus, love!

Appendix 1
ISIME CRITICAL TEXT

The Istituto storico italiano per il medio evo (ISIME) with the support of the Rome Province of the Dominican Order of Preachers recently published the first seventy-six letters of a multidisciplinary effort to develop a new critical text of Catherine's letters.[1] ISIME's project was conceived as a continuation of the work of Eugenio Dupré Theseider and bypasses the work of Antonio Volpato (for which no explanation is given). It is a literary-historical endeavor where linguists, philologists, and very specialized manuscript experts seek to apply new methodologies to the study of over sixty-seven manuscripts (including eight original and fifty-nine direct copies) from which Catherine's letters are derived. The project emphasizes the evolution of language from Catherine's Sienese, but also reexamines historical issues particularly the dating of the letters. Concluding that many cannot be dated, the project assigns new numbering to the letters based on an alphabetical order. As well, letters 371 and 372 are combined and four letters are further divided so that ISIME lists 386 rather than 383 letters.[2] The work of the team of experts—which includes the letters as they are published—is documented on its website, https://database.dekasisime.it.

It is beyond the scope of this appendix to analyze the differences in editorial judgment between Volpato—who worked with Dupré Theseider—and ISIME. Here I summarize differences in dating and content affecting the Letters published in this volume.

DATING

Coming up with dates for Catherine's undated letters is a matter of judgment using historical and literary clues. Noffke also used a linguistic methodology which ISIME specialists do not critique, though they prioritize their own analyses. Given Noffke's thorough familiarity with Catherine's history, her own work based directly on the various manuscripts from which she translated the letters, and her meticulous life-long scholarship on Catherine, I consider her judgment regarding dating of the letters highly credible. Given the foregoing, and the analysis that follows of Letter T49 (IS 21), I conclude that Noffke's judgment is in general as valid as that of ISIME, undoubtedly with variations from letter to letter. Accordingly, this volume's organization of Catherine's letters in broad historical order remains valid.

Twelve of the letters in this volume are included among the seventy-six just published. Noffke's dating of three of these varies by a year or more from that of ISIME; based on strong historical and linguistic evidence, she dates two letters that ISIME states cannot be dated. For the other seven letters, ISIME's dating and that of Noffke coincide exactly or within a few months.

As an example, in Letter T49 (IS 21) to Alessa, ISIME argues for an early 1374 date, while Noffke argues for a Fall 1377 date—a three-year difference. Noffke bases her estimate on similarities regarding a fountain metaphor between this letter and *The Dialogue* (chap. 64) and on her linguistic analysis, which "points emphatically" to Catherine's stay at Val d'Orcia in 1377.[3] She also cites a 1377 date in Dupré Theseider's unpublished notes which he had readied—before his untimely death—for the purpose of further dating the letters.[4] ISIME speculates that Catherine could have sent Alessa the advice about a routine for her life in 1374 when Alessa became a *mantellata*, and they note a similar reference to scripture in Letter 49 and a letter dated 1374. It is notable that ISIME does not take into consideration Dupré Theseider's notes. They cite Noffke only partially, stating her

ISIME Critical Text

dating is based only on linguistic evidence, and appear to give that evidence no weight.[5] In this case (Letter T49), I find Noffke's arguments more credible. I would add that the letter to Alessa could have been written at any time given Catherine's authoritative letters to her followers about how to live their life. Further, thirteen seventy-four as a date for Alessa's joining the *mantellate* is debatable.

CONTENT

Regarding variations in content, decisions regarding inclusions or exclusions of certain words or phrases from the available manuscripts in a final text are most often a matter of judgment. Having compared this volume's twelve letters included in the 2023 ISIME publication with Volpato's text, I found very few differences in content. The differences between the texts primarily reflect the very specialized ISIME textual work, namely, the spelling and versions of words, and the syntax and grammar of sentences. ISIME translations are likely to include word usage and style—Sienese fourteenth century rather than Tuscan or later centuries—that is more representative of Catherine's actual speech. These differences, however, mostly make no difference to an English rendition which requires changes in syntax and grammar; use of similes or the Italian spelling of words are not relevant to the translation. The few places where words were excluded and phrases added would make a minor difference to the translation, while not meaningfully modifying Catherine's message. For instance, in letter 33 (IS 1) I translated, "loving, tender, Word-Christ, sweet, good Jesus" noting that while dictating Catherine could multiply the appellations for her beloved Jesus. The ISIME version removes "loving Word." In Letter T 358 (Is 30) the ISIME text removes "*because in his breast shines this justice*" from "he brings about right-order *because in his breast shines this justice*. And he renders justice as one who has achieved discernment." In letter T127 (IS 66) the ISIME texts adds that we should not just "ride" the donkey of our humanity, but we should also "tame" it.

CATHERINE OF SIENA

In a personal communication, Antonio Volpato informs me that there are Letters—not included here—where differences of a phrase or sentence between his text and that of ISIME make a significant difference to Catherine's meaning. As ISIME publishes more Letters, such important variations may apply to Letters included in this volume.

Appendix 2

LETTERS IN NUMERICAL ORDER

Letter Number	IS Number	Correspondent	Page
1		Lapa, Mother	250
7		Cardinal Pietro of Ostia	166
13		Marco Bindi, Merchant	237
14		Catherine's Three Brothers	248
16		Important Prelate	161
26		Eugenia, Nun and Niece	47
33	1	Abbot of Monte Oliveto	110
36		Novices of Monte Oliveto	99
41		Friar Tommaso dalla Fonte	88
49	21	Alessa, *Mantellata*	72
51		Felice, Augustinian Hermit	104
73		Costanza, Nun	39
86	2	Abbess of Santa Maria, Florence	54
95		Young Men Mentored by Fr. Giovanni dalle Celle	219
99		Neri di Landoccio Pagliaresi, Lay Disciple	60
113	46	Bandecca Salimbeni, Widow	224
117		Lapa, Mother	250
120		Rabe, Wife of Francesco Tolomei	216
125		Nera, *Mantellata* Prioress	66

CATHERINE OF SIENA

Letter Number	IS Number	Correspondent	Page
127	66	Friars Bartolomeo Dominici and Tommaso d'Antonio	91
130		Ipòlito, Florentine Widower	209
131		Nicolò Soderini, Florentine Political Leader	173
132		Various *Mantellate*	63
134	67	Bartolomeo and Jacomo, Hermits	95
143		Giovanna, Queen of Naples	177
146	64	Friar Bartolomeo Dominici	91
149		Piero Gambacorta, Pisan Official	170
154		Francesco Tebaldi, Carthusian	114
181		Cardinal Nicola da Osimo	156
182	53	Bartalomea, Nun	43
185		Gregory XI	140
186		Neri di Landoccio Pagliaresi	86
213		Daniella of Orvieto, *Mantellata*	75
214		Caterina and Giovanna, *Mantellate*	68
219		Friars Raymond of Capua, Giovanni Terzo, and Felice	122
241		Giovanna, Mother of a Disciple	212
249		Francesco di Pipino, Tailor	243
252		Gregory XI	146
256		Niccolò, Prior of the Knights Hospitallers	198
266		Ristoro Canigiani, Florentine Politician	180
267		Raymond of Capua	126
272		Raymond of Capua	131
300	9	Monna Agnesa, Wife of Francesco di Pipino	243
305		Urban VI	151
307		Florentine Woman	232

Letters in Numerical Order

Letter Number	IS Number	Correspondent	Page
326		William Flete and Antonio da Nizza, Augustinian Hermits	108
347	20	Alberigo da Barbiano, Captain	204
358	30	Andrea Vanni, Painter, Political Leader of Siena	187
373		Raymond of Capua	132
374	57	Bartolomeo Smeducci, Knight	192
375		Unknown Layman	231

NOTES

PREFACE

1. Suzanne Noffke, OP (1937–2020), was a Racine Dominican, an independent scholar with a doctorate in linguistics.

NOTES ON TRANSLATION

1. Catherine of Siena, *Epistolario de Santa Catalina de Siena: Espíritu y doctrina*, ed. and trans. José Salvador y Conde, 2 vols. (Salamanca: San Esteban, 1982).

2. William of St. Thierry, *The Mirror of Faith*, trans. Thomas X. Davis (Kalamazoo, MI: Cistercian Publications, 1979), 95.

INTRODUCTION

1. She also wrote a book, *The Dialogue*, an expansion of themes that she described in Letter 272. *The Dialogue*, ed. and trans. Suzanne Noffke (New York: Paulist, 1980); and twenty-six prayers, *The Prayers of Catherine of Siena*, trans. Suzanne Noffke, 2nd ed. (San Jose, CA: Authors Choice Press, 2001).

2. "What strikes us most about the Saint is her infused wisdom. That is to say, lucid, profound, and inebriating absorption of the divine truths and the mysteries of the faith contained in the Holy Books of the Old and New Testaments. That assimilation was certainly favored by most singular natural gifts, but it was also evidently something prodigious, due to a charism of wisdom from the Holy Spirit, a mystic charism." Words of Paul VI in *L'Osservatore Romano*, English edition, October 15, 1970, 6–7; from the formal proclamation, Paul VI, *Mirabilis in ecclesia deus* (Rome: Vaticana Editrice, October 4, 1970).

3. The other four women doctors of the church were literate and had some form of education, and Edith Stein a doctorate in philosophy. The male doctors all had various levels of education.

4. Prophetic here does not refer to revealing future events but to proclaiming God's word, as did the Old Testament prophets. For a historian's

perspective of Catherine's prophetic vocation see André Vauchez, "Catherine de Sienne, prophétesse d'un renouveau spirituel," *Laboratoire italien* 21 (2018). https://doi.org/10.4000/laboratoireitalien.1842.

5. *Catherine of Siena: A Life of Passion and Purpose* (Mahwah, NJ: Paulist, 2018), 94.

6. The first critical edition is found in Catherine of Siena, *Lettere*, ed. Antonio Volpato, Opera omnia, testi e concordanze (Pistoia: Provincia Romana dei Frati Predicatori. Centro Riviste, 2002) and as a searchable CD-ROM that includes the critical edition of *The Prayers and the Dialogue* edited by Giuliana Cavallini. See *Santa Caterina da Siena: Opera omnia*, ed. Fausto Sbaffoni (Pistoia: Provincia Romana dei Frati Predicatori, 2002), CD-ROM. This first edition, with a few changes and annotations to some of the letters, is online, *Lettere, edizione critica e commento*, ed. Antonio Volpato (Rome: Centro internazionale di studi cateriniani, 2016), https://centrostudicateriniani.it/santa-caterina-da-siena/epistolario/. References to *The Letters* in this volume is to this online edition.

7. See "dating" below.

8. See, for instance (in this volume), Letter 219 to Raymond of Capua and Letter 127 to her close friend Bartolomeo Dominici.

9. Catherine of Siena, *The Letters of Catherine of Siena*, ed. and trans. Suzanne Noffke, 4 vols. (Tempe: Arizona Center for Medieval and Renaissance Studies, 2000–2008). References to these volumes will be to Noffke's editorial material and will be abbreviated as Noffke, vol:p.

10. For a well-documented and balanced contemporary biography of Catherine, see Donald Brophy, *Catherine of Siena: A Passionate Life* (New York: BlueBridge, 2010). Raymond of Capua's hagiography, on which most information about Catherine's life has been based, emphasized the extraordinary in line with the genre and with the goal of furthering her cause for beatification. See Raymond of Capua, *The Life of Catherine of Siena*, trans. Conleth Kearns (Wilmington, DE: Glazier, 1980). For a discussion of Raymond's intentions by the scholar who has recently produced a new critical edition of the original Latin, see Silvia Nocentini, "La Legenda maior di Raimondo da Capua: una eredità condivisa," in *Virgo digna coelo: Caterina e la sua eredità*, ed. Alessandra Bartolomei Romagnoli, Luciano Cinelli, Pierantonio Piatti (Rome: Libreria Editrice Vaticana, 2013), 103–18.

11. Antonio Volpato, a medieval historian and author of the critical edition of *The Letters*, affirms the importance of preaching for evangelization in medieval Siena, where sermons included popularization of Thomas Aquinas's theology (Letter 219n46).

12. For a scholarly account of her life highlighting her mystical experience, see Thomas McDermott, *Catherine of Siena: Spiritual Development in Her*

Notes

Life and Teaching (Mahwah, NJ: Paulist, 2008), 7–77. As already mentioned, Raymond of Capua's hagiography details Catherine's mystical experiences.

13. Ann King-Lenzmeier, *Hildegard of Bingen: An Integrated Vision* (Collegeville, MN: Liturgical, 2001), 4.

14. Giulia Barone, "Caterina o la liberazione della parola," in *Caterina da Siena e la vita religiosa femminile: Un percorso domenicano*, ed. Pierantonio Piatti (Rome: Campisano, 2020), 27–28.

15. It is notable that we have no information as to whether Catherine desired to enter a monastery, the usual way of dedicating one's life to God in her day. It is not known if her family could not or would not provide the required dowry, or whether she truly preferred the penitent life.

16. Penitent groups were also guided by the Franciscans and other monks or priests.

17. For a summary of the penitential lifestyle, see Maiju Lehmijoki-Gardner, ed., *Dominican Penitent Women*, Classics of Western Spirituality (Mahwah, NJ: Paulist Press, 2005), 16–21.

18. Historical material about the *mantellate* and how much their spirituality influenced Catherine's own practice and wisdom has not always been incorporated into an understanding of her spirituality.

19. For a more detailed discussion of Catherine's oral formation through church attendance see Suzanne Noffke, *Catherine of Siena: Vision Through a Distant Eye* (Collegeville, MN: Liturgical, 1996; repr., New York: Authors Press, 2006), chap. 3.

20. Lehmijoki-Gardner, *Penitent Women*, 22.

21. Lehmijoki-Gardner, *Penitent Women*, 24.

22. See Letters 213 and 300. For a discussion of Catherine's asceticism see Diana L. Villegas, "Fasting and Penance," last modified January 2023, https://catherineofsiena-spirituality.org/mystical-spirituality-and-holiness/.

23. Lehmijoki-Gardner, *Penitent Women*, 24.

24. Lehmijoki-Gardner, *Penitent Women*, 21.

25. After 1373 she lived on and off with Alessa, one of the *mantellate* belonging to the gentry. Raymond of Capua tells us that Catherine spent weeks and even months with Alessa in *The Life of Catherine of Siena*, trans. Conleth Kearns (Wilmington, DE: Glazier, 1980), sec. 299.

26. A brief hagiographical source, anonymously written by a contemporary, highlights Catherine's miraculous interventions in the community. See "The *Miracoli* of Catherine of Siena," in Lehmijoki-Gardner, *Penitent Women*.

27. Lehmijoki-Gardner, *Penitent Women*, 27.

28. Barone, "Liberazione della parola," 27.

29. Katherine Gill, "Women and the Production of Religious Literature in the Vernacular, 1300–1500," in *Creative Women in Medieval and Early Modern*

Italy, ed. E. Ann Matter and John W. Coakley (Philadelphia: University of Pennsylvania Press, 2016), 73.

30. Jane Tylus, "Mystical Literacy: Writing and Religious Women in Late Medieval Italy," in *A Companion to Catherine of Siena*, ed. Carolyn Muessig, George Ferzoco, and Beverly Mayne Kienzle (Leiden: Brill, 2012), 166.

31. Barone, "Liberazione della parola," 29.

32. Susan Groag Bell, "Medieval Women Book Owners: Arbiters of Lay Piety and Ambassadors of Culture," *Signs* 7, no. 4 (1982): 754.

33. Groag Bell, "Medieval Women Book Owners," 768.

34. Gill, "Women and Vernacular Literature," 73.

35. For example, see Letter 127nn11, 14, 16 and Letter 181n22.

36. André Vauchez asserts Flete influenced Catherine as early as 1367 when she was twenty years old. (*Life of Passion and Purpose*, 20).

37. See, for instance, Letters 267 and 373.

38. Catherine may have dictated her first letters as early as 1368. Noffke begins dating existing letters in 1372. (Noffke, I:1).

39. Catherine's spirituality regarding participation in the crusade is summarized in the introduction to Letter 374.

40. For a discussion of Catherine's involvement in ecclesiastical politics, see Diana L. Villegas, "Catherine of Siena's Spirituality of Political Engagement," *HTS Teologiese Studies/Theological Studies* 77, no. 2 a6319 (2021), https://doi.org/10.4102/hts.v77i2.6319; Diana L. Villegas, "Catherine of Siena's Crusade Letters: Spirituality and Political Context," *HTS Teologiese Studies/Theological Studies* 77, no. 2 a6499 (2021), https://doi.org/10.4102/hts.v77i2.6499. For a book-length analysis from the perspective of a medieval historian, see F. Thomas Luongo, *The Saintly Politics of Catherine of Siena* (Ithaca, NY: Cornell University Press, 2006).

41. Luongo, *Saintly Politics*, 70.

42. Letter 181. See also Villegas, "Catherine of Siena's Spirituality of Political Engagement," 3.

43. Raymond had served in Rome while Stefano della Cumba was provincial of the Roman Dominicans. (Noffke, I:256n26).

44. For two somewhat different views in English, see Jane Tylus, *Reclaiming Catherine of Siena: Literacy, Literature, and the Signs of Others* (Chicago: University of Chicago Press, 2009); Karen Scott, "'Io Caterina': Ecclesiastical Politics and Oral Culture in the Letters of Catherine of Siena," in *Dear Sister: Medieval Women and the Epistolary Genre*, ed. Karen Cherewatuk and Ulrike Wiethaus (Philadelphia: University of Pennsylvania Press, 1993), 106–7. For a foundational view from an Italian literature scholar, see Marina Zancan, "Lettere di Caterina da Siena. Il testo, la tradizione, l'interpretazione," *Annali d'italianistica* 13 (1995): 155.

Notes

45. Some interpretations about Catherine's intentions as writer miss the straightforward meaning of her beliefs and spiritual experience. For instance, Luongo interprets Catherine's description of her consolation in learning to write as "justifying her loquacity—and authorizing her writing—by comparing herself to the Psalmist, the very model of an inspired author." My interpretation is that Catherine was sharing her very significant experience with Raymond, her close friend, and had no intention of making any claims about her writing. Citation from F. Thomas Luongo, "Catherine of Siena, Auctor," in *Women Intellectuals and Leaders in the Middle Ages*, ed. Kathryn Kerby-Fulton, Katie Ann-Marie Bugyis, and John Van Engen (Cambridge: Boydell & Brewer, 2020), 108.

46. See, for instance, her "commands" to Gregory XI in Letters 185 and 252. For a discussion of the scolding she gave Raymond for not doing as she ordered since she was sure it was God's will, see Diana L. Villegas, "Examining Catherine of Siena's Controversial Discernments about Papal Politics," *HTS Teologiese Studies/Theological Studies* 77, no. 2 (2021): 2–3, https://doi.org/10.4102/hts.v77i2.6654.

47. Medieval form of address.

48. Letter 373. The Master is Giovanni Tantucci, an Augustinian hermit and disciple of Catherine. Bartolomeo Dominici and Tommaso dalla Fonte are Dominican friars members of her "family" and especially close friends. Messer Tommaso is a notary who worked at the papal court and was a disciple of Catherine's who also advised her.

49. For the views of a prominent medieval literature scholar, see Tylus, *Reclaiming Catherine*, 163–214. For that of a historian see Luongo, "Auctor," 108.

50. "The Writings of Catherine of Siena: The Manuscript Tradition," in *A Companion to Catherine of Siena*, ed. Carolyn Muessig, George Ferzoco, and Beverly Mayne Kienzle (Leiden: Brill, 2012), 296.

51. *Lettere*, 2016. Edits and annotations through October 2023 are included in this volume.

52. This summary is based on Suzanne Noffke's dating of the Letters; see "dating" below.

53. Catherine wrote about one third of her letters to women. In a comparative literature dissertation, Lisa Tagliaferri offers categorizations of Catherine's letter recipients, including illustrative charts. "Lyrical Mysticism: The Writing and Reception of Catherine of Siena" (PhD diss., CUNY, 2017), https://academicworks.cuny.edu/gc_etds/2154.

54. Catherine dictated her letters since she did not learn to write until the last couple of years of her life (and we don't know how well). In any case, dictating to scribes was common in the Middle Ages even for those who were literate. See Luongo, "Auctor," 100.

55. Noffke, "Manuscript Tradition," 296 and Raymond of Capua, *Life*, sec. 7.

CATHERINE OF SIENA

56. After Catherine's death, Neri and Barduccio became urban hermits and Stefano a Carthusian monk.

57. *Lettere 2016*, Introduction, 8–9. Such references would have been problematic in that the crusade failed and those interested in Catherine's canonization did not want to call attention to her great support for it nor to the legend that Catherine predicted the success of the crusade.

58. Noffke, "Manuscript Tradition," 297–98.

59. For a description and discussion regarding the manuscripts of the letters and their history, see Noffke, I:xxi–xxxviii; and Noffke, "Manuscript Tradition," 296–324. For information on the manuscripts being studied by ISIME, see https://database.dekasisime.it/index.html#home.

60. *Lettere 2016*, Introduction, 12. Noffke, "Manuscript Tradition," 302.

61. *Opere della serafica Santa Caterina da Siena*, ed. Girolamo Gigli, 4 vols. (Siena, Lucca, 1707–21).

62. *Sainte Catherine de Sienne: Essai de critique des sources II, Les oeuvres de Sainte Catherine de Sienne* (Paris: De Boccard, 1930).

63. Catherine of Siena, *Epistolario di Santa Caterina da Siena*, ed. Eugenio Dupré-Theseider, vol. 82, Fonti per la storia d'Italia, Epistolari secolo XIV (Rome: Reale Istituto Storico Italiano per il Medio Evo, 1940).

64. *Lettere 2016*.

65. Catherine of Siena, *Epistolario I A-B*, ed. Attilio Cicchella et al. (Rome: Istituto storico italiano per il medio evo, 2023). This group's work is documented online in https://database.dekasisime.it, where new versions of the letters are made available as they are published.

66. See appendix 1 for my assessment of possible differences between the new ISIME translations and Volpato's work.

67. *Le lettere di S. Caterina da Siena, ridotte a miglior lezione*, ed. Niccolò Tommaseo, 4 vols. (Florence: Barbera, 1860).

68. The new edition of the Istituto italiano per il medio evo (ISIME) has new numbering for the letters, indicated by IS. See appendix 2 for the IS numbers of letters in this volume.

69. In Noffke's translation and in scholarship on Catherine's letters, "G" next to a letter number indicates Gigli's numbering, "DT" indicates Dupré Theseider's, and "T" Tommaseo's. Since all letters in this volume use the Tommaseo numbering of the critical edition, no letters precede the numbers.

70. See her arguments in Noffke, I:xli–slvii. I have indicated the few very speculative dates in the notes for the relevant letters.

71. Volpato, author of the critical edition, has not commented on Noffke's dating. ISIME documents Noffke's dating but seems to offer their own analysis independent of her logic (see appendix 1).

Notes

72. Dates by Fawtier or Dupré Theseider that differ significantly from Volpato's will be indicated in a note.

73. Noffke refers to Dupré Theseider's unpublished notes dating 208 letters in Noffke, I:xl.

74. Biographical data for all volumes is available in appendix I, Noffke, IV:371–407.

75. *Saint Catherine of Siena as Seen in Her Letters* (London: J. M. Dent; New York: E. P. Dutton, 1905).

76. *I, Catherine: Selected Writings of Catherine of Siena* (London: Collins, 1980).

77. When Catherine means "in" she uses the Italian *nel*.

78. My translation is supported by a classical Italian literary study of Catherine's language and style, which states that *dolce* has multiple meanings. "It [*dolce*] instills an intimate and delicate note to her discourse and an effusion of motherly tenderness" (my translation), in Alvaro Bizziccari, "Linguaggio e stile delle Lettere di Caterina da Siena," *Italica* 53, no. 3 (1976): 337. Catherine also uses *dolce* in her letters with a number of connotations so that the English equivalent will vary depending on context.

79. "Paul, a servant of Jesus Christ, called to be an apostle" (Rom 1:1); "Paul and Timothy, servants of Christ Jesus" (Phil 1:1). Antonio Volpato calls attention to Paul's influence on Catherine's use of this term. See "Caterina da Siena, i suoi 'titoli' nelle Lettere e la sua missione apostolica," in *Caterina da Siena e la vita religiosa femminile: un percorso domenicano*, ed. Pierantonio Piatti (Rome: Campisano, 2016), 114.

80. "Caterina, i suoi 'titoli.'"

81. Major medieval literature scholars have given other interpretations to the phrase "in his precious blood," such as calling it Catherine's ink. I believe these readings are based on literary interpretations that do not sufficiently weigh Catherine's beliefs and her theology or are meant to be literary metaphors. See for instance Tylus, "Mystical Literacy," 169.

82. Bizziccari, "Linguaggio e stile," 328 (my translation).

83. This is a summary of Catherine's spirituality and does not seek to thematize her theology. For Catherine's theology see Suzanne Noffke's two-volume anthology of passages from Catherine's works; these are organized according to various topics, including theological themes. See *Catherine of Siena: An Anthology*, 2 vols., Medieval and Renaissance Texts and Studies (Tempe: Arizona Center for Medieval and Renaissance Studies, 2011–2012). Giuliana Cavallini, editor of the critical edition of *The Prayers and The Dialogue*, addresses some themes of Catherine's theology in *Catherine of Siena* (London: Chapman, 1998), 34–51, 67–108.

84. Bernard McGinn summarizes this anthropology in "The Human Person as Image of God: II Western Christianity," in *Christian Spirituality: Origins to the Twelfth Century*, ed. Bernard McGinn, John Meyendorff, and Jean Leclercq (New York: Crossroad, 2000); he tells us, "There can be no argument that the 12th century was fascinated with the mystery of the human person as *imago Dei* and brought to the study of this mystery a systematic ordering mentality not seen before....The great mystical theologies...were rooted in anthropology," 323.

85. I have also discussed central themes of Catherine's wisdom on the spiritual journey in Diana L. Villegas, "Catherine of Siena's Wisdom on Discernment and Her Reception of Scripture," *Acta Theologica* 32, no. 2S (2013), https://doi.org/10.38140/at.v0i17.2580 and in "Continuous Prayer in Catherine of Siena," *HTS Teologiese Studies/Theological Studies* 73, no. 3 (2017), https://doi.org/ 10.4102/hts.v73i3.4611.

86. Thomas McDermott thematizes Catherine's spirituality of knowledge of self and God in "Catherine of Siena's Teaching on Self-Knowledge," *New Blackfriars* 88, no. 1018 (2007): 637–48, https://doi.org/10.1111/j.1741-2005.2006.00130.x.

87. Catherine's language about sin also reflects medieval spirituality regarding sinfulness.

88. A systematic, contemporary version of this anthropology, namely, that God's love is the ground of being, can be found in Karl Rahner, *Foundations of Christian Faith* (New York: Seabury, 1978), 31–35, 51–61, 75–81, 116–33.

89. The soul is our core transcendent self; *affetto* of the soul in this case is God's love dwelling within us united to our own deepest movement of love.

90. *Dialogue* 1:25.

91. For a more detailed presentation see Villegas, "Continuous Prayer in Catherine of Siena"; and https://catherineofsiena-spirituality.org/time-in-cell-knowledge-of-god-and-knowledge-of-self/, accessed August 2023.

92. The concept of *affetto* in the history of spirituality was most developed by the Cistercians in the twelfth century. The classic article on this concept is Antoine Guillomont, Louis Cognet, and Jean Chatillon, "Cor et Cordis Affectus," in *Dictionnaire de spiritualité* (Paris: Beauchesne, 1953), 2278–2308. See also *affetto* in Notes on Translation.

93. *Confessions*, I:1.

94. Augustine of Hippo classically said, "Hence, this trinity of the mind [*mens*] is not on that account the image of God because the mind remembers itself, understands itself, and loves itself, but because it can also remember, understand, and love Him by whom it was made." *On the Trinity: Books 8–15*, ed. Gareth B. Matthews, trans. Stephen McKenna, *Augustine on the Trinity* (Cambridge: Cambridge University Press, 2002), 14:12.15.

Notes

95. *Dialogue* 4:32.

96. For an interpretation of Catherine's wisdom in the key of Aquinas's moral theology, see Grazia Mangano Ragazzi, *Obeying the Truth: Discretion in the Spiritual Writings of Saint Catherine of Siena* (Oxford: Oxford University Press, 2014).

97. See, for instance, McDermott, *Catherine: Spiritual Development*, and Cavallini, *Catherine of Siena*, 22–33.

98. See the final argument of Raymond of Capua's hagiography urging Catherine's canonization. (*Life*, 359. Reference is to numbered sections rather than page number).

99. *Dialogue* 1, my translation, my highlight.

100. We must remember that Catherine's views and language reflect her intuitive wisdom and not a systematic or philosophical point of view about truth.

101. See Villegas, "Continuous Prayer in Catherine of Siena," 7.

102. *Summa Theologiae*, II–II, q. 104, ad. 5.

103. See also the discussion in the introduction to Letter 213, and Diana L. Villegas, "Discernment in Catherine of Siena," *Theological Studies* 58, no. 1 (1997); Villegas, "The Spirituality of Catherine of Siena," https://catherineofsiena-spirituality.org/discernment/, accessed October 2023.

1. NUNS

1. Following the Old Testament understanding of blood as symbolic of life, so a life was sacrificed when all blood was shed.

2. Memory, one of the three powers of the soul. Catherine exhorts Costanza to hold in her consciousness Jesus's giving of self (the blood).

3. Grounded in consciousness of God's love evidenced in Jesus's giving of his life for us.

4. "The place" is God, source of all and at the same time the space of consciousness where we encounter God. "Wall" refers to the body of Christ as container/structure that enfolds God and holds the blood, which is also the fluid of grace. The metaphor of Christ as wall is clearer in Letter 318, "His [Christ's] humanity was a wall that held within it the eternal Godhead that was united to his humanity. He spilled the fire of divine charity through the open wall of Christ crucified." See also Noffke, I:304.

5. Although in difficult, convoluted metaphors this paragraph communicates Catherine's mystical understanding of the union of God and Christ and how this mystery manifests itself for a person's transformation.

6. When Catherine says, *which is within you, cell*, she is addressing Costanza as cell, that is as dwelling where God is present. We "are cell," because

God dwells within us and, therefore, have a capacity to connect to God, who both holds us in being and is present to us through the Spirit.

7. Catherine uses the word *fatten* as a metaphor that indicates nourishing and feeding to foster growth; she is probably thinking of fattening an animal (something with which she would be familiar given her father's wool business and the raising of sheep in the area around Siena).

8. This is not a philosophical or theological position; it is a metaphor to express Catherine's intuitive experience of all that is encompassed in the will.

9. My interpretation of this metaphor is that through our virtuous, ordered acts we participate in God's love, this would be the glory; the fruit would be the good effect in human life of our virtuous acts.

10. "She" now refers to the soul or person.

11. That is, being able to eat one's fill without physical distress, a metaphor probably related to Catherine's own experience with difficulties keeping down food.

12. The implied meaning is something akin to: "don't slip back into self-centeredness or lack of virtue or to living your life in such a way that you do not remain constantly connected to God's love."

13. See "continuous prayer" in the general introduction.

14. *Affetto* of the soul: in this case the motivation that emerges from the core of self where God's love dwells.

15. God's love desiring that we respond to that love becomes "food" when one connects intentionally in prayer to this reality.

16. From the context Catherine is referring to an ecstatic experience of God, where spiritual consciousness is disconnected from bodily consciousness; however, she may be referring to life after death.

17. Part of memory, understanding, and will.

18. Referring to the fact that animals eat on the ground (like sheep) and not up high on the tree of the cross. Also, animals were not capable of reason and of conscious connection to God's love.

19. *Margarita*, medieval Italian for luminous star, bright light.

20. *Particular friendships* is a term used in religious life—mostly in the past—to refer to exclusive relationships seen as disruptive to life in community.

21. In contemplative orders visiting rooms were separated by a wall. On one side was the cloister, on the other the public space. There was a grated opening in this wall (the grille) through which the contemplative nun could visit while remaining in the cloister.

22. A hedgehog curls up into a ball for protection, so the metaphor suggests being wary and ready to protect oneself.

23. Love of God emerging from the depth of self where God's love for us dwells and draws out our capacity to love God.

Notes

24. Mental prayer is related to but not equivalent to continuous prayer. The former is a contemplative prayer, where the person is wordlessly absorbed in God; continuous prayer is the capacity to be easily conscious of God's presence throughout the day. By "mother of prayer" Catherine usually means continuous prayer, because it "gives birth to" the capacity to connect to God's presence. However, in this letter, unusually, both contemplative and continuous prayer are labelled "mother."

25. Here "angelic food" is our desire for God unlike at the beginning of the letter where it is God's desire for us.

26. Christ's breast.

27. "She" throughout this paragraph refers to the metaphor, "mother love." This is the love offered by God through Jesus as milk-bearing mother.

28. Referring to those who waste time chitchatting about superficially pious topics.

29. Catherine's spirituality of obedience as a virtue is rooted in her interpretation of Jesus's obedience to the Father that led to our salvation.

30. Referring to the virtue of discernment. See Letters 213 and 358.

31. Fear of the reactions of others.

2. *MANTELLATE* AND CLOSE LAY MALE DISCIPLES

1. Italics indicate Catherine shifts from addressing the correspondent to addressing God.

2. *Continua memoria*, literally "continuous memory," refers to memory as one of the three powers of the soul and is a dimension of continuous prayer. See next note.

3. "Here" seems to refer to placing oneself at the foot of the cross in prayer and to a state of continuous conscious attention to God's presence, especially as Christ on the cross. On continuous prayer see general introduction and Letters 26 and 154.

4. Understanding, one of the three powers of the soul.

5. Christ's life poured out for our salvation.

6. "Eating souls" refers to prayer and work for the salvation of others.

7. Literally "what I can't do visibly, I do invisibly."

8. Catherine was addressed as "mamma" by her disciples.

9. *Misera, miserabile*, a rhetorical expression of humility.

10. She means she will offer penance and prayer to atone for Neri's sins; atoning for sins was an ascetical practice in imitation of Jesus's atoning for our sins.

11. Through Christ we are saved making us ready to enter into eternal life, so he is the wedding garment making us apt for the celebration of our ultimate union with God.

12. This most likely refers to Catherine's expectation that she and some of the *mantellate* could join the crusade. For more on Catherine's crusade spirituality, see Letter 256.

13. One of Catherine's titles for the pope.

14. Volpato notes the ambassador was not primarily concerned with issues of the crusade as Catherine was made to believe. Letter 132n22.

15. Noffke notes that there is a question as to whether Nera was the prioress at this time (Noffke, II:443n2). The significance of this letter from the point of view of Catherine's spirituality is the way she writes to the leader of her penitent group, someone undoubtedly significantly older than she is; therefore, the precise identity of the prioress is not as relevant.

16. Though writing to her prioress, Catherine uses the example of a male superior, thus the masculine pronouns.

17. One of the three powers of the soul.

18. The church.

19. In other words, don't seek to avoid suffering.

20. It is unclear to what extent Catherine believed this and to what extent it was part of her rhetoric.

21. With "blood" here meaning the sacraments, Catherine is referring to the papal interdicts against the offering of the sacraments; these interdicts were used to punish cities that would not yield to the Papal League.

22. Equivalent to "cell."

23. The identity of this woman is unclear.

24. Reference to Matt 12:43–45.

25. Hold in memory, the power of the soul.

26. Rhetorical expressions of humility.

27. Catherine's teaching here and elsewhere in this letter follows her wisdom on the virtue of discretion, that is, living according to the right ordered measure, a fruit of transformation. See Letters 213 and 358.

28. The bedroom of a nun or monk.

29. Literally, glory, meaning a blessing or gift.

30. Latin words for "my fault," part of the act of contrition of the Mass.

31. See discussion in the general introduction.

32. See also Letter 358. Summaries of Catherine's teaching on discernment are found in Diana L. Villegas, "Discernment in Catherine of Siena," *Theological Studies* 58, no. 1 (1997); Diana L. Villegas, "The Spirituality of Catherine of Siena," https://catherineofsiena-spirituality.org/discernment/.

33. *Affetto dell'anima* literally means affection of the soul.

Notes

34. The branches are well-ordered behavior toward God, self, and others.

35. Servile fear is fear of the reactions of others.

36. Catherine ministered to many members of the nobility, so it is not surprising that she applies her wisdom about the fruit of discernment to their life situation.

37. Catherine shifts within the same sentence from the metaphor of picking fruit to that of fishing, namely, throwing out a hook to "catch" persons for God.

38. Continuous prayer is a multifaceted concept in Catherine. Most essentially it is a way of being in life where the person has reached such transformation and closeness to God that her consciousness easily and frequently connects to the presence of God within her. See general introduction, "continuous prayer."

39. The discipline and hairshirt were common medieval instruments of penance, and such physical penance a common form of spiritual practice. See discussion of penitent spirituality, general introduction.

40. Literally, "killing."

41. The change in subject from the person, "she," to the direct address, "you" reflects Catherine's rhetorical shifts during dictation.

42. God's mercy and the cross are made one with the image of opening one's arms *on* God's mercy.

43. Continuous desire is longing for God's love and what is ordered in God's love; this grows as God's light shines upon our inner self, leading us to recognize and experience the immensity of God's boundless love in Christ's giving of his life for us.

44. Christ's love revealed in his giving his life—all his blood—for us.

45. Christ's love is both fire and blood.

46. About discernment as ordered love.

47. The three powers of the soul.

3. FRIARS AND MONKS

1. The "Caterina" here is one of two other *mantellate* with this name. Catherine sends Tommaso greetings from herself and several *mantellate* under his direction.

2. This is a nonsacramental confession to Tommaso, who was away.

3. Catherine literally says, "united and transformed into God." This is not a theological statement but one of her rhetorical flourishes to emphasize her point.

4. "Young man" and "father" both refer to Christ. See Letter 41n11.

5. See general introduction "knowledge of God and self."

6. One of the powers of the soul.

7. Memory and understanding, of the three powers of the soul.

8. Though the reference is unclear, it probably refers to the love of Christ. For instance, in Letter 86 Christ is a mother who has breasts through which we receive the milk of love.

9. Meaning members of Saint Agnes's religious order.

10. The last sentence, "l'altra (cagione) si è quando altri si fusse abbattuto in luogo che fusse cagione di riduciarsi a se medessimo" is translated quite differently by Noffke (into English) and by Salvador (into Spanish). My translation of this puzzling sentence is yet different from theirs, as I interpret and translate it based on the nature of Catherine's relationship with Tommaso.

11. According to Volpato, Giovanna was most likely Giovanna di Capo, one of Catherine's early scribes, who would have added the last sentence requesting prayers for herself and the epithet applied to her "pazza," crazy. The reason for this epithet is unclear (Letter 41n29, Noffke, I:10n24).

12. Form of signature that is found in only a few early letters (Letter 41n30).

13. Form of address used for priests; rarely used by Catherine.

14. The Dominican friars of Catherine's parish, San Domenico, Siena and their superior at the time, most likely Tommaso dalla Fonte.

15. Catherine uses the word *fattens* as a metaphor that indicates nourishing and feeding to foster healthy, solid growth, as when referring to fattening an animal (something with which she would be familiar given her father's wool business and the raising of sheep in the area around Siena).

16. Most likely Catherine refers to an inner revelation (Letter 127n18).

17. The comparison between humans and animals and the use of the donkey as the animal with which the comparison is made was not uncommon to some medieval authors, including Aquinas (Letter 127n21).

18. One of Catherine's titles for God.

19. Volpato asserts that this refers to Catherine's inner revelation rather than to the Scripture passage (Letter 127n23).

20. Metaphor for the side of Christ.

21. Referring to Birgitta of Sweden and her spiritual guide.

22. Catherine considered the crusade a pilgrimage during which one might have the great grace to die as a martyr. She wanted to go on this pilgrimage herself and desired this "grace" for her followers. It is unclear here how these permissions were related to her and her disciples.

23. "Blessed brigade" (*bella brigata*) was the term Catherine used for her "family"—she and her closest followers—when referring to joining the crusade.

Notes

24. Noffke believes the appellation "Martha" refers to Catherine herself Noffke (I:41n19). I agree with Volpato (Letter 127n41) that this is a reference to one of the other Catherines who were part of the "family."

25. Spelling of Tommaso in critical text.

26. Form of address used for priests (Letter 146n1); rarely used by Catherine.

27. In *The Dialogue* (72:134–135) Catherine teaches about the stages of growth in love. An advanced stage involves the capacity to look with love into the heart of the bestower of love.

28. Another reference to the dynamics of the three powers of the soul, memory, understanding, and will. See general introduction.

29. Cecca, a *mantellata*, is the scribe who inserts her voice sending her greetings to Bartolomeo. Describing herself as "plain" is part of the rhetoric of humility congruent with the culture.

30. Rare example of a signed letter.

31. *Camposanto* [contemporary Italian] means cemetery. The critical text spells the word *Campo santo*.

32. Catherine is urging these hermits to join the crusade as an opportunity for martyrdom.

33. Referring to giving up one's life for Christ, becoming martyrs.

34. Referring to St. Lawrence, martyred by fire.

35. Anger against injustice. Catherine uses the word hatred, here meaning anger.

36. *Facessero vendetta*, to seek punishment. That the animals should do so is a metaphor to highlight just how thorough is the need for justice.

37. Punishment for one's sins.

38. Referring to the three powers of the soul.

39. Reference to going on crusade risking one's life for the salvation of the unbelievers.

40. The metaphor of the cross as table.

41. On the cross.

42. Metaphor for nourishing ourselves on the blood (life) of Christ in a continuous fashion, as sheep continuously graze.

43. Noffke names several novices and believes they were at the monastery near Bologna. However, the critical text chooses the earliest rubric of address, which simply mentions the name of the religious order, no location. See Noffke, II:125.

44. *Summa Theologiae*, II–II, q.104, a.5. See Noffke, II:129n30.

45. Literally "obedience." A term used in religious life to designate a task that must, in obedience, be accomplished.

46. "I have eagerly desired to eat this Passover with you before I suffer." (Luke 22:15; NRSV).

47. Referring to the metaphorical wall made of stones mortared with a mixture that includes Jesus's blood.

48. Lode and channel are mining metaphors, that is, the source of the metal and the channel through which it is mined.

49. This was an Augustinian order of hermits, not the Augustinian canon regulars.

50. The eye of understanding, where the latter is one of the powers of the soul.

51. Here *affetto* means both the will—of the three powers of the soul—and the depth of affective motivation that emerges from the core of self; that is, *affetto* becomes alive to consciousness and effective in powering the person's capacity to choose.

52. Changes in pronoun reflect changes in the subject from soul, feminine, to the male correspondent.

53. Work for the salvation of others.

54. Rural area near Siena where there was a monastery of Augustinian hermits (different from the better-known Augustinian canons). Today it houses Augustinian nuns.

55. For an analysis of Catherine's discernment of God's will when it contradicted that of persons such as William and Raymond, see Diana L. Villegas, "Examining Catherine of Siena's Controversial Discernments about Papal Politics," *HTS Teologiese Studies/Theological Studies* 77, no. 2 (2021). https://doi.org/10.4102/hts.v77i2.6654.

56. Referring to the servants waiting in vigil for their master (Luke 12:35–40).

57. See Noffke's discussion (III:270) about the possible identity of the abbot and of Pietro, the monk.

58. In this paragraph and the next, love (charity) is personified.

59. Literally, a daisy (*margarita* or *margherita*), which in medieval Italian was also a luminous celestial event.

60. Light is God's love as power of the Spirit dwelling in the person and guiding her.

61. *Odio verso se medesima*, literally self-hatred, but meaning hatred for selfish self-love.

62. The ransom theology of redemption was common in Catherine's medieval Italy.

63. Catherine sometimes multiplied the appellations of Jesus; while they sound awkward in English, I translate these literally because they reflect

Notes

Catherine's love of Jesus and her sense of intimacy with him as it is spontaneously expressed in her dictation.

64. That is, accepting troubles and suffering.

65. *Affetto* here is also personified.

66. By "doctrine of truth" Catherine does not mean a set of precepts, but rather the way of God's love when it means the truth from God's perspective about life and relationships.

67. Critical text spelling; current spelling is Tebaldi, a surname and town.

68. Fawtier and Dupré Theseider both date this letter between late 1378 and the end of 1379.

69. Catherine makes a distinction between the path of religious life with vows of poverty, chastity, and obedience and the perfection to which all the baptized are called.

70. "She," the soul, feminine in Italian; "he" is the correspondent.

71. Reason is feminine in Italian.

72. One of the powers of the soul.

73. The fire of divine love mentioned at the beginning of the paragraph.

74. In *The Dialogue* there is a section on levels of tears indicating the level of transformation of love and *affetto*. *Dialogue* 88–94:161–74.

75. Continuous prayer is a multifaceted concept in Catherine. It is form of consciousness, where the reality of God is never far from consciousness, and a way of living according to God's will. See general introduction.

76. *Affetto* of God is God's love toward us, and in this case the person's *affetto* is the person's movement of love toward God arising from her core.

77. Connection to inner consciousness and the presence of God experienced there.

78. Catherine speaks of different levels of love depending on the transformation of the person. There is mercenary love, love of faithful servant, love of friend, and finally filial love. While reference to one or another of these forms of love appear in many letters, her complete, ordered presentation of progression in forms of love is in the section on the steps of Christ's body and Christ as Bridge in *Dialogue* 60–79:113–46.

79. Power of the soul.

80. Time in which to do God's will. This meaning culled from Catherine's wisdom about time in other letters.

81. Rhetorical expressions of humility.

82. Catherine's closest followers, whom she called her family.

83. See general introduction, "political engagement and letter writing" for more details about Raymond.

84. The title "master" indicated he was a graduate in theology and could teach at a university.

85. Expression used in fourteenth-century Tuscany. Literally, "bad-pocket," alluding to the devil "pocketing" someone.

86. Referring to better times for the church.

87. The merchants are church leaders and pastors leading disordered lives.

88. John the Baptist, unique in closeness to Jesus.

89. All her followers.

90. Those with God in heaven.

91. From the *Exsultet* proclamation at the Easter liturgy proclaiming the "happy fault of Adam."

92. The church.

93. Referring to the renewal of the church and her pastors and leaders rather than any personal future.

94. The pope.

95. Rhetorical expression of humility.

96. See the account of Gardner, *Saint Catherine of Siena: A Study in the Religion, Literature, and History of the Fourteenth Century in Italy* (New York: E. P. Dutton, 1907), 223–27. This classic work remains a source of details regarding Catherine's political engagement.

97. See a discussion of this aspect of Catherine's discernment in Villegas, "Examining Catherine of Siena's Controversial Discernments about Papal Politics," 4–5.

98. Catherine is referring to herself.

99. Referring to prayer that emerges from the core of the person.

100. The rebellious city-states.

101. In this paragraph Catherine suddenly starts addressing Gregory XI directly, then halfway through turns to the plural pronoun. It is unclear if this was intended rhetoric (my assumption) or part of the inconsistencies in a dictated text.

102. Referring to Rome, to which Gregory XI had returned from Avignon.

103. This is a reference to the crusade. Catherine believed the pope should stop warring with others in Europe and instead dedicate his resources to reconquering and protecting the Holy Sepulcher through a crusade.

104. In this paragraph Catherine again returns to addressing the pope directly, perhaps expecting Raymond to read these messages to Gregory.

105. She seems to suggest she is considering going to Rome.

106. While some early scholars questioned the authenticity of this postscript, contemporary scholars consider it authentic. See Noffke, II:505n51. See

Notes

F. Thomas Luongo's discussion of this postscript in *The Saintly Politics of Catherine of Siena* (Ithaca, NY: Cornell University, 2006), 193–96.

107. Tears of consolation.

108. Rhetorical expression of humility.

109. Catherine refers to a vision of Aquinas and John the Evangelist modeling for her how to write.

110. Usually she addresses Raymond as "friar" though here she uses the title *maestro*, master, for someone with a degree that entitles him to teach at a university.

111. The martyrs, whom she envied, for she saw martyrdom as the ideal in terms of giving one's life in imitation of Jesus, for the good of God's people and the church.

112. Referring to the relative isolation of Urban VI.

113. The troubling spiritual experiences which she then relates.

114. The liturgical feast of January first on the liturgical calendar of the time.

115. One of the Sundays before Lent prior to the changes made after Vatican Council II.

116. Most likely the three cardinals that remained ambivalent about supporting Clement VII.

117. Young Florentine layman who became one of Catherine's disciples and scribes and one of the "family." He became an editor of one of the extant manuscripts that includes *The Dialogue* and some of Catherine's letters.

118. Understanding, memory, desire (will), the three powers of the soul.

119. Catherine's closest followers, some of whom lived in the same house with her in Rome.

120. Raymond.

121. Catherine's way of expressing humility, where she faulted herself in situations in which she was not likely to be at fault.

122. Concern for the salvation of people and for the good of the church.

123. Terce and vespers are hours of the Liturgy of the Hours or Divine Office.

124. Catherine identifies with a depiction of St. Peter in the boat with Jesus.

125. Refers to Urban VI's political situation.

126. Referring to previous mystical experience of God holding her in an encircling embrace to give her support and strength.

127. If God should choose to take her to heaven.

128. Another term for the inner cell. See general introduction, "cell of self-knowledge."

129. The Master is Giovanni Tantucci, an Augustinian hermit and disciple of Catherine. Bartolomeo Dominici and Tommaso dalla Fonte are the Dominican friars members of her "family."

130. Tommaso Petra is a notary who worked at the papal court and was a disciple of Catherine's who also advised her.

4. ECCLESIASTICAL AUTHORITIES

1. The popes resided in Avignon, France, from 1307 to 1377.

2. See Diana L. Villegas, "Catherine of Siena's Spirituality of Political Engagement," *HTS Teologiese Studies/Theological Studies* 77, no. 2 a6319 (2021): 3, https://doi.org/10.4102/hts.v77i2.6319.

3. While Catherine has been credited with persuading Gregory XI to start a crusade, this is not the case, as he wanted a crusade even before being consecrated pope. Catherine did, however, believe very strongly in the importance of the crusade for the good of the church. See Villegas, "Catherine of Siena's Spirituality of Political Engagement," 2–4.

4. The preferred medieval cure.

5. Love includes aversion for all that is not of love. The knife is a metaphor for the radical manner in which selfish self-love must be excised.

6. *Prelate* refers to bishops or archbishops.

7. Allusion to the pope and his spiritual isolation [from Catherine's perspective].

8. They cannot bear life-giving fruit.

9. The Italian is *rappiastrare*, applying, in this case, a salve; this relates to the metaphor that follows about applying medication to sores.

10. *Babbo*, term of endearment, daddy, papa.

11. Referring to the preceding metaphor, "wound."

12. Bishops and other ecclesiastical authorities under the leadership of the pope.

13. To cauterize and cut out the sores, that is, the misbehaving pastors.

14. Allusion to the Papal League's loss of authority among the Italian city-states.

15. The Tuscan city-states that refused allegiance to the Papal States.

16. The crusade.

17. Raising the standard of the cross here refers to starting the crusade as knights carried standards representing Christianity.

18. Piero Gambacorta, leader of Pisa who advocated in favor of the pope.

19. Fear of God as in the Old Testament, meaning "with respect" for God; e.g., Gen 20:11; also used by Paul (Rom 3:18).

20. See introduction to Letter 181.

Notes

21. Corneto, now Tarquinia, is the port where Gregory XI arrived on his return to Rome from Avignon.

22. On virtue tested and strengthened by its opposite, see *Dialogue*, 8:38–39.

23. Fear of what others will do or say.

24. The children are the citizens of the city-state of Siena, which had joined Florence, also an independent city-state, in an alliance against the Papal States. Catherine had considered this a sinful disloyalty to the pope and advocated against it. Now she wants the pope to entice Siena to ask for his forgiveness.

25. She is urging the pope not to delay at Corneto but to move quickly to Rome.

26. Annotation at the end of the letter.

27. In this letter truth does not refer to a set of beliefs or doctrines but to the reality of God's unfathomable love that illuminates human beings. Thus, sometimes in this letter truth is personified, meaning God; in these cases, I capitalize truth.

28. One of three powers of the soul.

29. The cardinals rebelling against Urban VI.

30. The plan to elect another pope, who was in fact elected on December 21st, three days after this letter was written. This election of Clement VII was the beginning of the Schism.

31. The curial cardinals.

32. Charging for sacraments performed.

33. *Barattarie*, the word used by Catherine, referred in medieval times to a betting booth set up in the public square.

34. Catherine's word is *margarita* or daisy, which is a medieval Tuscan word with a number of meanings, among them "a bright star."

35. Cardinals of the curia.

36. Members of religious orders and others who are faithful advisors, like Catherine herself.

37. Catherine is saying that Urban VI needs the light of God's love to illuminate his heart and mind so that he is able to discern who is behaving in a virtuous manner and who in a disordered manner and, in this way, to know how to deal with each.

38. Spelling in critical edition.

39. A protonotary was an official who compiled and registered documents in the courts of royalty, of the nobility, and of the papal court.

40. See general introduction, "Political Engagement and Letter Writing."

41. Translation based on Letter 181n13.

42. Referring to blood as the liquid used to prepare the mortar that holds the stones of the building together.
43. The three powers of the soul.
44. Raising the standard of the cross refers to calling forth a crusade.
45. Protests and rebellions in Rome against the papacy (Letter 181n52).
46. Pilgrimage to the Holy Land or the crusade.
47. Raymond would have made this recommendation to Catherine. Friar Stefano had been controversial among Dominicans due to the severity of his local reforms and application of the rules. He was not elected Master General (Letter 181n66).
48. The papal curia or court of Urban V, then in Rome.
49. *Prelate* here means a cardinal or bishop whose name is purposefully left out due to the charges Catherine implies against him (Volpato, Letter 16n1).
50. Metaphor referring to John 4:34, where Jesus says, "my food is to do the will of him who sent me." Catherine is suggesting that this high church official should desire (i.e., hunger for) the spiritual well-being of his fellow human beings and those under his care.
51. Catherine refers to herself in the third person.
52. Here desire is infinite love; thus, Jesus suffered from seeing how far removed human persons were from their potential holiness. It is the suffering of seeing a person one loves fall short of their potential.
53. NRSV: "I have eagerly desired to eat this Passover."
54. Humanity would be saved through the cross.
55. The church.
56. Referring to the advice she is offering in this letter.
57. Noffke interprets this as a reference to the coming of spring (II:113), while Volpato (Letter 16n48) points out that Catherine has used the metaphor of a flower opening to refer to the beginning of the crusade; I concur with Volpato's interpretation.
58. Starting the crusade.
59. Dupré Theseider dates the letter in January of 1377. Noffke's arguments for her dating seem most reliable and credible to me. See Noffke, II:260–61.
60. An official who has a diplomatic leadership position representing the pope and Papal States.
61. There is an untranslatable play of words here. Bond is "legame" and to be bound is "legato," so she wants Pietro, the Legato of the pope, to be *legato* (bound) with the *legame* (bond) of love.
62. The cross (feminine in Italian) is here personalized by Catherine.
63. Most likely a reference to the Rule of Benedict since the cardinal was a Benedictine.

Notes

64. "It" is selfish self-love which Catherine personalizes.
65. That is, going on crusade.

5. CIVIL AUTHORITIES

1. The name usually appears as Gambacorta but is Gambacorti in the critical text.
2. This metaphor, used in *The Dialogue* as well, points to the fact that *affetto* is that which moves the whole person forward, toward a goal (*Dialogue* 63:118). In *The Dialogue* the feet are at times equal to *affetto* (*Dialogue* 26:64).
3. Referring to the virtue of discernment. See introduction to Letter 213.
4. Women in his family, especially Gambacorta's daughter Tora, who eventually became one of Catherine's disciples and a Dominican nun.
5. Rhetorical expression of humility.
6. Some of her followers were opposed to her trip (Letter 149n27). At times in Siena there was negative gossip about a single young woman travelling as did Catherine.
7. The women in Gambacorta's family.
8. Spelling in critical text; this name is usually spelled with two *c*'s.
9. Refers to money-lending practices where it was said time made money as interest accrued.
10. That is, the person will honor the Father when he joins God in heaven after death. This is an unusual application of the parable of the return of the prodigal son and is an example of one of Catherine's spontaneous metaphors.
11. Catherine at times referred to the crusade as a wedding feast, that is, a celebration from multiple perspectives. Knights would be on a pilgrimage that involved prayer and asceticism rather than fighting one another and some could become martyrs; the unbelievers would be converted; the Holy Land would be returned to the church.
12. Willingness to be a martyr.
13. Noffke, IV:540.
14. This reference to circumcision is likely based on an Old Testament story (Gen 34:1–26) used in medieval sermons (Letter 143n5). Catherine's adaptation is an example of her appropriation of content from sermons to create her metaphors.
15. Referring to the custom in Jesus's day of sacrificing a lamb or calf to celebrate a wedding.
16. Medieval image, see Letter 143n10.
17. Catherine had in mind the crusade. See also Letter 143n19.
18. Giving blood for blood refers to seeking martyrdom in the crusade pilgrimage.

19. This family title was, by Catherine's time, an "empty honorific." Thomas F. Luongo, *The Saintly Politics of Catherine of Siena* (Ithaca, NY: Cornell University, 2006), 88n85.

20. Rhetorical expression of humility.

21. The eye of understanding or understanding, one of the three powers of the soul.

22. Rendering that which is due to God, neighbor, and self is fruit of the virtue of discernment, a virtue that is an outcome of love. See Letters 213 and 358.

23. The virtues, faith, hope, charity, humility, and fortitude, temperance, prudence, and justice were common themes of medieval spirituality.

24. Catherine teaches that requests that are mere words and are not seasoned with heartfelt love are ineffective.

25. Mercy is a response to repentance from the depth of one's being; words of repentance that are not filled with heartfelt conviction do not elicit mercy.

26. Catherine could be referring to Prov 26:11 or 2 Pet 2:22, or both.

27. "And indeed, your heavenly Father knows that you need all these things. But strive first for the Kingdom of God and his righteousness, and all these things will be given to you as well. So do not worry about tomorrow, for tomorrow will bring worries of its own. Today's trouble is enough for today" (NRSV, Matt 6:32b–34).

28. Reason as a key part of "understanding," one of the powers of the soul.

29. Depth of desire when fully ordered and transformed by God is that which gives direction to a person's choices and acts; it is ordered love.

30. Feeling unworthy in a false manner.

31. There is a confusing change of subject, from will to the person himself; these inconsistencies are inevitable in a dictated text. Catherine's point is that the person, having understood and affectively appreciated God's mercy and infinite love, and having seen through false humility, is able to experience contrition as she receives communion.

32. What follows is a convoluted metaphor referring to the Exodus account about the Passover.

33. The corded belt worn over a religious habit.

34. Referring to birth and final entry into God's presence and the fullness of God's mercy after death.

35. Accordingly, in several instances in this letter, "justice" is rendered as "right-order."

36. Metaphor for sitting in judgment in the role of judge.

Notes

37. Right-ordered behavior is a fruit of the ordering of the three powers of the soul.

38. Sexual license.

39. Sacraments mediate the blood, i.e., salvation.

40. In memory, power of the soul.

41. The critical text includes this "etc."; it is unclear to what it refers.

6. KNIGHTS, MILITARY LEADERS

1. *Della pace* (peace), title given by one of Catherine's scribes, most likely due to a peace insignia placed on his standard when he fought against foreign warriors. See Noffke, I:184n2; Letter 374n2.

2. Many knights of small locations such as San Severino were soldiers for hire, a reputable occupation. Bartolomeo was considered particularly successful.

3. Catherine had a whole spirituality of crusade that is evidenced in this letter. For a documented and detailed discussion of this, see Diana L. Villegas, "Catherine of Siena's Crusade Letters: Spirituality and Political Context," *HTS Teologiese Studies/Theological Studies* 77, no. 2 a6499 (2021), https://doi.org/10.4102/hts.v77i2.6499.

4. Since Bartolomeo is a knight and not a priest, *reverend father* is a respectful form of address.

5. Slavish fear is the motivation to please God out of fear of punishment instead of out of love. In other places this term refers to fear of the opinion and reactions of others.

6. Here adversaries are the flesh, the world, and the devil, who threaten salvation. See Letter 374n5.

7. Pronouns in this letter are masculine as the letter is addressed to a man, except when referring to the soul, feminine in Italian.

8. According to the honor of chivalry.

9. Catherine appeals to the principles of chivalry whereby a son was required to avenge the unnatural death of his father (Letter 148n24).

10. Rendering what is due to someone is language related to the virtue of discernment, which involves rendering what is ordered to God, self, and others. See Letters 213 and 358.

11. The translation of this ambiguous passage is based on manuscript notes included in the critical edition (Letter 374ns) and significantly differs from prior translations.

12. Giving one's blood in this context refers to willingness to become a martyr in pursuit of the crusade.

13. In several places Catherine compares the crusade to a wedding feast; see also Letter 144.
14. Original crusade spirituality expected the pilgrimage to have a major penitential component.
15. God IS, sin *is-not*.
16. Founded in Jerusalem in the eleventh century, this order of religious knights has changed names and canonical status over history. It still exists, since 1961 called the Knights Hospitallers of St. John of Jerusalem, now dedicated to humanitarian works and headquartered in Rome.
17. See introduction to Letter 374.
18. In contrast to humans, animals were guided by instinct and need and not by reason and reflection.
19. Angelic state referred to celibacy.
20. Mud, a condition in which animals lived. Catherine is undoubtedly thinking of farm animals, like the sheep whose wool her family dyed and sold.
21. The battle for the Holy Land and the conversion of the unbelievers.
22. Analogy to the horse of a knight.
23. Catherine mixes her metaphors, mixing biblical images of mockery such as the crown of thorns or the reed placed in Christ's hand, and spurs and gloves, parts of a knight's uniform.
24. The food of honor of God and salvation of human persons; quarry referred to booty taken in battle.
25. Allusion to memory and the three powers of the soul. Holding in consciousness the honor of God and the salvation of persons empowers action.
26. As a martyr during a crusade pilgrimage.
27. *Caporali*, literally corporals. The context indicates that the letter is meant for the leader of the company, Alberigo, and all its members, whom she addresses explicitly as knights in the letter; therefore, the translation of corporals would be misleading.
28. Catherine's absolute clarity that Urban VI was God's true representative could be questioned, offering insight into the process of discernment. See Diana L. Villegas, "Examining Catherine of Siena's Controversial Discernments about Papal Politics," *HTS Teologiese Studies/Theological Studies* 77, no. 2 (2021), https://doi.org/10.4102/hts.v77i2.6654.
29. Grace and salvation.
30. Willingness to be a martyr.
31. Earnings from the battle.
32. Referring to the cardinals who first elected Urban VI and then later advocated for and elected Clement VII.
33. The blood here represents the sacraments. The pope as head of all clergy and the church has been given authority over the distribution of the

Notes

sacraments and, therefore, sacramental grace. Since Catherine believed the sacraments were necessary for salvation, the key to the blood is also the key to salvation.

7. OTHER LAYMEN AND WOMEN

1. Spelling of Ipòlito in the critical text.
2. Fawtier dates the letter in 1375; Dupré Theseider considers it not dateable. (Noffke, II:276n2).
3. Referring to Matt 19:29, Mark 10:30.
4. Island off the coast of Pisa where a new Carthusian monastery was founded with support from Pope Gregory XI. Catherine visited this monastery and established a correspondence with its founding prior.
5. Literally, "will be the life of your soul."
6. Critical text spelling of Corrado.
7. God endowed human persons with being/existence, out of the freedom of love. He had no need or obligation to do so.
8. Based on Luke 14:26 and Matt 10:37.
9. Memory, understanding, and will, the three powers of the soul that reveal the trinitarian structure of human consciousness; so connecting to these three powers, the person connects to the image of God within. See general introduction.
10. Giovanna's husband.
11. The metaphor of progression along the stairs of Christ's body is developed in *The Dialogue* in the section, The Bridge, beginning with chap. 26 and especially in chaps. 49–64.
12. The metaphor of *affetto* as "carrying the soul" expresses in an image the more abstract formulation of *affetto* as the motivation that moves our desires, thoughts, and actions and that arises from the core of the person. Through the metaphor of the stairs, Catherine teaches about the transformation of *affetto*, that is, the ordering of such motivation according to the law of love.
13. "Full" in the sense of having eaten plenty.
14. The spelling of Matteo in the critical text.
15. Friars were required to travel with at least one known companion.
16. Most likely referring to gossip about Catherine's relationship with the Salimbeni and how that might be to the detriment of the Tolomei.
17. Spelling in critical text. Usually "dalle."
18. Location of the Sienese Salimbeni family castle just outside Siena.
19. Catherine uses the singular masculine pronoun, though her correspondents are three young men.
20. Soul, feminine in Italian.

21. Retribution (deserved punishment) is intended to radically change behavior.

22. This awkward sentence has been translated with its repetitions, as they reveal a significant emphasis Catherine intended, and which probably worked better when stated orally.

23. Literally "all bad roots."

24. This name appears as *Benedetta* in some letter collections and *Bandecca* is rendered in some texts as *Bandeçça*. The critical text has *Bandecca*.

25. See Noffke II:333, 675.

26. One of the powers of the soul.

27. While desire as moving force of the will can be united to God and move toward goodness, it can be subject to sin and thus move toward what is sinful. See discussion of the three powers of the soul in the general introduction.

28. The benefits of acting lovingly and virtuously; God desires for us such quality of life.

29. We are made by God through a free act of love and for this reason we belong to God and are part of God's creation; God does not create us out of need, for God does not have needs.

30. Our motivation and desire arising from our core is united to God, whose *affetto*/love also exists in the depth of our consciousness.

31. Allusion to Luke 9:62.

32. Suzanne Noffke and ISIME, unlike Antonio Volpato, give validity to the two (of over 50 manuscripts) that identify the recipient as Samuello da Rimine, lawyer. See Noffke II:617 and https://database.dekasisime.it/index.html#/lettera/375, accessed August 2, 2024.

33. Motivation and desire as part of the will, as that which moves the will to choose and act.

34. *Affetto* here is God's love dwelling in the person and empowering the person's deepest motivation.

35. For Catherine's teaching on discernment, see Letters 213 and 358 and the general introduction.

36. The fruit is the transformation that can take place when suffering is lived in union with God.

37. Referring to the turmoil in Rome related to the election and papacy of Urban VI.

38. Dupré Theseider considers the letter undatable; in my judgment Noffke's dating of this letter is possible but quite uncertain.

39. Not meant to be demeaning but to express the opposite of possessed by reason.

40. The rhetorical purpose of Catherine's shift in pronouns from "we" to "I" is, in this case, not discernible.

Notes

41. See introduction to Letter 307 on Catherine's belief in punishment for our sins.

42. Play on words in Italian: abandon what is earthly (worldly) and don't eat earth. In Italian soil and earth are "terra."

43. That is, in this life as opposed to in eternal life.

44. Memory here refers to the power of the soul that keeps God present in consciousness.

45. A rebellion against those supporting the Papal League occurred while Catherine was in that city. She had to move from the home of her politically involved hosts to the home of Francesco and Agnesa.

46. Using the discipline (a knotted cord) to hit oneself was a widespread medieval practice based on devotion to the passion of Christ. It was a way to intercede for others uniting oneself with the sufferings of Christ and also served to curve sinful passions. See "penitent spirituality" in the general introduction.

47. This sentence begins "E Centa, voglio," where Volpato following prior scholars has capitalized *Centa*, implying the nickname of a woman. My translation agrees with Noffke's interpretation, namely, that *centa*, which can also mean a cord used as a belt, is the more likely meaning as it fits the context. (See Noffke, III:281n5).

48. Agnesa's son.

49. Given her oral reception of Scripture, Catherine's biblical citations are not always precise. Volpato points out that the first citation is actually from Jas 1:12 and the second from 2 Tim 2:5.

50. Since temporal and spiritual suffering and temptations born in union with God's grace work onto our transformation, then metaphorically, those causing these are assisting in this process, which leads us to union with God in heaven (the crown).

51. Most likely the general indulgence common in medieval times.

52. Ellipsis in critical text. Gostanzia is the spelling here for Costanza.

8. FAMILY

1. *Apetito disordinato*, "disordered desires," is a moral category in Thomas Aquinas's *Summa Theologiae* I–II, q. 77.

2. Catherine refers to the most important (first) and ultimate (last) directives to which Jesus calls us. In *The Dialogue* (54:107–108), in the voice of Jesus speaking to Catherine, we are told that loving God above all else and our neighbors as ourselves is the beginning, middle, and end of the commandments. See also Noffke I:30n10.

3. Sienese widow, member of the nobility who accompanied Catherine on most of her journeys and served as scribe for her early letters. Three of Cecca's sons were Dominican friars.

4. Cecca's daughter who eventually joined the monastery of Montepulciano.

APPENDIX 1: ISIME CRITICAL TEXT

1. Catherine of Siena, *Epistolario I A–B*, ed. Attilio Cicchella et al., Fonti per la storia dell'Italia medievale (Rome: Istituto storico italiano per il medio evo, 2023).

2. *Epistolario I A–B*, clxii–clxiii.

3. Noffke, II.600.

4. Noffke, I.xxxvii n50.

5. *Epistolario I A–B*, 123.

BIBLIOGRAPHY

CRITICAL EDITIONS

Catherine of Siena. *Epistolario I A–B* in *Fonti per la storia dell'italia medievale*. Edited by Attilio Cicchella, Francesca de Cianni, Cristina Dusio, Diego Parisi, and Silvia Serventi. Rome: Istituto storico italiano per il medio evo, 2023.

———. *Lettere, edizione critica e commento*. Edited by Antonio Volpato. Rome: Centro internazionale di studi cateriniani, 2016. Last accessed October 2023. https://centrostudicateriniani.it/santa-caterina-da-siena/epistolario/.

OTHER EDITIONS AND TRANSLATIONS

Catherine of Siena. *Epistolario de Santa Catalina de Siena: Espíritu y doctrina*. Translated by José Salvador y Conde. 2 vols. Salamanca: San Esteban, 1982.

———. *Epistolario di Santa Caterina da Siena* in *Fonti per la storia d'Italia, Epistolari secolo XIV*. Edited by Eugenio Dupré-Theseider. Rome: Reale Istituto Storico Italiano per il medio evo, 1940.

———. *Le lettere di S. Caterina da Siena, ridotte a miglior lezione*. Edited by Niccolò Tommaseo, 4 vols. Florence: Barbera, 1860.

———. *The Letters of Catherine of Siena*. Edited and translated by Suzanne Noffke. 4 vols. Tempe, AZ: Arizona Center for Medieval and Renaissance Studies, 2000–2008.

———. *Opere della serafica Santa Caterina da Siena*. Edited by Girolamo Gigli. 4 vols. Siena, Lucca, 1707–21.

OTHER WORKS OF CATHERINE OF SIENA

Catherine of Siena. *Il Dialogo della divina provvidenza ovvero Libro della divina dottrina*. Edited by Giuliana Cavallini. Siena: Cantagalli, 1995. [*The Dialogue*, critical edition]
———. *The Dialogue*. Classics of Western Spirituality. Edited and translated by Suzanne Noffke. New York: Paulist, 1980.
———. *Obras de Santa Catalina de Siena: El Diálogo, oraciones y soliloquios*. Translated by José Salvador y Conde. Madrid: Biblioteca de Autores Cristianos (BAC), 2011. [*Dialogue and Prayers*, Spanish edition]
———. *Le orazioni*. Edited by Giuliana Cavallini. Rome: Cateriniane, 1978. [*The Prayers*, critical edition]
———. *The Prayers of Catherine of Siena*. Translated by Suzanne Noffke. San Jose, CA: Authors Choice Press, 2001. First published 1983 by Paulist Press.
———. "Santa Caterina da Siena: Opera omnia." Edited by Fausto Sbaffoni. Pistoia: Provincia Romana dei Frati Predicatori, 2002. CD-ROM. Includes Antonio Volpato's critical edition of the Letters as well as Giuiliana Cavallini's critical edition of *The Dialogue* and *The Prayers*.

LIFE OF CATHERINE OF SIENA

Brophy, Donald. *Catherine of Siena: A Passionate Life*. New York: BlueBridge, 2010.
"The *Miracoli* of Catherine of Siena." In Maiju Lehmijoki-Gardner, ed., *Dominican Penitent Women*, 65–89. Mahwah, NJ: Paulist, 2005.
Raymond of Capua. *Legenda maior*. Edited by Silvia Nocentini. Florence: SISMEL-Edizioni del Galluzzo, 2013. [critical edition of the original Latin]
———. *The Life of Catherine of Siena*. Translated by Conleth Kearns. Wilmington, DE: Glazier, 1980.

GENERAL BIBLIOGRAPHY

Augustine of Hippo. *On the Trinity: Books 8–15*. Translated by Stephen McKenna. Cambridge: Cambridge University Press, 2002.
Barone, Giulia. "Caterina o la liberazione della parola." Chap. 1 in *Caterina da Siena e la vita religiosa femminile: Un percorso domenicano*, edited by Pierantonio Piatti. Rome: Campisano, 2020.

Bibliography

Bizziccari, Alvaro. "Linguaggio e stile delle Lettere di Caterina da Siena." *Italica* 53, no. 3 (1976): 320–46.

Cavallini, Giuliana. *Catherine of Siena*. London: Chapman, 1998.

Fawtier, Robert. *Sainte Catherine de Sienne: Essai de critique des sources II, Les oeuvres de Sainte Catherine de Sienne*. Paris: De Boccard, 1930.

Foster, Kenelm, and Mary John Ronayne. *I, Catherine: Selected Writings of Catherine of Siena*. London: Collins, 1980.

Gardner, Edmund G. *Saint Catherine of Siena: A Study in the Religion, Literature, and History of the Fourteenth Century in Italy*. New York: E. P. Dutton & Co., 1907.

Gill, Katherine. "Women and the Production of Religious Literature in the Vernacular, 1300–1500." Chap. 4 in *Creative Women in Medieval and Early Modern Italy*, edited by E. Ann Matter and John W. Coakley. Philadelphia: University of Pennsylvania Press, 2016.

Groag Bell, Susan. "Medieval Women Book Owners: Arbiters of Lay Piety and Ambassadors of Culture." *Signs* 7, no. 4 (1982): 742–68.

Guillomont, Antoine, Louis Cognet, and Jean Chatillon. "Cor et Cordis Affectus." In *Dictionnaire de spiritualité*, 2278–2308. Paris: Beauchesne, 1953.

King-Lenzmeier, Ann. *Hildegard of Bingen: An Integrated Vision*. Collegeville, MN: Liturgical, 2001.

Lehmijoki-Gardner, Maiju, ed. *Dominican Penitent Women*, Classics of Western Spirituality. Mahwah, NJ: Paulist Press, 2005.

Luongo, F. Thomas. "Catherine of Siena, Auctor." In *Women Intellectuals and Leaders in the Middle Ages*, edited by Kathryn Kerby-Fulton, Katie Ann-Marie Bugyis, and John Van Engen, 97–112. Cambridge: Boydell & Brewer, 2020.

———. *The Saintly Politics of Catherine of Siena*. Ithaca, NY: Cornell University Press, 2006.

Mangano Ragazzi, Grazia. *Obeying the Truth: Discretion in the Spiritual Writings of Saint Catherine of Siena*. Oxford: Oxford University Press, 2014.

McDermott, Thomas. *Catherine of Siena: Spiritual Development in Her Life and Teaching*. New York: Paulist, 2008.

———. "Catherine of Siena's Teaching on Self-knowledge." *New Blackfriars* 88, no. 1018 (2007): 637–48. https://doi.org/10.1111/j.1741-2005.2006.00130.x.

McGinn, Bernard. "The Human Person as Image of God: II Western Christianity." In *Christian Spirituality: Origins to the Twelfth Century*, edited by Bernard McGinn, John Meyendorff, Jean Leclercq, 312–30. New York: Crossroad, 2000.

Nocentini, Silvia. "La *Legenda maior* di Raimondo da Capua: una eredità condivisa." In *Virgo digna coelo: Caterina e la sua eredità*, edited by Alessandra

CATHERINE OF SIENA

Bartolomei Romagnoli, Luciano Cinelli, Pierantonio Piatti, 103–18. Rome: Libreria Editrice Vaticana, 2013.

Noffke, Suzanne. *Catherine of Siena: An Anthology*. Medieval and Renaissance Texts and Studies. 2 vols. Tempe: Arizona Center for Medieval and Renaissance Studies, 2011–2012.

———. *Catherine of Siena: Vision through a Distant Eye*. Collegeville MN: Liturgical, 1996. Reprint: Scholars Press 2006. Page numbers refer to Liturgical Press edition.

———. "The Writings of Catherine of Siena: The Manuscript Tradition." Chap. 12 in *A Companion to Catherine of Siena*, edited by Carolyn Muessig, George Ferzoco, and Beverly Mayne Kienzle, 295–337. Leiden: Brill, 2012.

Rahner, Karl. *Foundations of Christian Faith*. New York: Seabury, 1978.

Scott, Karen. "'Io Caterina': Ecclesiastic Politics and Oral Culture in the Letters of Catherine of Siena." In *Dear Sister: Medieval Women and the Epistolary Genre*, edited by Karen Cherewatuk and Ulrike Wiethaus, 87–121. Philadelphia: University of Pennsylvania Press, 1993.

Scudder, Vida Dutton. *Saint Catherine of Siena as Seen in Her Letters*. New York: E. P. Dutton, 1905.

Tagliaferri, Lisa. "Lyrical Mysticism: The Writing and Reception of Catherine of Siena." PhD diss., CUNY Academic Works, 2017. https://academicworks.cuny.edu/gc_etds/2154.

Tylus, Jane. "Mystical Literacy: Writing and Religious Women in Late Medieval Italy." In *A Companion to Catherine of Siena*, edited by Carolyn Muessig, George Ferzoco, and Beverly Mayne Kienzle, 155–183. Leiden: Brill, 2012.

———. *Reclaiming Catherine of Siena: Literacy, Literature, and the Signs of Others*. Chicago: University of Chicago Press, 2009.

Vauchez, André. *Catherine of Siena: A Life of Passion and Purpose*. Mahwah, NJ: Paulist, 2018.

———. "Catherine de Sienne, prophétesse d'un renouveau spirituel," *Laboratoire italien* 21 (2018). https://doi.org/10.4000/laboratoireitalien.1842.

Villegas, Diana L. "Catherine of Siena's Crusade Letters: Spirituality and Political Context." *HTS Teologiese Studies / Theological Studies* 77, no. 2 a6499 (2021). https://doi.org/10.4102/hts.v77i2.6499.

———. "Catherine of Siena's Spirituality of Political Engagement." *HTS Teologiese Studies/Theological Studies* 77, no. 2 a6319 (2021). https://doi.org/10.4102/hts.v77i2.6319.

Bibliography

———. "Catherine of Siena's Wisdom on Discernment and Her Reception of Scripture." *Acta Theologica* 32, no. 2S (2013): 209–27. https://doi.org/10.38140/at.v0i17.2580.

———. "Continuous Prayer in Catherine of Siena." *HTS Teologiese Studies/ Theological Studies* 73, no. 3 (2017). https://doi.org/ 10.4102/hts.v73i3.4611.

———. "Examining Catherine of Siena's Controversial Discernments about Papal Politics." *HTS Teologiese Studies / Theological Studies* 77, no. 2 (2021). https://doi.org/10.4102/hts.v77i2.6654.

———. "The Spirituality of Catherine of Siena." Last modified January 2023. https://catherineofsiena-spirituality.org.

Volpato, Antonio. "Caterina da Siena, i suoi 'titoli' nelle Lettere e la sua missione apostolica." In *Caterina da Siena e la vita religiosa femminile: un percorso domenicano*, edited by Pierantonio Piatti. Rome: Campisano, 2016.

Zancan, Marina. "Lettere di Caterina da Siena. Il testo, la tradizione, l'interpretazione." *Annali d'italianistica* 13 (1995): 151–61.

INDEX

abbess of Santa Maria delli Scalzi, 54
abbott of Monte Oliveto, 110
admonishment, 67
affeto, 30, 31, 32, 44, 48, 51, 77, 79, 95, 106, 113, 119, 170, 171, 185, 270n92, 289n12
Agnes, Saint, 90
Agnesa, 243
Alberigo da Barbiano, 204
Alessa dei Saracini, 29, 72, 91, 94, 255, 256
Andrea, 69, 70
Andrea di Vanni, 187
angelic food. *See under* God
animal, 200
anthropology, theological, 29–30, 48, 161, 270n84
asceticism, 5–6
Augustine of Hippo, 29, 30, 218, 270n94
authority of Catherine, 13–14, 66, 104, 110, 114
Avignon, 133

Babbo, 143, 147, 149, 150, 154
Bandecca, 224
Barduccio, 135
Barduccio di Piero Canigiani, 16
Bartalo, 246
Bartalomaea, 43
Bartolomeo (brother), 248, 250

Bartolomeo (Pisa hermit), 95–96
Bartolomeo Dominici, 14, 63, 91, 94, 138
Bartolomeo Smeducci di San Severino, 192
battle, 199–203. *See also* Crusades
bed, 39–40, 42
Benincasa, 248, 250
Birgitta of Sweden, 140
body, the, 79–81, 135–37
bond, 171–72, 220, 222
Boniface VIII, Pope, 6
Book of Hours, 10
Bride of Christ, 129, 130–31
building, 157–60
business, 174, 175

Caffarini. *See* Tommaso d'Antonio da Siena
canonization of Catherine, 16
Carthusians, 212
Castel Sant'Angelo, 204
Caterina dello Spedaluccio, 68
Cavalca, Domenico, 10
Cavallini, Giuliana, 34
Cecca, 251, 253
cell, the, 3, 26–29, 42, 56–57, 58, 73–74, 89, 104, 114, 120, 138, 212, 225, 271n6
cemeteries, 95–96
chivalry, 199

church, 108, 109, 122, 124, 126, 129–30, 140, 149–50, 154, 160, 165
Clement VII, Pope, 133, 152, 177, 204
communion, 180–81, 182, 184–86, 190. *See also* sacraments
Company of Saint George, 204, 208
confession, 50–51, 206–7
consciousness as writer, Catherine, 13–14
consolation, 102–3
contrition, 182
conversation, 73, 75, 138
conversion, 166
corded belt, 244, 245
Corneto, 146, 147
Costanza, 28–29, 39, 247, 291n52
Council of the Wise, 108
cross/crucifixion: Christ, 27, 42–43, 51, 56, 62, 74, 96, 97, 162–63, 165–66, 172, 201–2, 240; food, 96, 112; holy desire, 161–63; love, 161, 167, 220; and sin, 172; spirituality of Catherine, 27; virtues, 167
Crusades, 65, 141, 174, 176, 177, 179–80, 192–93, 195, 198–99, 276n22, 282n3, 285n11

Daniella of Orvieto, 75
darkness, 41
death of Catherine, 133
desire, 29–30, 32, 47–48, 76, 79, 123, 163–64, 170, 229, 290n27
Dialogue, The (Catherine), 11, 35, 131, 138
discernment, 36–37, 72, 75–85, 170, 187, 209, 233, 233, 234–35
discipline, 222, 245, 291n46
discretio, 75–76, 274n27
doctors of the church, 1, 263n3

Dominic, Saint, 124
Dominicanism, 8–9, 11
Dupré Theseider, Eugenio, 16, 17, 18, 254, 255

eagle, 98
early life of Catherine, 4–5
education of Catherine, 4
eternal life, 241–42
Eugenia, 47
evil one, 41, 51–52, 67, 71, 102–3, 116, 121, 128, 135, 136
exhortation, 20, 21–22, 147
eye. *See under* soul

faith, 239
family, 213–14
fasting, 244
fattening, 272n7, 276n15
Fawtier, Robert, 16, 17
fear, 193
Felice, 104–5, 122
fire, metaphor of, 23, 39, 40, 41, 92, 97, 116–17, 144
Flete, William, 10–11
Florence, 126–27, 173, 209, 232
flowers, 227–28
food, 48–49, 55, 96, 110, 111. *See also* God: angelic food
Foster, Kenelm, 18
Francesca, 65
Francesco di Pipino, 243–44
Francesco Tedaldi, 114
Francesco Tolomei, 216
fruit, 77–78, 229–30

garment, 44
garden, 227–28
Gigli, Girolamo, 16
Giovanna di Capo, 68, 91, 91n11
Giovanna di Corrado Maconi, 212–13

Index

Giovanna of Anjou, 177–78
Giovanni dale Celle, 219
Giovanni Terzo (Tantucci), 122
Giustina, 253
God: *affeto*, 30, 119; angelic food, 26, 47, 48–49, 51, 53; anger, 69–70; as bed, 39–40, 41–42; binding/bond, 167, 220, 222; breast, 54, 55; and communion, 181; and creatures, 111–12, 152–53, 174, 178, 182–83, 227–28, 239–40; desire, 47–48; and discernment, 77, 78–79; experience of, 5; Father, 159; fear of, 235; fire, 23, 92; "God-is," 25–26, 53; goodness, 42, 70, 149, 213–14, 240; grace, 183–84; honor, 66–67, 79; and humanity, 29, 30–31; insults to, 194; knowledge of, 24, 26–27, 29, 74, 104, 189–90; love, 26, 28, 54, 62, 64, 72–73, 74, 86, 87, 90, 91–92, 94–95, 96, 97, 106–7, 111–12, 123, 153, 161, 164, 179, 194–95, 213–14, 225–26, 229–30, 233–34, 249; and patience, 239; reign, 184; responds, 182–83; Son, 159, 181–82; and soul, 97; stonemason, 159; and suffering, 240–41; and three powers of the soul, 30–31, 212–13; union with, 47, 89, 91, 119, 249; vision of, 122, 123–24; will, 65, 89–90, 97, 108–9
Gorgona, 114
Gostanzia. *See* Costanza
gratitude, 71
Gregory, Saint, 125
Gregory XI, Pope, 11, 12, 13, 104, 122, 126–27, 140–41, 146–47, 156, 166, 177, 192, 198, 282n3
Guelphs, 173, 180

hermits, 95–96
He-Who-Is, 53, 142, 158, 227
Hildegard of Bingen, 6
holiness, 126
Holy Sepulcher, 93, 195
Holy Spirit, 158, 214
Hospitallers. *See* Knights Hospitallers
humility, 33, 68, 74, 95, 105, 193–94, 215, 221, 234

illness, 9, 84, 133, 135–37
illumination, 110
imitation of Christ, 8, 110
Ipòlito, 209
Isola della Rocca, 132
Istituto italiano per il medio evo (ISIME), 16, 254–57

Jacomo, 95–96
Jesus Christ: blood, 20, 39, 40–41, 70, 71, 96, 152, 195–96; breast, 57, 58; bride of, 8; and creatures, 112; cross/crucifixion, 27, 42–43, 51, 56, 62, 74, 96, 97, 112, 162–63, 165–66, 172, 201–2, 240; and Crusades, 201; death, 203; desire, 229; devotion to, 8; and donkey, 91, 92–93; giving life for, 195, 205; as God, 40–41; humanity, 54, 55; knight, 201–2; lamb, 185–86; letters dedicated to, 18–20; love, 56, 67, 96–97, 98, 101–4, 162, 163, 195; mediator, 101; mother, 22, 55; obedience, 100; sacrifice, 100–101; safety, 194; side, 122, 124, 245; and sin, 125; spouse, 49–50, 71; staircase, 216, 217–18; stonemason, 158; suffering, 8, 49, 112, 161, 162; tree, 150; union with, 61, 62, 63,

98, 144, 150; as wall, 271n4; will, 123; Word, 95, 98, 112
Job, 241
John the Unique, 124
justice, 57–58, 96, 97, 187, 189, 190–91

knighthood, 199–202, 204, 205
Knights Hospitallers of St. John of Jerusalem, 198, 288n16
knowledge: cell, 114–15, 120; discernment, 187; of God, 24, 26–27, 29, 74, 104, 106, 189–90; self, 52, 57, 74, 104, 106, 111, 114–16, 119–20, 142, 189–90, 215; soul, 106, 115–16, 189–90

lamb, Passover, 185–86
Lapa, 250
laypeople, 9, 50, 78
legate, 167, 168
Leonardo, 210
letters: authenticity, 17; *carissimo*, 19; Christ, dedicated to, 18–20; collections, 16–18; conclusion, 20; content, 256; dating, 15, 17, 132, 255–56; exhoration, 20, 21–22; ISIME, 254–57; linguistic analysis, 254–56; Mary, dedicated to, 18–19; ministry of Catherine, 13, 15; numbering, 17, 254, 268n69, 268n71; parts, 18–20; recipients, 1–2, 13–14, 16, 18–19; scribes, 15–16, 60; *servant and slave*, 19–20; style, 2–3, 14, 15–16, 21–23, 269n78; translations, 17–18
light, 153–54, 156, 181–82, 205, 224, 225–26, 236–37, 239
literacy, 10, 14–15, 131, 132, 267n45
Liturgy of the Hours, 4
Lorenzetti, 187

Lorenzo, 97
loss, 238
love: and *affeto*, 185, 214; binding, 167, 168–69; Christ, 56, 67, 96–97, 98, 101–4, 162–63, 168, 195; and cross, 161, 167, 220; and discernment, 77, 79, 84; as fire, 39, 40, 41, 116, 144; forms, 279n78; garment, 44, 45; God, 26, 28, 54, 62, 64, 72–73, 74, 86, 87, 90, 91–92, 94–95, 96, 97, 106–7, 111–12, 123, 153, 161, 164, 179, 181–82, 194–95, 213–14, 225–26, 229–30, 233–34; Holy Spirit, 214; and humility, 105; imitation of, 110; and justice, 57–58; metaphors for, 22–23, 39; moderation, 72–73; neighbor, 58, 63, 107, 229, 230; perfect, 111; and prayer, 52; prelates, 142–43; progression, 216–17; queen, 231; self, 24–25, 46, 62, 94, 116, 127, 141, 142–44, 153, 154, 164–65, 169, 181, 195, 207, 210–11, 216, 218, 221; self-ordering, 188; soul, 97–98, 220, 234; and suffering, 55–56; and superiors, 113; tree, 226–27; and truth, 34–35, 234; understanding, 220–21; and virtue, 33, 43, 52, 154, 221; weapon, 199; and will, 95, 113, 232
loyalty, 207
Lucca, 146

Malatasca, 123
mantellate, 8–9, 10, 14, 63–64, 66, 250
Marco, 237–38
martyrdom, 127, 152, 192–93, 205
Mary, 9, 18–19, 207–8, 253
Mass, 136
Master General, 159, 160

Index

Mateio, 216, 218–19
McDermott, Thomas, 34
McGinn, Bernard, 270n84
memory, 31, 159
merchandise, 175
metaphors, 21–23, 39, 224
milk, 54, 55, 56, 58
ministry of Catherine, 9, 13, 15
Mirror of the Cross (Cavalca), 10
moderation, 72–73
monasticism, 220
Monte Oliveto, 99, 110
mother, Catherine as, 64
mystical experiences of Catherine, 5, 15, 21, 122

Naples, 177
Nera, 66, 274n15
Neri di Landoccio Pagliaresi, 16, 60–61, 86
Niccolò (Knights Hospitallers), 198–99
Niccolò Soderini, 173–74, 212, 285n8
Nicola da Osimo, 12, 146, 156
Nicolò Soderini. *See* Niccolò Soderini
Noffke, Suzanne, 15, 17, 132, 251, 255–56

obedience, 57, 78, 99, 100, 102–4, 119–20, 134, 222–23
order, 188–91
Orsa, 246

papacy, 11, 12, 109, 128–31, 133, 134, 151–52, 160, 176, 204, 283n24
Papal League, 126–27, 147
parenthood, 210, 211
Passover, 100

patience, 33–34, 68, 69, 81, 238–39, 243, 250, 252, 253
Paul, Apostle, 159, 243, 246
Paul VI, Pope, 263n2
penance, 80–83, 244
penitents, 8
perfection, 73
persecution, 70, 124, 128–29, 134
Piero, 170
Pietro, Pierre, 166
pilgrimage, 241, 244, 245–46. *See also* Crusades
Pisa, 95–96, 146, 147
politics and Catherine, 12, 147
Pòlito. *See* Ipòlito
pope, the, 93. *See also specific popes*
prayer, 35–36, 48, 51–53, 54, 84, 115, 116, 118–19, 184, 273n24, 275n38
prelates, 78, 142–43
pride, 236
providence, 240
punishment, 233, 234, 242

Rabe di Francesco di Tato Tolomei, 216
Raymond of Capua, 2, 11–12, 14, 34, 122, 126–27, 131, 132–33, 140, 151, 156, 160–61, 176, 180, 181, 264n10
reason, 116
receptivity, 86–87
reconciliation, 251
reform, 109, 126, 151–52, 154
religious life, 7, 36, 99, 209, 219, 223
rhetoric, 68–69, 96, 127
ring, marriage, 178
Ristoro Canigiani, 180
Ronayne, John, 19
royal dress/garment, 43–44, 45–46

sacraments, 94, 152, 180, 288n33
Saint Antimo, 223

Saint Mary of Monte Oliveto, order of, 99
salvation, 240
Scudder, Vida Dutton, 18
self-centeredness/selfishness, 24–25, 45, 46, 49, 62, 66–67, 77, 115–16, 127, 141, 160, 164–65, 169, 181, 189, 195, 207, 210–11, 216, 218, 221
self-knowledge. See under knowledge
self-will, 82–83, 85
sensuality, 116, 148–49, 189, 194–95, 226, 239
servants of God, 155
Sexagesima Sunday, 134
shame, 44
she is not, 52, 84, 142, 195, 213
she-who-is, 3
Siena, 6–7, 9–10, 147, 150–51, 187
silence, 165
Simeon, 125
sin, 68–69, 70–71, 125, 171–73
soul: *affeto*, 77, 289n12; cell, 26–29; discernment, 234–35; eye, 105–6; fire, 117; food, 26, 48–49, 51, 53, 55; and garden, 228; garment, 44; and God, 97; judgments, 235; knowledge, 106, 115–16, 189–90; light, 182; love, 97–98, 220, 234; purification, 63; three powers, 29–31, 76, 86, 188, 212–13, 220, 231, 232; and truth, 153, 234, 235–36; well-being, 79
spirituality of Catherine: *affeto*, 30, 31; the cell, 27–29; the cross, 27; desire, 29–30, 32; discernment, 36–37; Dominicanism, 8–9; goals, 60; knowledge of God, 24, 26–27, 29; knowledge of self, 24–26, 29; obedience, 36, 99;

prayer, 35–36; and theology, 269n83; three powers of the soul, 30–31; truth, 34–35; virtue, 32–34; will of God, 108
sponge, 225, 229
spouse, God/Christ as, 49–50, 57
Stefano (brother), 248, 250
Stefano (Giovanna's son), 212
Stefano della Cumba, 12, 160
Stefano Maconi, 16
suckling, 54, 55
suffering, 8, 45, 49, 55–56, 161, 162–64, 206, 240–43

terror, 135
Thomas Aquinas, 36, 99, 132
three powers of the soul, 39, 40, 41
Tommaseo, Niccolò, 17
Tommaso da la Fonte, 88
Tommaso d'Antonio da Siena, 14, 16, 91
Tommaso Petra, 138, 139
tongue, the, 74–75
transformation, 13, 35, 36–37, 68, 76, 104, 110, 141, 147, 170, 193, 216
treasure, 175–76
tree, 141–42, 150, 224–25, 226–27
truth, 34–35, 152–54, 234, 235–36
Tuscany, 141

understanding, 31, 105–6, 110, 112–13, 214, 220–21, 227, 234
Urban VI, Pope, 11, 12, 108, 133, 151, 177, 204, 205, 206, 208

Vauchez, André, 2
vernacular literature, 10
vicar of Christ, 128–29, 149. See also papacy
vice, 82, 154, 182, 200

Index

virtue: battling, 200; and cross/crucifixion, 167; discernment, 76, 79–80, 81, 83–85; food, 48, 55; growth, 147–49; and love, 33, 43, 52, 154, 221; pope, 148–49; reign of God, 184; self-knowledge, 119–20; spirituality of Catherine, 32–34; treasure, 176
visions of Catherine, 5, 122
vocation of Catherine, 4–6, 12, 13, 250–51
Volpato, Antonio, 16, 17, 19–20, 254, 256, 257
vows, 56–57, 119, 223

we-are-not, 25, 89–90, 221, 227, 242
wedding, 197
Western Schism, 133, 151–52
will, 31, 32, 44, 49, 64, 65, 82, 87, 89–90, 95, 97, 101, 103, 108–9, 112–13, 120–21, 123, 208, 214–15, 232
William Flete, 108
wolves, 165
women, 6
worldliness, 44, 61–62, 171–72, 217, 226, 241

you-are-not, 52, 172, 251

Other Volumes in This Series

Abraham Isaac Kook • THE LIGHTS OF PENITENCE, LIGHTS OF HOLINESS, THE MORAL PRINCIPLES, ESSAYS, LETTERS, AND POEMS
Abraham Miguel Cardozo • SELECTED WRITINGS
Abū al-Ḥasan al-Shushtarī • SONGS OF LOVE AND DEVOTION
Albert and Thomas • SELECTED WRITINGS
Alphonsus de Liguori • SELECTED WRITINGS
Anchoritic Spirituality • ANCRENE WISSE AND ASSOCIATED WORKS
Angela of Foligno • COMPLETE WORKS
Angelic Spirituality • MEDIEVAL PERSPECTIVES ON THE WAYS OF ANGELS
Angelus Silesius • THE CHERUBINIC WANDERER
Anglo-Saxon Spirituality • SELECTED WRITINGS
Apocalyptic Spirituality • TREATISES AND LETTERS OF LACTANTIUS, ADSO OF MONTIER-EN-DER, JOACHIM OF FIORE, THE FRANCISCAN SPIRITUALS, SAVONAROLA
Athanasius • THE LIFE OF ANTONY, AND THE LETTER TO MARCELLINUS
Augustine of Hippo • SELECTED WRITINGS
Bernard of Clairvaux • SELECTED WORKS
Bérulle and the French School • SELECTED WRITINGS
Birgitta of Sweden • LIFE AND SELECTED REVELATIONS
Bonaventure • THE SOUL'S JOURNEY INTO GOD, THE TREE OF LIFE, THE LIFE OF ST. FRANCIS
Cambridge Platonist Spirituality
Carthusian Spirituality • THE WRITINGS OF HUGH OF BALMA AND GUIGO DE PONTE
Catherine of Genoa • PURGATION AND PURGATORY, THE SPIRITUAL DIALOGUE
Catherine of Siena • THE DIALOGUE
Catherine of Siena • SELECTED LETTERS
Celtic Spirituality
Classic Midrash, The • TANNAITIC COMMENTARIES ON THE BIBLE
Cloud of Unknowing, The •
Devotio Moderna • BASIC WRITINGS
Dominican Penitent Women
Earliest Franciscans, The • THE LEGACY OF GILES OF ASSISI, ROGER OF PROVENCE, AND JAMES OF MILAN
Early Anabaptist Spirituality • SELECTED WRITINGS
Early Dominicans • SELECTED WRITINGS
Early Islamic Mysticism • SUFI, QUR'AN, MI'RAJ, POETIC AND THEOLOGICAL WRITINGS
Early Kabbalah, The
Early Protestant Spirituality
Edith Stein • SELECTED WRITINGS
Elijah Benamozegh • ISRAEL AND HUMANITY
Elisabeth Leseur • SELECTED WRITINGS
Elisabeth of Schönau • THE COMPLETE WORKS

Other Volumes in This Series

Emanuel Swedenborg • THE UNIVERSAL HUMAN AND SOUL-BODY INTERACTION
Emergence of Evangelical Spirituality, The • THE AGE OF EDWARDS, NEWTON, AND WHITEFIELD
Ephrem the Syrian • HYMNS
Fakhruddin 'Iraqi • DIVINE FLASHES
Farid ad-Din 'Attcr's Memorial of God's Friends • LIVES AND SAYINGS OF SUFIS
Fénelon • SELECTED WRITINGS
Francis and Clare • THE COMPLETE WORKS
Francis de Sales, Jane de Chantal • LETTERS OF SPIRITUAL DIRECTION
Francisco de Osuna • THE THIRD SPIRITUAL ALPHABET
George Herbert • THE COUNTRY PARSON, THE TEMPLE
Gertrude of Helfta • THE HERALD OF DIVINE LOVE
Gregory of Nyssa • THE LIFE OF MOSES
Gregory Palamas • THE TRIADS
Hadewijch • THE COMPLETE WORKS
Hasidic Spirituality for a New Era • THE RELIGIOUS WRITINGS OF HILLEL ZEITLIN
Henry Suso • THE EXEMPLAR, WITH TWO GERMAN SERMONS
Hildegard of Bingen • SCIVIAS
Ibn 'Abbād of Ronda • LETTERS ON THE ṢŪFĪ PATH
Ibn Al'-Arabī • THE BEZELS OF WISDOM
Ibn 'Ata' Illah • THE BOOK OF WISDOM AND KWAJA ABDULLAH ANSARI: INTIMATE CONVERSATIONS
Ignatius of Loyola • SPIRITUAL EXERCISES AND SELECTED WORKS
Isaiah Horowitz • THE GENERATIONS OF ADAM
Jacob Boehme • THE WAY TO CHRIST
Jacopone da Todi • THE LAUDS
Jean Gerson • EARLY WORKS
Jeanne Guyon • SELECTED WRITINGS
Jeremy Taylor • SELECTED WORKS
Jewish Mystical Autobiographies • BOOK OF VISIONS AND BOOK OF SECRETS
Johann Arndt • TRUE CHRISTIANITY
Johannes Tauler • SERMONS
John Baptist de La Salle • THE SPIRITUALITY OF CHRISTIAN EDUCATION
John Calvin • WRITINGS ON PASTORAL PIETY
John Cassian • CONFERENCES
John and Charles Wesley • SELECTED WRITINGS AND HYMNS
John Climacus • THE LADDER OF DIVINE ASCENT
John Comenius • THE LABYRINTH OF THE WORLD AND THE PARADISE OF THE HEART
John Donne • SELECTIONS FROM DIVINE POEMS, SERMONS, DEVOTIONS AND PRAYERS
John Henry Newman • SELECTED SERMONS

Other Volumes in This Series

John of Avila • AUDI, FILIA—LISTEN, O DAUGHTER
John of the Cross • SELECTED WRITINGS
John Ruusbroec • THE SPIRITUAL ESPOUSALS AND OTHER WORKS
Jonathan Edwards • SPIRITUAL WRITINGS
Julian of Norwich • SHOWINGS
Karl Barth Spiritual Writings
Knowledge of God in Classical Sufism • FOUNDATIONS OF ISLAMIC MYSTICAL THEOLOGY
Late Medieval Mysticism of the Low Countries •
Luis de León • THE NAMES OF CHRIST
Luther's Spirituality
Margaret Ebner • MAJOR WORKS
Marguerite Porete • THE MIRROR OF SIMPLE SOULS
Maria Maddalena de' Pazzi • SELECTED REVELATIONS
Maximus Confessor • SELECTED WRITINGS
Mechthild of Hackeborn • THE BOOK OF SPECIAL GRACE
Mechthild of Magdeburg • THE FLOWING LIGHT OF THE GODHEAD
Meister Eckhart • THE ESSENTIAL SERMONS, COMMENTARIES, TREATISES AND DEFENSE
Meister Eckhart • TEACHER AND PREACHER
Menahem Nahum of Chernobyl • UPRIGHT PRACTICES, THE LIGHT OF THE EYES
Miguel de Molinos • THE SPIRITUAL GUIDE
Nahman of Bratslav • THE TALES
Native Meso-American Spirituality • ANCIENT MYTHS, DISCOURSES, STORIES, DOCTRINES, HYMNS, POEMS FROM THE AZTEC, YUCATEC, QUICHE-MAYA AND OTHER SACRED TRADITIONS
Native North American Spirituality of the Eastern Woodlands • SACRED MYTHS, DREAMS, VISIONS, SPEECHES, HEALING FORMULAS, RITUALS AND CEREMONIALS
Nicholas of Cusa • SELECTED SPIRITUAL WRITINGS
Nicodemos of the Holy Mountain • A HANDBOOK OF SPIRITUAL COUNSEL
Nil Sorsky • THE COMPLETE WRITINGS
Nineteenth-Century Salesian Pentecost, The • THE SALESIAN FAMILY OF DON BOSCO, THE OBLATES AND OBLATE SISTERS OF ST. FRANCIS DE SALES, THE DAUGHTERS OF ST. FRANCIS DE SALES, AND THE FRANSALIANS
Nizam ad-din Awliya • MORALS FOR THE HEART
Norbert and Early Norbertine Spirituality
Origen • AN EXHORTATION TO MARTYRDOM, PRAYER AND SELECTED WORKS
Philo of Alexandria • THE CONTEMPLATIVE LIFE, THE GIANTS, AND SELECTIONS
Pietists • SELECTED WRITINGS
Pilgrim's Tale, The •
Pseudo-Dionysius • THE COMPLETE WORKS

Other Volumes in This Series

Pseudo-Macarius • THE FIFTY SPIRITUAL HOMILIES AND THE GREAT LETTER
Pursuit of Wisdom, The • AND OTHER WORKS BY THE AUTHOR OF THE CLOUD OF UNKNOWING
Quaker Spirituality • SELECTED WRITINGS
Rabbinic Stories
Richard of St. Victor • THE TWELVE PATRIARCHS, THE MYSTICAL ARK, BOOK THREE OF THE TRINITY
Richard Rolle • THE ENGLISH WRITINGS
Robert Bellarmine • SPIRITUAL WRITINGS
Safed Spirituality • RULES OF MYSTICAL PIETY, THE BEGINNING OF WISDOM
Scandinavian Pietists • SPIRITUAL WRITINGS FROM 19TH-CENTURY NORWAY, DENMARK, SWEDEN, AND FINLAND
Schleiermacher • CHRISTMAS DIALOGUE, THE SECOND SPEECH, AND OTHER SELECTIONS
Seventeenth-Century Lutheran Meditations and Hymns
Shakers, The • TWO CENTURIES OF SPIRITUAL REFLECTION
Sharafuddin Maneri • THE HUNDRED LETTERS
Søren Kierkegaard • DISCOURSES AND WRITINGS ON SPIRITUALITY
Sor Juana Inés de la Cruz • SELECTED WRITINGS
Spirituality of the German Awakening, The
Symeon the New Theologian • THE DISCOURSES
Talmud, The • SELECTED WRITINGS
Teresa of Avila • THE INTERIOR CASTLE
Theatine Spirituality • SELECTED WRITINGS
Theologia Germanica of Martin Luther, The
'Umar Ibn al-Fāriḍ • SUFI VERSE, SAINTLY LIFE
Valentin Weigel • SELECTED SPIRITUAL WRITINGS
Venerable Bede, The • ON THE SONG OF SONGS AND SELECTED WRITINGS
Vincent de Paul and Louise de Marillac • RULES, CONFERENCES, AND WRITINGS
Walter Hilton • THE SCALE OF PERFECTION
William Law • A SERIOUS CALL TO A DEVOUT AND HOLY LIFE, THE SPIRIT OF LOVE
Wycliffite Spirituality
Zohar • THE BOOK OF ENLIGHTENMENT

The Classics of Western Spirituality is a ground-breaking collection of the original writings of more than 100 universally acknowledged teachers within the Catholic, Protestant, Eastern Orthodox, Jewish, Islamic, and Native American Indian traditions.

To order any title, or to request a complete catalog, contact Paulist Press at 800-218-1903 or visit us on the Web at www.paulistpress.com.

ALSO OF INTEREST

Growing in Love with Catherine of Siena
Diana L. Villegas: *Illustrated by Paula A. Gomez*
This book is a selection of passages of Catherine of Siena's wisdom presented with meditations and prayer exercises.
5759-4 $24.95

Speaking with Authority
Catherine of Siena and the Voices of Women Today
Mary Catherine Hilkert
Reflects on the person and impact of Catherine of Siena as a means to examine the challenges facing contemporary women of faith.
4586-7 $15.95

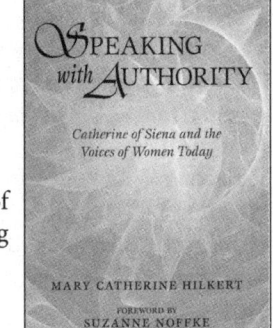

Catherine of Siena:
A Life of Passion and Purpose
André Vauchez
A historical and spiritual biography of Catherine of Siena, highlighting her as a visionary, a mystic, and a prophet.
5341-1 $24.95